Aristotle's Empiricism

Aristotle's Empiricism

MARC GASSER-WINGATE

OXFORD
UNIVERSITY PRESS

OXFORD
UNIVERSITY PRESS

Oxford University Press is a department of the University of Oxford. It furthers
the University's objective of excellence in research, scholarship, and education
by publishing worldwide. Oxford is a registered trade mark of Oxford University
Press in the UK and in certain other countries.

Published in the United States of America by Oxford University Press
198 Madison Avenue, New York, NY 10016, United States of America.

© Oxford University Press 2021

Library of Congress Control Number: 2021932106

ISBN 978-0-19-756745-6

DOI: 10.1093/oso/9780197567487.001.0001

1 3 5 7 9 8 6 4 2

Printed by Integrated Books International, United States of America

Acknowledgments

The questions animating this project are ones I became interested in while working on my doctoral thesis at Harvard. I am deeply grateful to my advisors, Mary Louise Gill, Rusty Jones, Alison Simmons, and Gisela Striker, for their comments and guidance during those years.

Papers discussing various arguments developed in the book were presented at conferences and workshops at Brown University, Dartmouth College, Harvard University, Northwestern University, the University of Pennsylvania, Providence College, the University of Sheffield, Temple University, the University of Toronto, and at the 2018 Eastern APA, the 2018 SAGP Annual Meeting, the 2018 Boston Summer Workshop, the Tahoe Ancient Philosophy Workshop, and the Orange Beach Epistemology Workshop. I am thankful to the audiences at these events for their criticism and feedback. Thanks are also due to my wonderful colleagues at Boston University, who generously commented on early, unpolished drafts of this material; to the Boston University Center for the Humanities, whose Junior Faculty Fellowship provided me with a critical semester of research leave; and to the CABAL and its associates for the supportive and stimulating philosophical community they help create. As Aristotle reminds us, we can all do philosophy alone, but we do it better with friends.

For helpful discussions about the central ideas developed in this book, I thank: David Charles, Sukaina Hirji, Robert Howton, Dhananjay Jagannathan, Colin King, Emily Kress, Jim Lennox, Hendrik Lorenz, Keith McPartland, Katy Meadows, Benjamin Morison, Jessica Moss, Christiana Olfert, Evan Rodriguez, David Roochnik, Susan Sauvé Meyer, and Jacob Stump. I also wish to thank Katja Vogt and an anonymous reader for Oxford University Press, who provided very detailed and careful comments on every part of the manuscript. The book owes much to their efforts. Finally, I am especially thankful to David Bronstein, whose thoughtful and always generous comments greatly improved the central arguments in the book; to Doug Kremm, for his steady philosophical spirit and for always being a willing interlocutor; to Patricia Marechal, for countless, invariably helpful conversations about nearly every aspect of the book; and to Whitney Schwab, for looking at early chapter drafts and keeping me honest during research leave.

Some parts of chapters 1 and 2 draw on "Conviction, Priority, and Rationalism in Aristotle's Epistemology," copyright ©2020 Journal of the History of Philosophy, Inc. This article was first published in *Journal of the History of Philosophy* 58(1), 2020, 1–27. The excerpts are reprinted with permission by Johns Hopkins University Press. Chapter 3 is a revised and expanded version of "Aristotle on Induction and First Principles," *Philosophers' Imprint* 16(4), 2016, 1–20. Some parts of chapter 4 draw on "Aristotle on the Perception of Universals," copyright ©BSHP. This article was first published in *British Journal for the History of Philosophy* 27(3), 2019, 446–67. The excerpts are reprinted by permission of Taylor & Francis Ltd, http://www.tandfonline.com on behalf of BSHP. I wish to thank these presses for permitting the inclusion of the relevant materials. I also wish to thank Peter Ohlin, my editor at Oxford University Press, for his sound advice and his interest in this project, and Zara Amdur, for her help compiling the book's index. Any errors are of course my own responsibility.

Above all I thank my partner, Amanda, for her patient, loving, and insightful support. I owe her more than I can express.

Contents

Acknowledgments   v

Introduction   ix

1. Perception, Knowledge, and Understanding in
   Aristotle's Epistemology   1
   1.1 Aristotle's Epistemic Terminology   4
   1.2 Understanding and Demonstration   11
   1.3 Rationalism and First Principles   22
   1.4 Understanding and Priority   26
   1.5 Understanding and Conviction   33
   1.6 Justification and Epistemic Value in Aristotle   40

2. Plato and Aristotle on Our Perceptual Beginnings   47
   2.1 Aristotle on Learning   48
   2.2 Perceptual Beginnings: A Platonic View   53
   2.3 Perceptual Beginnings and Our Epistemic Ascent   64
   2.4 Perceptual Foundations and Perception's
       Epistemic Value   70

3. Understanding by Induction   73
   3.1 Demonstrative Understanding and νοῦς   75
   3.2 Learning in *APo* II.19: Some Preliminaries   77
   3.3 Learning in *APo* II.19: Induction   82
   3.4 The First Stand: Perception to Universal Knowledge   88
   3.5 Subsequent Stands: Universal Knowledge to νοῦς   94
   3.6 Induction and Universal Knowledge   97

4. Perception and Perceptual Contents   105
   4.1 Perceptual Objects and Contents: A Broad View   108
   4.2 Perception and Rationality: A Nontransformative View   119
   4.3 Perceptual Experience and Conceptual Resources   126
   4.4 Particularity and Universality: *APo* I.31   133

4.5 The Perception of Universals   138
4.6 Discrimination, Recognition, and Compound Universals 148

5. Perception, Experience, and Locomotion: Aristotle
    on Nonrational Learning   158
    5.1 Discrimination, Pleasure, and Desire   160
    5.2 Perception and *Phantasia*   176
    5.3 Animal Experience, Human Experience, and Rationality 188

6. Perception in Aristotle's Ethics   197
    6.1 Strong Particularism: Ethics and Rules of Conduct   199
    6.2 Against Strong Particularism   205
    6.3 Perception, Experience, and Practical Wisdom   216

7. Final Thoughts   230

Bibliography   233
Index-Locorum-Aristotle   243
Index-Locorum-Plato   250
Index Nominum   251
Thematic-Index   253

Introduction

Aristotle is famous for thinking that all our knowledge comes from perception. Of course, we acquire knowledge in many different ways—we learn from our teachers, parents, colleagues, and friends, or from accumulated personal experience, or through various forms of reasoning, or indeed out of mere force of habit. But all these forms of learning, Aristotle thinks, rest on some sort of prior knowledge—the knowledge of our teachers, say, or of the premises in our arguments, or of our own past experiences. And generally this prior knowledge will itself depend on further prior knowledge. Where does the regress end? With *perceptual* knowledge—the only sort of knowledge that is not itself derived from anything prior. Perception is thus supposed to provide a bedrock for our learning, by supplying us with knowledge in a way that doesn't depend on our already having some knowledge at our disposal.

This view of our cognitive beginnings plays a central role in Aristotle's epistemology. He's sometimes considered the first empiricist for having held it. But it's not immediately clear what the view is meant to entail. It's not clear, for instance, what the knowledge perception supplies would contribute to the more advanced states that Aristotle takes to derive from it—states like experience (ἐμπειρία), craft knowledge (τέχνη), or scientific understanding (ἐπιστήμη). Nor is it clear how we should understand the nature of its contribution—what it might *mean* for various forms of knowledge to be "based on" or "derived from" perceptual knowledge. Indeed, to some ears it will already sound puzzling that there could be such a thing as perceptual knowledge, or that any form of knowledge would emerge directly from perception, without any sort of inference, or any (perhaps implicit) reliance on our existing beliefs or conceptual resources. My aim in this book is to shed some light on these questions: to give an account of the sort of empiricism Aristotle espoused, and of his broader conception of perception's place in our cognitive lives.

Of course empiricism is a slippery label. To say that all our knowledge issues from perception is not yet to say that perception itself plays a more than incidental role in our learning. Plato's middle dialogues provide a good illustration of this point: perception is presented as a necessary starting point for our learning because it prompts a form of recollection that supplies us with expert knowledge. But perception isn't itself characterized as an epistemically valuable state: it prompts recollection by perplexing us, "summoning thought" and "awakening the intellect" into recovering knowledge already present in our souls, and which might serve to sort out what perception alone could not make clear.[1] On this kind of view perception does serve as a starting point for all our learning, insofar as it *occasions* the rest of our cognitive development. But it doesn't provide an *edifice* for more advanced forms of knowledge, or supply the basic materials from which these forms of knowledge would be derived.

Even if perception did serve as some sort of edifice, one might wonder just how much it could teach us on its own. For Aristotle often emphasizes that our capacity to perceive is a capacity we share with all animals, and which yields a form of knowledge far removed from the sort of theoretical understanding he takes as his cognitive ideal—as he puts it in the *Metaphysics*, "to perceive is common to all, and therefore easy, and nothing wise" (A2 982a11–12). In particular perception doesn't tell us *why* anything is the case, or why it *must* be so, or even how things are when we are not actively perceiving them. Given these limitations, it's natural to think that Aristotle must have attributed any significant epistemic achievement to some other, non-perceptual cognitive capacity—a *rational* capacity, perhaps, or at least a capacity that would allow for more advanced modes of thought. Thus perception might do more than awaken our intellect, and yet still be thought to not have much to contribute of its own.

Nor indeed would taking a broad view of perception's contributions necessarily make Aristotle an empiricist. For some empiricists would

---

[1] *Republic* 524d1–5; see also *Phaedo* 75a–b. More on these passages below.

reject the very terms in which these contributions are being assessed—
terms that suggest a division between basic forms of perceptual
cognition, on the one hand, and more advanced forms of rational
thought, on the other. One might insist, for instance, that rational
thought is in fact nothing above the operation of perception, memory,
and some perceptually based associative capacities, or at least that
rational thought, whatever exactly its nature, does not make us any
more reliable or trustworthy than perception alone, and so should not
be taken to mark any substantive advance in our epistemic condition.
This is arguably the view of the first empiricists to bear the name.[2]
On this view there is simply no question of perception's *contribution*
to more advanced forms of thought. For all worthwhile thought is, at
bottom, perceptual.

Now, it's quite plain that Aristotle would reject these more radical
versions of empiricism.[3] He takes perception and perceptually based
forms of experience to be fundamentally distinct from theoretical
knowledge, and thinks his predecessors were confused precisely
because they conflated the two.[4] We perceive particulars, as he
often reminds us, while theoretical knowledge deals with universal
causes and essences, and the inferential and explanatory connections
between them. But it's also plain that he is influenced by the basic
insight that perception and memory are powerful practical guides,
even without the corrective assistance of the intellect: he recognizes
that nonrational animals can engage in highly complex, reasonable
behavior, and takes them to share in the same form of experience
we rely on in many of our human practices. While reason remains a
distinct and distinctively human capacity, it is not a capacity we need
to develop sophisticated and reliable forms of knowledge, or in terms
of which we would understand the value of the knowledge we develop
by nonrational means. Or so I will be arguing.

---

[2] I have in mind here the ancient empiricist doctors. In portraying them this way I
am following the interpretive line defended in Frede (1987, 243–60) and Frede (1990,
227–34).

[3] It's unlikely that Aristotle had access to the formulation of empiricism sketched
above, which is mostly based on Galen's report of certain Hellenistic debates of unclear
origins. But he probably did have access to views that were similar in spirit—see
e.g. Lorenz (2006, 4–7) and the passages cited below for some evidence to this effect.

[4] See *Met* Γ5 1009b12–13, *An* I.2 404a25ff, or *An* III.3 427b6ff.

Whether this makes Aristotle an empiricist will, unsurprisingly, depend on what we take empiricism to require. My aim is not to defend the label. What I hope to show is that Aristotle had an interesting conception of perception's role as a starting point for our learning, and of its relation to various more advanced forms of practical and theoretical knowledge. This is already a point worth defending—a number of prominent commentators have thought that Aristotle had nothing (or nothing good) to say about what perception teaches us, or how much we can learn on its basis.[5] It's easy enough to motivate this sort of criticism, since as far as we know Aristotle never explicitly discussed perception's epistemic contributions, at least as some philosophers might conceive of them today. Concerns about which beliefs perception might justify, and how, for instance, are simply never addressed. But it would be a mistake to conclude from this that Aristotle had a simplistic or naïve conception of our perceptual beginnings. To the contrary: I'll be arguing that a coherent and philosophically rich view of perceptual knowledge can be found in the various texts in which Aristotle describes perception's role in animal life, its interaction with more advanced modes of apprehension, and the cognitive resources on which it does and does not depend. As I understand it, the view is driven by three main insights.

The first insight is that perception can solicit behavior: we don't just perceive some state of affairs, but rather perceive things as things to be avoided, or pursued, or reacted to in some other, more complex manner. Thus when attacked by a bear you might perceive a brown ursine shape moving toward you, but it will also be part of your experience that the bear is something *to be avoided* or *to be run away from*. Perception suggests a response to your situation, and its affective profile motivates you to act as it suggests—and it does this without your deliberating or engaging in any sort of rational thought, and thus in a manner available to humans and nonrational animals alike.

---

[5] Barnes, for instance, tells us that "we need an account, which Aristotle nowhere gives, of how such concepts as *man* are derived from the data of perception" (1993, 266), Burnyeat characterizes Aristotle's treatment of perceptual learning as "perfunctory in the extreme" (1981, 133), and Irwin takes Aristotle to display a "rather naïve attitude to observation and induction" (1988, 137; see also 32–36).

The second insight is that perception can be *trained*: we can expand the range of things we recognize perceptually and the range of actions perception solicits from us. And again, we can do this without relying on rational modes of thought, using only perception and some auxiliary perceptual capacities—in particular, our capacity to retain what we perceive and associate some occurrent perception with the perceptions we've retained.[6] Together, these perceptual capacities provide the basis for a complex form of practical experience (ἐμπειρία). To have such practical experience is to be disposed to respond appropriately to a range of situations without understanding the appropriateness of one's response—to recognize what some situation calls for without knowing why it calls for it. Thus an experienced doctor might reliably cure malarial patients without being able to explain why her treatments work, or how she comes to her diagnoses. On Aristotle's view such a doctor would *perceive* some given malarial patient as someone to be leeched, despite not recognizing that the patient is malarial, and to be leeched for that reason. Trained perception of this sort serves as a reliable nonrational guide in our various practices, medical or otherwise, and in the pursuits and goal-directed behaviors of all but the most basic of animals.

The third insight is that this perceptually grounded form of practical experience provides a basis for more advanced, *causal* forms of knowledge—and, ultimately, for the cognitive ideal that is scientific understanding. It provides this basis because the domains in which we can become experienced are precisely those that can be investigated in theoretical terms: the fact that some doctors are reliably successful at curing malarials is a sign that malaria is a disease that admits of theoretical treatment, that is, a disease whose effects and relation to other diseases we might come to understand scientifically. Aristotle takes this to follow from the fact that we can be perceptually responsive to certain universal causes even if we cannot perceive the universals themselves. We do so by reliably discriminating the features perceptible entities possess because they instantiate the universals

---

[6] The auxiliary capacities I have in mind are those provided for by perceptual *phantasia*. Below I will examine in more detail the role Aristotle takes perceptual *phantasia* to play in animal cognition, and the sense in which it serves as an auxiliary to perception.

in question—e.g. by discriminating the symptoms of malaria in our patients, though we cannot perceive the universal *malaria* itself.

Aristotle therefore thinks we can be perceptually responsive to certain universals without recognizing them as such: perceptible particulars possess certain features because they instantiate certain universals, and perception allows us to discriminate these features and experience them as action-guiding aspects of our environment. Perception, so understood, serves as a basis for the development of a perceptually grounded form of practical experience. And practical experience, in turn, serves as a basis for advanced causal knowledge— knowledge that treats in explicit terms the explanatory structure that underpins the reliably successful practice of those with experience, and whose objects are therefore universals, and recognized as such.[7] Aristotle calls the cognitive development leading from perception to such advanced knowledge *induction*, and intends his inductive account of our learning as an alternative to certain innatist views he finds absurd—the contrast depending in large part on the role he assigns perceptual knowledge in our inductive progress.

Taken together, these three insights yield an interesting, moderate kind of empiricism. This is a kind of empiricism in that our perceptual powers (unassisted by the intellect) afford us an epistemically valuable form of knowledge, which itself serves as a basis for the development of advanced causal knowledge. This empiricism is moderate in that rational reflection on our perceptual knowledge is required to develop any such advanced causal knowledge. And this empiricism is interesting both on purely philosophical grounds and because of its interpretive implications. Indeed, Aristotle often seems rather quick to dismiss innatist views of our learning. Understanding his empiricism will help illuminate what exactly his alternative to these views is meant to be, and give us a better sense of the background zoological and psychological considerations motivating this alternative. It will also help illuminate some critical parts of his moral psychology— in particular, the view that perception is central to the development

---

[7] Where the resulting knowledge is either craft knowledge (if it aims at producing something) or scientific understanding (if it aims at working out what is the case). I will also be considering the case of practical wisdom, and argue we should think of it on the model of craft knowledge.

and deployment of practical wisdom, and that virtuous agents must ultimately *perceive* what to do in the various situations they face. Finally, it will help illuminate Aristotle's conception of our humanity: articulating the difference between rational and perceptual forms of knowledge tells us which parts of our cognitive life we share with other animals, and what is distinctive about the modes of thought that separate us from them.

Here, in outline, is how all this will be defended. I begin chapter 1 with some ground clearing: I argue that talk of perceptual knowledge is not a complete nonstarter, and explain how I will be using various knowledge terms to capture the different cognitive states that feature in Aristotle's epistemology. I then offer an account of scientific understanding (Aristotle's epistemic ideal) as a form of theoretical expertise requiring a synoptic, reflective appreciation of the explanatory structure of some domain, and in particular of the role the truths comprising that domain might play in a special kind of demonstration. I offer this account early on in order to resist views that make scientific understanding the sole locus of justification, and conclude from this that perception could not itself play any significant epistemic role. I argue that, for all his remarks about demonstrative principles being "most convincing" and "primitive," Aristotle did not consider them an ultimate or unique source of justification. However I also raise some concerns about invoking talk of justification in this context, and suggest an alternative, pluralistic conception of epistemic value that I think better fits Aristotle's epistemology. In doing so I hope to explain why we should resist dismissive takes on our perceptual accomplishments based on Aristotle's descriptions of his epistemic ideal. But I also hope to articulate the terms in which I think we should understand Aristotle's account of our cognitive development, and perception's place within it.

In chapter 2 I consider the Platonic background for Aristotle's account of our cognitive development, such as we find it in some of Plato's middle dialogues. I argue that, on the surface, the Platonic view agrees with Aristotle's claim that all advanced knowledge must come "from" perception: it's from perception that we are prompted to think of our perceptual shortcomings, and refer our perceptions to the knowledge of Forms we go on to recollect. But the knowledge we recollect is not meant to be derived on the basis of what we perceive. For our knowledge of Forms is something we're already meant to possess, in some latent form, before we perceive anything at all—and perception contributes to our recovering this knowledge only by compelling us to reflect on its own deficiencies. So the fact that we must begin from perception is a lamentable consequence of our embodied existence, not something that would supply us with any valuable form of knowledge, or be useful except as a means to recollect. Aristotle explicitly presents his account of the perceptual origins of our learning as an alternative to this sort of view. He does so, I argue, precisely because he takes perception to be an epistemically valuable capacity—a capacity whose exercise supplies us with sophisticated forms of knowledge even without the intervention of the intellect. What this shows is that Aristotle did not take perception to be foundational in an etiological sense only, as a causal precursor to the rest of our learning. Perception is indeed such a causal precursor, but it is also a source of knowledge that we can safely rely on in our learning and practical pursuits.

In chapter 3 I argue that we learn scientific first principles by induction. This is what Aristotle says, but few take him at his word. I offer a reading of the last chapter of the *Analytics* on which this claim makes sense. It involves conceiving of induction as a somewhat more robust process than is commonly thought—roughly, as a form of cognitive progress from a range of particular truths to some universal explanation why all these truths hold. I argue there are good grounds to think this is what Aristotle has in mind in the *Analytics*, and I go through some examples where he seems to be displaying just this sort of progress in his own scientific works. One upshot of this view is that we don't need to think that Aristotle gave up on induction as a path toward principles, invoking some kind of rational intuition or some other set of methods to remedy its deficiencies. Another upshot is that the knowledge perception provides plays a central role in our inductive learning of principles, supplying the basic body of facts these principles are meant to explain.

In chapter 4 I consider in greater detail the role perception is meant to play in the early stages of this inductive process. I begin by defending an expansive reading of perceptual objects and contents, on which we perceive not just colors, sounds, and so on, but also Callias, lyres, and loaves of bread, and whether Callias is near, the lyre well-tuned, and the loaf baked. I consider what relationship this broad perception has to the characterization of sense-perception we find in *De Anima*. I argue that for Aristotle, *per se* perceptibles (the objects of one or more sense modality) are fundamental in a psychological sense: they serve to define the sensory powers whose operation underlies all perceptual activity. But I further argue that they are not fundamental in an epistemological sense: our knowledge of these *per se* perceptibles should not be taken to provide a "given" that would serve as an exclusive basis for all our learning. I also consider whether or not broad perception would implicitly depend on our conceptual resources or some sort of "cognitive penetration" from the intellect, and argue against views on which our perceptual powers are inherently transformed by the rational part of our soul. Finally, I consider in more detail Aristotle's take on perceptual learning, focusing on his claim that our perceptions are "of universals" even though we perceive particulars, his broader conception of particular and universal cognitive states, and his portrayal of our pretheoretical apprehension of "compound" universals we might seek to define more precisely. I argue that Aristotle thought we could be perceptually responsive to universals we do not yet recognize as such, and that we can be so responsive even though we only perceive particulars—and that this view informs his generous conception of the sort of knowledge possessed by those with nonrational, perceptually grounded forms of experience.

In chapter 5 I examine the zoological and psychological views that account for the perceptual learning discussed in chapter 4. These views, I argue, are motivated by two key ideas developed in Aristotle's account of animal locomotion. The first is the idea that perception can solicit some behavior from a perceiving subject: we and other animals perceive how things are, but also perceive how to act in the various situations we face. This is possible because we perceive things as pleasant and painful, and thus as objects of some of our appetites, and also perceive the means necessary to fulfill these appetites—so that perception has both cognitive and affective dimensions, the combination of which allows it to play a key motivational role. The second idea is that perceptual *phantasia* makes possible the retention of past perceptions as memories, and the association of past memories with some occurrent perception. This mechanism allows past perceptions to inform what we recognize perceptually, and accounts for the development of the complex, goal-directed dispositions that characterize the state of experience—as we find it in both humans and nonrational animals. I end by contrasting the state of experience with forms of knowledge that do depend on our rational powers, and considering the limits of Aristotle's empiricism.

In chapter 6 I examine what implications this account has for Aristotle's moral epistemology. My main question here is how Aristotle's empiricist views bear on our understanding of the role perception plays for the virtuous—and whether or not, as is often thought, they point toward a certain form of ethical particularism, according to which universal rules could never adequately codify virtuous conduct. I argue they do not. While it might be inexpedient for virtuous agents to attempt to articulate universal rules of conduct with any sort of precision, this is not because it is in principle impossible to do so, or because the subject matter of ethics does not admit of theoretical treatment. Still, while ethical theorizing is possible, perception and perceptually grounded experience play an indispensable role in the development and deployment of practical wisdom. For ethical theorizing, while possible in principle, does not itself provide any guidance how to act: our learning to be virtuous depends on first-hand, personal experience that theoretical modes of thought could not provide. I argue that this is simply a consequence of the fact that ethics is a *practical* subject matter: an analogous point could be made (and is arguably made by Aristotle) about a doctor's knowledge of medicine. If this is right, ethics is not an exceptional subject matter, different in kind from those that admit of universal treatment—even if practical wisdom does require accumulated personal experience in a way our knowledge of some purely theoretical discipline does not. I end by considering what a practically oriented, universal treatment of virtuous conduct would look like, and how we might conceive of its ethical significance.

1

Perception, Knowledge, and Understanding in Aristotle's Epistemology

The topic of this book is Aristotle's conception of perceptual knowledge—what this knowledge amounts to, how we acquire it, and how we should understand the relationship between this knowledge and the other, more advanced forms of knowledge we might develop on its basis. To some this will sound like a nonstarter: there is simply no such thing as perceptual knowledge in Aristotle, and so there is no question what sort of knowledge it is, or how this knowledge might contribute to our learning. One might of course allow that perceiving things would, in some cases, result in our developing some kind of knowledge about the things we perceive. But the resulting knowledge in such cases, the objection goes, is not supplied by perception alone. For some sort of mediation is needed to turn our perceptions into knowledge, and this mediation is something perception alone could not provide.

Objections of this sort can be motivated in a number of different ways. Some will argue that perception, for Aristotle, doesn't itself justify anything, or provide any grounds for rational conviction—and that it therefore could not be taken to provide us with any knowledge on its own. Others will point out that perception, for Aristotle, has particular, contingent objects, while knowledge paradigmatically concerns itself with necessary, universal truths, and the explanatory relations between them. Others yet will note that perceptual modes of cognition, for Aristotle, are shared with even the most primitive nonrational animals, and argue that these primitive animals couldn't rightly be said to know anything, because their cognitive lives are too impoverished to form the sorts of states that would constitute

Aristotle's Empiricism. Marc Gasser-Wingate,
Oxford University Press (2021). © Oxford University Press.
DOI: 10.1093/oso/9780197567487.003.0001

knowledge. In all these cases the thought is that knowledge is supposed to be some sort of epistemic accomplishment, and that perception, as Aristotle describes it, is just too limited to yield anything that would qualify as such.

My aim in this chapter is to dispel some of these initial concerns and to consider, more broadly, how we should approach questions about the relationship between perception and the more advanced cognitive states that appear in Aristotle's descriptions of our learning. I'll begin with a preliminary argument against the view that talk of perceptual knowledge is a nonstarter. The argument is simple: perception is (or yields, when successfully exercised) a kind of γνῶσις; γνῶσις, as Aristotle uses the term in his account of our learning, is factive cognition; and factive cognition is something we might plausibly take to constitute knowledge. If this is right, it establishes that perception yields a kind of knowledge—at least on one philosophically defensible characterization of what knowledge is.

Now, this is a modest claim, aimed primarily at those who would put down the book one sentence in. We might of course dispute that knowledge is factive cognition, or insist that knowledge requires a kind of reflection about the contents of our experiences or beliefs which perception could not provide. For the purposes of my broader argument, however, it won't matter much whether or not we are right to call perceptual γνῶσις a form of knowledge. That will inevitably depend on what we take knowledge to require, and there isn't much to gain by terminological intransigence.[1] What will matter is that perception is sufficient to yield epistemically valuable cognitive states, rather than merely serving as a causal precursor to such states, which

---

[1] I find overly restrictive conceptions of knowledge implausible, and especially out of place in the context of Aristotle's epistemology. So part of the reason I find it appropriate to render γνῶσις as "knowledge," and present perceptual γνῶσις a specific kind of knowledge, is that I think this captures Aristotle's generous conception of the cognitive accomplishments attributable to the perceptual part of our soul, and thus available (as I will be arguing) to both rational and nonrational animals. But this choice of translation is not meant to be prejudicial: the central question is what these accomplishments amount to, and how we should understand their value and the relationship they bear to more sophisticated forms of understanding. If you agree with me on these points but nonetheless wish to call perceptual γνῶσις something else, and reserve "knowledge" for some more exalted cognitive state, I am happy to give up the label.

would prompt their development by other, intellectually involved means.

And this is precisely what a number of commentators would deny ("rationalists," as I'll be calling them). On the rationalist view, ἐπιστήμη is, for Aristotle, the sole locus of epistemic value: anything that falls short of ἐπιστήμη does not strictly speaking constitute any form of knowledge, or any sort of epistemically valuable state. Since Aristotle is clear that perception alone never yields ἐπιστήμη, it follows that perception alone never yields any epistemically valuable state. Perception might of course remain a necessary prerequisite to the development of such states, and perhaps help explain the psychological underpinnings of this development—but it would not itself supply the basic knowledge we might use as a foundation for the development of further, more advanced forms of knowledge and understanding. For, as the point is typically put, perception cannot provide the sort of *justification* Aristotle's conception of knowledge requires: that sort of justification must issue from our rational intuition of certain principles, and nothing else, and is therefore available only to someone with ἐπιστήμη.[2]

As I understand them, rationalist interpretations along these lines are motivated by background views about the role justification and conviction play in Aristotle's epistemology, and what it would take for some cognitive state to count as an epistemically valuable one. In this chapter and the next, I will be arguing that these views are mistaken— or at least that they are not supported by Aristotle's discussions of the nature and development of ἐπιστήμη. I will also be defending an alternative conception of epistemic value, which I think better fits Aristotle's description of our learning, and sheds some light on the different epistemic accomplishments he describes, and in particular those accomplishments he attributes to the perceptual part of the soul.

---

[2] For such views see in particular Frede (1996, 172) and Irwin (1988, 132–36). Some rationalist views are more nuanced, and allow that states other than ἐπιστήμη might count as epistemically valuable insofar as they approximate ἐπιστήμη to a sufficient degree (see e.g. Fine (2010, 152–55)). But even these more nuanced views assume that ἐπιστήμη provides the sole standard against which epistemic value is to be measured. In what follows I will argue against this assumption, and defend a more expansive, pluralistic conception of epistemic value.

In doing so I hope to explain why we should resist the dismissive take on perception endorsed by rationalist interpreters. But I also hope to articulate the terms in which we would best understand Aristotle's account of our learning, perception's role in this account, and the contrast between various perceptual and intellectual forms of knowledge.

1.1 Aristotle's Epistemic Terminology

Before taking on rationalist readings of Aristotle's epistemology, let me return to a modest point: talk of perceptual knowledge is not a complete nonstarter in this context. It's not a complete nonstarter because perception, as Aristotle frequently emphasizes, is a kind of γνῶσις, and γνῶσις, as Aristotle uses the term in his discussions of our learning, can reasonably be taken to constitute knowledge— to have γνῶσις of X (or to γιγνώσκειν or γνωρίζειν X) is to know X, on at least some philosophically plausible conceptions of knowledge.

That perception is a γνῶσις is, I take it, uncontroversial. Here are the texts where Aristotle articulates the point most clearly:[3]

[1] To see is something we prefer over almost everything else—not just with a view toward action, but even when we aren't setting out to do anything. The reason is that seeing makes us γνωρίζειν most of all the senses, and reveals many differences between things. (*Met* A1 980a24–27)

[2] We do not regard any of the senses as wisdom; yet surely these give the most authoritative γνώσεις of particulars. But they do not tell us the "why" of anything—e.g. why fire is hot; they only say that it is hot. (*Met* A1 981b10–13)

---

[3] See also *Top* V.3 131b23–28 and the further references in Burnyeat (1981, 114). Here and henceforth, unattributed translations are my own.

[3] The function of an animal is not just to generate: that is common to all living things. All animals partake in a kind of γνῶσις; some more, some less, some very little indeed. For they have perception, and perception is a kind of γνῶσις. (*GA* I.23 731a30–34)

[4] Of what is present there is no memory, but rather perception. For by the latter we do not γνωρίζειν what is future or past, but what is present only, whereas memory is of the past. (*Mem* 449b13–15)

[5] We must γνωρίζειν magnitude and motion by means of the same capacity by which we γνωρίζειν time. So it's clear that it's by the primary faculty of perception that there is γνῶσις of these. (*Mem* 450a9–11)

Perception, in these passages, is advanced as something that either *yields* some sort of γνῶσις (as in [1] and [2]), or something *by which* we γνωρίζειν, or by which there is γνῶσις (as in [4] and [5]), or something that simply *is* a kind of γνῶσις (as in [3]). I take it these different formulations reflect the different ways we might conceive of perception itself: as a power whose use results in some sort of cognitive state, or as the cognitive state resulting from the successful use of this power. When conceived of as a power, perception is something that yields a kind of γνῶσις, or through the use of which we γνωρίζειν. When conceived of as the state resulting from the successful use of this power, perception just is a kind of γνῶσις. In fact γνῶσις itself is used in both of these ways: in [2] and [5] it picks out a cognitive state, while in [3] it picks out the means by which this state is normally brought about. So perception can be taken to count as a γνῶσις both *qua* power or *qua* state.[4]

Now, γνῶσις and its cognates are terms that resist easy translation. Aristotle uses them to cover an extremely broad range of states and modes of apprehension, in a number of different contexts—so that some translators opt for the (presumably more neutral) "cognition"

---

[4] I will be following Aristotle in using "perception" to denote both the power to perceive and the perceptual experience or state resulting from the use of this power—in context it will be clear which is invoked. For more on Aristotle's terminology in these cases, see pp. 48–49.

rather than "knowledge." Thus some might agree that perception is a kind of γνῶσις, but deny that perception yields any kind of knowledge: our perceptual powers might be taken to allow for some sort of awareness of the world unavailable to plants, yet still fall short of supplying us, on their own, with any sort of knowledge.

In his discussions of our learning, however, Aristotle does not use γνῶσις to pick out mere awareness. For something to count as a γνῶσις it must be a case of *factive* cognition, that is, cognition that links agents to truths.[5] This is a point Bronstein has recently defended in great detail, and I take his arguments to this effect to be decisive.[6] To my mind, it's a point that should come as no surprise. For Aristotle's main account of our learning is framed as an answer to the question how we might come to γνωρίζειν certain principles, and what prior forms of γνῶσις must be there for our γνῶσις of principles to be brought about (*APo* II.19 99b17–30). And what he is attempting to explain is not how some potentially mistaken cognition or awareness of principles would be possible, but rather how we might come to *know* these principles, and understand them for what they are. Anything less would not really constitute an explanation how we learn principles: to learn we must end up with the truth.[7] So γνῶσις might be used more broadly in other contexts, but when it is invoked to describe our learning, it picks out factive cognition, specifically.

---

[5] Nowadays factivity is often understood in propositional terms—a cognitive state is factive when an agent's bearing it toward *p* entails that *p* is true. For Aristotle, however, things can be true or false which are not propositions: he tells us the perception of *special* perceptibles is always true (*An* III.3 427b11–12), or, somewhat more cautiously, that it admits of falsehood the least (428b18–19), and this sort of perception does not involve any sort of predicative combination or propositional structure (cf. 4.3 n37). I intend factivity to cover those cases as well. For more on perception and its contents, see 4.1.

[6] See Bronstein (2016a, 16–21). The view that γνῶσις is factive in the context of Aristotle's discussions of our learning (though perhaps not in general) is also implicit in a good deal of scholarship on Aristotle's epistemology, where the term is rendered as "knowledge." See, for instance, Ackrill (1981), Barnes (1993), Bolton and Code (2012), Burnyeat (1981, 2011), Karbowski (2016), Kosman (1973), or Taylor (1990). For a dissenting view, see Fine (2010), and also Ferejohn (1991, 68–69) and LaBarge (2006, 38).

[7] Note on this point the phrasing at *APo* II.19 99b28–29, where Aristotle asks about principles πῶς ἂν γνωρίζοιμεν καὶ μανθάνοιμεν ἐκ μὴ προϋπαρχούσης γνώσεως. See also *Met* A1 980a27–b25, where different forms of perceptual γνῶσις are said to allow for different forms of learning (μανθάνειν, 980b23–24). I take it μανθάνειν is factive in these passages, and therefore so is γνῶσις.

One might object here that γνῶσις cannot be factive cognition because perception is a γνῶσις, and not all our perceptions are true. But we can hold that perception is a way to γνωρίζειν things without holding that every single perceptual state counts as a γνῶσις. To call perception a γνῶσις, as I see it, is to say that perception is a capacity whose exercise *reliably* yields factive cognition—a view Aristotle thinks warranted on broadly zoological grounds, as I will be arguing below (see in particular chapter 5). It's compatible with this view that perception might in certain cases fail to yield factive cognitive states, or present things in an inaccurate way, so long as it does not normally mislead.[8] It's also compatible with this view that perception would reveal to us only a limited portion of reality—and in particular that it would not reveal to us any of the causes that would explain what we perceive, and which Aristotle considers "more true" than what they serve to explain (cf. *EE* I.6 1216b26–35, *Met* α1 993b19–31, and section 4.6). Perceptual γνῶσις, after all, is meant to belong to even the most basic animals (cf. [3]).

So the exercise of our perceptual powers reliably yields a kind of γνῶσις, and γνῶσις, in this context at least, is factive cognition. This does not yet establish that perception yields a kind of knowledge. For one might deny that factive cognition constitutes knowledge—one might think that knowledge requires justification, or at least some sort of reflective appreciation of the epistemic standing of our beliefs or other cognitive states. Note, however, that at this point I am arguing only that talk of perceptual knowledge isn't a nonstarter. And the view that unreflective factive cognition constitutes knowledge, while of course up for dispute, isn't a nonstarter. Consider, for instance, the sort of animal knowledge Sosa distinguishes from its more reflective counterpart:

---

[8] Aristotle does of course seek to explain perceptual error in his psychological works. But he doesn't do this in order to explain the role perception might play as a starting point for our learning, nor does he take as epistemically basic the sort of perception he considers least fallible (on which point see pp. 124–25). I take it this is because his account of our learning is not primarily intended as a recipe for the secure aggregation of truths, and takes for granted the reliability of some of our cognitive powers—for instance, in [2], the reliability of perception in reporting that fire is hot.

One has *animal knowledge* about one's environment, one's past, and one's own experience if one's judgments and beliefs about these are direct responses to their impact—e.g., through perception or memory—with little or no benefit of reflection or understanding.

One has *reflective knowledge* if one's judgment or belief manifests not only such direct response to the fact known but also understanding of its place in a wider whole that includes one's belief and knowledge of it and how these come about.[9]

Or, in a similar vein, the notion of knowledge Kornblith adopts from cognitive ethologists:

the notion of knowledge which cognitive ethologists are interested in, namely, true belief which is the product of a reliable process, does not in any way exclude [reflection about our beliefs]; it merely fails to require it. And the vast majority of human belief is surely arrived at unreflectively. The cognitive ethologist's account of knowledge is equally applicable to human beings, and it carves out a category of beliefs which is just as interesting in the case of human beings as it is in other animals, and for just the same reasons.[10]

In both cases a form of knowledge is presented which does not require any reflection about our judgments or beliefs, and is thus available to nonhuman animals. Such knowledge simply results from the successful operation of reliable cognitive processes—just as perceptual γνῶσις, for Aristotle, results from the successful operation of our

---

[9] Sosa (1985, 241–42).

[10] Kornblith (1999, 335). See further Goldman (1976, 791), Nozick (1981, 178), Sartwell (1991), or Williamson (2000, 38). There are of course a number of disagreements among these authors on a number of different points—but they all agree that knowledge need not be a reflective achievement.

reliable perceptual powers.[11] But it remains a case of knowledge nonetheless—because (I submit) it is case of factive cognition.

So Aristotle describes perception as a kind of γνῶσις, that is, as a power whose exercise reliably yields a kind of factive cognition. And such factive cognition can reasonably be taken to constitute knowledge, even in subjects who cannot take a reflective stance on their cognitive states. Of course on Aristotle's view there are many other forms of γνῶσις besides the perceptual—some of them far more advanced, and requiring a good deal of reflective intellectual work. Thus perception, memory, and experience, as I will be arguing, are forms of γνῶσις available to both humans and nonrational animals, while craft knowledge, practical wisdom, and scientific understanding are rational forms of γνῶσις, available to humans only.[12] Whether or not one agrees with such a broad conception of knowledge, it isn't a nonstarter, and so neither is talk of perceptual knowledge in the context of Aristotle's epistemology.

As I see it, then, and as Aristotle himself suggests in *APo* II.19, γνῶσις is a generic term that would cover all sorts of factive cognition, from our most rudimentary perceptions to the highest forms of scientific understanding. It's worth noting that Aristotle also uses γνῶσις and its cognates more narrowly, to pick out ordinary, non-explanatory knowledge, specifically. So γνῶσις is both a generic term for knowledge (understood as factive cognition) and a term that

---

[11] Kornblith, Sosa, and others put the point in terms of the true *beliefs* that would result from such processes. It might thus be objected that knowledge must at least entail true belief, and that since Aristotle explicitly denies δόξα to nonrational animals (*An* III.3 428a18ff) he should *a fortiori* be taken to deny them knowledge (for this view see Fine (2010, 153) or Fine (2014, 189)). But it's in fact doubtful δόξα should be understood as belief in this context. For Aristotle denies nonrational animals δόξα because he thinks δόξα results from rational conviction, and nonrational animals cannot be rationally convinced. But we do not typically think all our *beliefs* follow from rational conviction. So δόξα is probably not belief. (This is a point Bolton presses against Fine in unpublished work. For a broader argument against assimilating belief and δόξα, see Moss and Schwab (2019).)

[12] This is not an exhaustive list. The former, more basic forms of knowledge are developed just by retaining and associating various perceptions, while the latter, more advanced forms of knowledge involve some amount of reflection, and a synoptic grasp of some explanatory structure—on which contrast see 5.3. Still, some advanced knowledge requires perception even after it has been acquired, and some of our perceptions can be informed by advanced knowledge we already possess, as I argue in 4.2 and 6.3.

picks out knowledge that is not advanced—where this would include perceptual knowledge, as well as knowledge acquired through the use of our mnemonic and associative powers, but exclude explanatory forms of knowledge and understanding I will be considering in more detail below.[13]

Now, I don't want to put too much weight on these terminological preliminaries. The interesting question, to my mind, is not whether or not we are right to call perceptual γνῶσις a form of knowledge, but rather how we should understand the contribution perceptual γνῶσις makes to the development of the other, more advanced kinds of γνῶσις we find in Aristotle's epistemology. I've noted here that Aristotle considers perception a reliable guide to the truth, which is of course always a good start—but that doesn't yet distinguish perception from any other form of knowledge, nor does it make clear how these other forms of knowledge would depend on the knowledge we get from perception. For one might agree that perception is a guide to the truth and nonetheless disagree substantially on a number of key points. For instance, one might disagree about the range of truths we might learn perceptually, or about the respective contributions our perceptual and intellectual capacities make to our learning, or about the relation perceptual knowledge bears to the various forms of knowledge that are said to depend on it.

I will be arguing in what follows that perception plays a number of key epistemic roles—apart from being a reliable guide to the truth. In particular, I will be arguing (in this chapter) that perception serves as a source of conviction and as an authority to which even our highest forms of understanding must be responsive, and (in the next) that perception supplies us with forms of knowledge that are valuable in themselves, quite apart from their serving as a means

---

[13] Ordinary knowledge is itself a broad category, and includes more than the forms of knowledge that issue from perception and mnemonic association—which I single out here because of their role in Aristotle's account of our learning. Sometimes Aristotle substitutes εἰδέναι for γνωρίζειν to pick out our knowing something in this ordinary way (see for instance *APo* I.2 71b31, I.2 72a25, I.3 72b13, I.6 75a32, I.13 79a16, or I.22 83b35). Sometimes he substitutes εἰδέναι for γνωρίζειν in its generic sense (see for instance *Met* α1 993b23–24). For more fine-grained accounts of the use Aristotle makes of γνωρίζειν, γιγνώσκειν, and εἰδέναι, see Bronstein (2016a, 19–20) and Burnyeat (2011, 21–22).

to the development of more advanced explanatory knowledge. That Aristotle assigns perception these roles shows that he considers it an epistemically valuable, though nonrational and therefore limited, form of cognition—and that he takes perception to serve not only as a prompt for our learning, but also as a foundation for it, in a sense I will seek to articulate below.

Before presenting these arguments, however, it will be necessary to consider in more detail the cognitive state that constitutes Aristotle's epistemic ideal (ἐπιστήμη). This is necessary because Aristotle's description of this ideal is sometimes taken to rule out the possibility of perception serving as a source of knowledge or non-instrumental epistemic value. Indeed, for rationalist readers ἐπιστήμη is the sole locus of epistemic value, and is grounded only in our rational intuition of certain basic principles—which intuition is itself not grounded in anything further, and so in particular not grounded in any form of perceptual knowledge. I will be engaging in some detail with the motivation for such readings, and the notion of grounding their formulation requires—because they have been fairly influential, but also because they seem to me to illustrate just the sort of dismissive view of perception Aristotle opposes.

1.2 Understanding and Demonstration

Aristotle's ideal cognitive state is the state possessed by someone with an expert theoretical grasp on some body of knowledge. An expert astronomer, for instance, is someone who knows all astronomical facts, and why these facts obtain, and what, in turn, they might serve to explain. An expert astronomer also knows how to prove all this within a regimented deductive system, providing explanatory demonstrations for all truths that admit of explanation, and recognizing those that don't as explanatory primitives. It's doubtful Aristotle thought anyone had fully achieved this kind of mastery, in astronomy or any other field. But he plainly thought of it as an ideal we might reasonably strive to achieve.

This ideal cognitive state is what Aristotle calls ἐπιστήμη, or ἐπιστήμη *simpliciter*, and which he defines in the following passage:[14]

[6] We think we understand (ἐπίστασθαι) something *simpliciter*, and not in the sophistical, incidental manner, when we think we know (γινώσκειν) of the explanation why something is the case that it is its explanation, and also [know] that it's impossible for it to be otherwise. (*APo* I.2 71b9–12)

A few things are clear from this passage. First, ἐπιστήμη is a state associated with a grasp of *explanations* (αἰτίαι): to have ἐπιστήμη is to know the explanation *why* something holds.[15] Second, ἐπιστήμη is a state we bear toward facts we grasp as *necessary*: to have ἐπιστήμη is to know of something why it *must* hold. Finally, Aristotle's definition invokes a kind of knowledge different from ἐπιστήμη: to ἐπίστασθαι *x* is to γιγνώσκειν or γνωρίζειν why *x* must be the case.[16] As I noted above, this other kind of knowledge can be understood in one of two ways—either as a generic or as knowledge in an everyday sense. If Aristotle has the former in mind here, his definition has a familiar genus-differentia form. If he has the latter in mind, his definition invokes an ordinary cognitive state to define an extraordinary cognitive achievement—much as we might invoke the state of belief when attempting a definition of knowledge.

---

[14] Following Barnes (1993, 90) in taking the final clause as dependent on γινώσκειν (on the alternative reading, we might understand something necessary without recognizing it as such). The rest of this section should make clear why this reading gives the better sense, but, as Barnes notes, there's already some evidence in its favor at 71b15, where Aristotle infers from his definition that if we understand something, it can't be otherwise. Aristotle's inference would be redundant if it was already part of the definition that the objects of understanding are necessary truths. On the reading suggested here the inference rests on the fact that knowing is a factive state.

[15] In what follows I will be rendering αἰτία as "explanation" and "cause" interchangeably. Aristotle does not specify which of his four types of cause he has in mind in [6], but his examples in *APo* generally involve formal causes, which at times also seem to include an efficient cause—on which point see Bronstein (2016a, 96–101) and Charles (2010). At *APo* I.24 85b27–35 we also find a case involving final causes. For a broader account of the relationship between Aristotle's causes and his demonstrative system, see Robin (1942, 425–37).

[16] For formulations of the definition with γνωρίζειν, see the parallel passages at *Phys* I.1 184a12 or *Met* A3 983a26 (Aristotle also uses εἰδέναι, e.g. at *APo* I.2 71b31).

In what follows I'll be using "understanding" or "scientific understanding" for ἐπιστήμη, as I've done in the translation above.[17] To my ears, knowledge does not require any grasp of explanations—we can, for instance, know that fire is hot without yet having any idea why fire is hot (cf. [2]). In fact Aristotle thinks this is precisely how our learning typically proceeds: we begin with the knowledge that things are some way, and eventually come to understand why they must be so.[18] Thus on the translation I'm adopting understanding is a kind of knowledge, but not all knowledge qualifies as understanding—understanding is a state we must achieve on the basis of prior, less advanced forms of knowledge, through the sort of inductive learning I will be describing in chapter 3.

Now, in passage [6] and most of *APo* Aristotle focuses on understanding as a state an individual might bear toward the particular *truths* belonging to some scientific domain. Thinking of understanding this way makes possible the sort of demonstrative account Aristotle offers in the rest of *APo* I.2:

[7] We'll say later whether there is another kind of understanding; we do claim here that there is knowing through demonstration.[19]
By "demonstration" I mean a scientific deduction, and by "scientific"

---

[17] See Burnyeat (1981) for a defense of this translation, which he takes Lyons (1963) to support, and see also Kosman (1973) and Barnes (1993, 82) for similar views. Alternative translations include "scientific knowledge," or "expert knowledge," or simply (but, I think, misleadingly) "knowledge." There are admittedly some issues with "understanding" as a translation—to my mind the main one is that Aristotle doesn't seem to think that *incidental, non-simpliciter* understanding (or ἐπιστήμη ὅτι, understanding *that*) requires any knowledge of explanations (cf. *APo* I.13), whereas we must presumably grasp some sort of explanation to count as understanding that something is the case. Still, "understanding" seems to me the best we can do—keeping in mind that understanding something, for Aristotle, is a specific way of knowing it.

[18] See in particular *APo* II.1-2 on knowing the fact that something holds (τὸ ὅτι) before seeking the reason why it does (τὸ διότι), or see *APo* II.19 and *Met* A1 on our path to universal knowledge "why" from more basic forms of knowledge "that," on which more below.

[19] The nondemonstrative understanding alluded to here is presumably our understanding of the indemonstrable principles from which our demonstrations begin—i.e. νοῦς. For νοῦς as a species of understanding, see for instance *APo* I.3 72b18-21. (It's admittedly possible to read Aristotle's remarks in a way that would not make νοῦς *identical* to non-demonstrative understanding—but that will not affect my argument here.)

[deduction] I mean [the sort of deduction] by possessing which we understand [something]. So if to understand is what we've posited it to be [in 71b9–12], demonstrative understanding must be from [premises] that are true, primitive, and immediate, and better known than, prior to, and explanatory of their conclusion; for it's in this way that the principles will be appropriate to what's being proved. There can be a deduction even when these conditions aren't met— but no demonstration, since [such a deduction] won't produce understanding. (*APo* I.2 71b16–25)

On Aristotle's view, then, a demonstration is a deduction that provides the person who grasps it with an understanding of its conclusion: we understand the things we can demonstrate. To count as a demonstration, a deduction must begin from premises which are true, primitive, and immediate. It's clear enough why Aristotle would want these initial premises to be true. To require that they also be *immediate*, or *unmiddled things* (ἄμεσα) is to require that they not have an explanatory "middle term," that is, given some premise *AaC*, that there be no term *B* such that *AaB* and *BaC* where *B* explains why *AaC*.[20] And to require that these premises be *primitives* (πρῶτα) is to require that our understanding of these premises not depend, in some way, on our understanding of prior premises. In what follows I will be spelling out the sense of priority and dependence at play in more detail. But to put my cards on the table, I think the priority in question is just a form of explanatory priority: our understanding of primitives does not depend on any prior understanding because primitives cannot be explained.

In addition to these three requirements, Aristotle tells us that demonstrative premises must be better known than, prior to, and explanatory of their conclusions. Though he doesn't make the point clearly here, Aristotle conceives of demonstrations as chains of explanatory syllogisms, and strictly speaking these last three requirements should be read as requirements on each of the

---

[20] Thus "All planets are non-twinkling" would not be an *immediate* premise, as Aristotle makes plain in *APo* I.13. For *nearness to the earth* explains why planets don't twinkle—as is made clear in the demonstration I reconstruct below. For the precise sense in which a term might explain a demonstrative conclusion, see 2.1 n5.

syllogisms that appear in the context of a demonstration, rather than requirements on the demonstration as a whole. Read this way, his claim is that the premise pairs in each of the syllogisms appearing in a demonstration will have to *explain* that syllogism's conclusion— so that the middle term *B* in the premise pair *AaB*, *BaC* will have to explain why *AaC*, the middle term *C* in the premise pair *AaC*, *CaD* will have to explain why *AaD*, and so on for all syllogisms in a deduction beginning from an initial premise *AaB* and ending with some demonstrated conclusion *AaX* (for some term *X*). The premises in each of these premise pairs will moreover have to be *better known than* (γνωριμώτερα) and *prior to* (πρότερα) their corresponding conclusions—and our demonstrations will thus begin with the premises that are *most* prior (i.e. primitive) and *best* known.[21]

These explanatorily basic, primitive, and best known premises are the *first principles* (ἀρχαί) proper to some scientific domain, and the first principles Aristotle focuses on most in his epistemological writings are *definitions*.[22] Definitions state the essence of the natural kinds studied by some science—so for instance "triangles are three-sided rectilinear figures" might be a geometrical principle, if indeed this is what triangles are essentially, and something no further geometrical fact could explain. Since first principles cannot be explained and demonstrations explain their conclusions, first principles cannot be demonstrated. We therefore understand principles in a

---

[21] All these relations are asymmetric and transitive. I'll be discussing the "better known" relation in more detail below; for now it's enough to note that, as it's being used here, the relation tracks explanatory priority.

[22] At I.2 72a15ff Aristotle tells us that first principles also include *axioms* (ἀξιώματα) and *suppositions* (ὑποθέσεις). Axioms include the sorts of things anyone must assume to demonstrate anything whatsoever, like basic logical laws, and the sorts of premises that might be relevant in a range of different domains, like the claim that equals removed from equals leaves equals (cf. *APo* I.10 76a41). Aristotle's discussion of suppositions is hard to follow—he seems to think of suppositions as existential statements corresponding to some definition (e.g. the statement that triangles are three-sided rectilinear figures, where this is contrasted with a definition expressing only what it is to be a triangle), but it's clear from elsewhere that definitions have existential import (*APo* II.7 92b17–19) and are expressed in subject-predicate form (*APo* II.3 90b3–4). In what follows I'll be considering definitional principles only, since these are the ones that play a central role in Aristotle's account of our learning.

nondemonstrative way—in Aristotle's terminology we "intuit" or have νοῦς of principles.[23]

This demonstrative treatment of scientific understanding gives us a clear picture of what it takes to understand the various propositions that make up some scientific domain: begin with the truths in this domain that can't be explained, and demonstrate those that can through a series explanatory syllogisms meeting the conditions outlined above. But this shouldn't obscure the fact that a holistic understanding of some domain is required before we can understand the individual truths belonging to that domain. For while we can understand specific truths by demonstrating them, we cannot do so in a piecemeal manner, with each demonstration yielding some independent piece of understanding: our ability to demonstrate some proposition depends on a prior understanding of the broader domain to which this proposition belongs.

To see why, consider what it would take for us to understand the conclusion of some demonstration—for instance, the conclusion that planets don't twinkle. As Aristotle tells us in [6], this will require knowledge of the reason *why* planets don't twinkle, and knowledge that it's *necessary* that planets not twinkle, and, as Aristotle tells us in [7], we know both of these things when we grasp a demonstration meeting certain formal requirements. Here is the relevant demonstration in this case:[24]

---

[23] The fact that νοῦς grasps principles doesn't in itself tell us anything about the role νοῦς plays in our *learning* these principles: it only tells us that once we know them in the right way we have νοῦς. Rendering νοῦς as "intuition" can obscure this fact, but I will use this traditional translation for lack of a better alternative (I will also speak of our "noetic grasp" of principles). Thus intuition results from, but does not contribute to, the sort of inductive learning that begins from perception—on which point see Barnes (1993, 267–70) and Lesher (1973, 63–65). It remains the case that νοῦς in a broader, non-technical sense ("thought") does contribute to our learning—on which see 3.6.

[24] See *APo* I.13 78a31ff for this example. To simplify things I'm assuming here that the domain of discourse is restricted to celestial bodies, and that the minor premise is an astronomical first principle and the major premise something that has already been demonstrated (using other principles). If that's right this explanatory syllogism does indeed complete a demonstration meeting the requirements presented in [7]. One might also allow that the minor premise be demonstrated from a principle expressing the definition of planet—nothing hangs on this.

[AaB]   Non-twinkling belongs to everything near the earth
[BaC]   Near the earth belongs to every planet
[AaC]   So non-twinkling belongs to every planet

It's clear enough how this syllogism would yield knowledge of the reason why planets don't twinkle: the explanatory middle term here is "near the earth," and so anyone who recognizes it as a middle term will recognize that planets don't twinkle *because* they're near the earth. It's perhaps a little less clear how this syllogism would yield knowledge that it *must* be the case that planets not twinkle—but the general thought is that the demonstrated proposition involves a reference to the essence of its subject, and so the demonstration as a whole reveals an attribute it must have if it really is to be the kind of subject it is. So in this case if a celestial body really is a planet, then it must be near the earth, and so must not twinkle (since no celestial body near the earth twinkles, which I'm treating here as a demonstrated truth).[25]

Note, however, that the syllogism above supplies us with an understanding why planets don't twinkle only on the condition that we grasp it *as part of a demonstration*, that is, on the condition that we recognize the middle term as providing the explanation for the syllogism's conclusion, the minor premise as expressing an essential fact about its subject, and the major premise as something that was itself demonstrated from astronomical principles. Naturally someone could grasp the demonstration without recognizing the theoretical role played by its premises (or by the terms within its premises), but on Aristotle's view such a person wouldn't *understand* its conclusion:

---

[25] Aristotle would say that non-twinkling belongs to every planet *per se* (καθ' αὐτό), because it follows from essential planetary attributes. It should be clear that Aristotle's *per se* predication isn't our modern notion of necessity—there are many things we would count as necessary today which don't follow from any claims about the essence of their subject. For treatments of the sort of necessity Aristotle did have in mind and its connection with the role definitional principles play as explanations, see Angioni (2014), Angioni (2016), Bronstein (2016a, 43–50), Charles (2000, 245–73), or Charles (2010). As I read Aristotle everything we can understand is necessary, but the conclusions of demonstrations are not of the form "A belongs to every B *in itself*" or "A *must* belong to every B." Demonstrative conclusions are universal affirmative statements—grasping a demonstration in the right sort of way makes clear their necessity.

she might see that the conclusion is true, but wouldn't know why it must be so.[26]

So a demonstration yields understanding of its conclusion only for someone who grasps it in a *theoretically sensitive* manner, as a deduction meeting the requirements presented in [7]. And it's clear that this sort of grasp is possible only for someone who understands the scientific domain pertinent to the demonstrated conclusion. For in order to see that a deduction is in fact a demonstration, one has to recognize its initial premises as explanatorily primitive first principles, and all the middle terms appearing in the demonstration's series of syllogistic inferences as explanations for the conclusion drawn from them. But this is possible only for someone who knows all the truths in the relevant scientific domain, and the explanatory relations between them—that is, someone who understands the relevant scientific domain *as a whole*. In the demonstration above, for instance, we will understand why planets don't twinkle only if we recognize the minor premise as an astronomical first principle. So we have to know that no astronomical fact explains why planets are near the earth. And this requires an appreciation of all other astronomical facts, and what these facts explain.[27]

Two caveats. First, it may be (for all Aristotle tells us) that an expert could know that nothing explains her primitives without knowing, of each fact in her domain of expertise, that that fact doesn't explain her primitives. But some appreciation of the domain's explanatory structure would be required nonetheless—even if it does not quite amount to, say, *de dicto* knowledge of the explanatory role played by each and every fact that comprises that domain. Second, Aristotle allows that we could provide imperfect definitions based on an

---

[26] She would, in other words, find herself in much the same position as someone inferring that planets are near from the fact that they don't twinkle, and that things that don't twinkle are near (i.e. switching the A and B terms in the syllogism above). As Aristotle explains in *APo* I.13, this person only understands her conclusion in a derivative sense (she has ἐπιστήμη ὅτι, not ἐπιστήμη τὸ διότι), because she doesn't grasp the explanation *why* planets are near, even though her inference does allow her to know *that* they are near. See also Kosman (1973, 283–84) on this point.

[27] I side here with Kosman (1973, 389) and McKirahan (1992, 243), *contra* Ferejohn (2009, 78–79). A further defense of the claim that knowing principles requires recognizing them as explanatory primitives will be given in chapter 3.

incomplete set of facts (see e.g. *An* I.1 402b22–403a2). So even if, in the ideal case, we would have all the domain-specific facts at our disposal, we can achieve some degree of astronomical understanding based on an incomplete set of astronomical facts, or perhaps with all the facts but an incomplete grasp of their explanatory relations (e.g. an understanding why *planets* move as they do without the corresponding understanding of the motions of comets and other celestial bodies).[28] Indeed it seems plausible, though Aristotle never directly suggests this, that any complete understanding of some domain would be developed on the basis of imperfect forms of understanding of this sort. Even in these non-ideal cases, however, understanding some specific proposition will require an understanding of the broader domain of which that proposition is part, and an appreciation of its explanatory role in that domain.

This holistic conception of understanding is something Aristotle inherits from Plato.[29] In the *Theaetetus*, for instance, it's agreed that someone who *knows* how to spell "Theaetetus" but thinks "Theodorus" must start with a τ does not in fact understand the first syllable of either name (207e5–208a5). It's further agreed that this argument can be repeated for each of the syllables in Theaetetus' name, so that even someone who knows the ordering of each of its letters (and knows why this ordering must proceed as it does) would nonetheless fail to *understand* its spelling if she could not also spell similar names like "Theodorus." In other words, someone must understand *spelling* before she can properly be said to understand the spelling of any specific word, even if she is correct about that specific word's spelling, and knows why that word must be spelled as it is.[30] An account

---

[28] In fact right after his account of demonstration Aristotle tells us that an expert could know "some or all principles" (*APo* I.2 75a28). As I understand this claim, an *actual* expert would have to know all the principles relevant to her domain, but we could nonetheless ascribe some degree of understanding to someone who can produce demonstrations using only some of these principles.

[29] On this point see also Burnyeat (1981, 135–36). On holistic epistemology in Plato, see for instance Harte (2002, 148–49, 206–7), Nehamas (1985, 20), or Smith (1998, 159–61).

[30] At *Philebus* 18c7–d2 Socrates says that the god who invented letters saw that "none of us could gain any knowledge of a single one of them, taken by itself, without understanding them all," and called "the one link that somehow unifies them all" the craft of literacy (γραμματικὴ τέχνη).

of what it takes to understand the spelling of specific words could surely be given—but it would assume a prior understanding of spelling itself, a craft applicable to words of any sort. Likewise, Aristotle's demonstrative account explains what it takes to understand specific conclusions—but assumes a prior understanding of the domain to which these various conclusions belong.

In this respect Aristotle's treatment of scientific understanding is similar to his treatment of the moral virtues. Just as virtues like courage or generosity, Aristotle thinks of understanding as an excellent state or disposition (a ἕξις) we might develop in our souls. In the practical case, the virtuous person has a disposition to decide and be motivated to act in certain ways when facing certain circumstances. In the theoretical case, the virtuous person has a disposition to explain a range of facts by demonstrating them—in the ideal case, by demonstrating them from their most basic explanatory grounds. Thus Aristotle characterizes understanding as a "disposition to demonstrate (ἕξις ἀποδεικτική)" at EN VI.3 1139b31–32, and moral virtue as a "disposition to decide (ἕξις προαιρετική)" at EN II.2 1106b36 (cf. also EE II.10 1227b5–11).[31] It remains true, of course, that a morally virtuous person will *know* what to do in a range of particular situations, and why to do it; and likewise an intellectually virtuous person will *know* a range of propositions pertinent to some domain, and why these propositions must hold. But such knowledge is best seen as a manifestation of their respective virtues; and these virtues best conceived as relations borne toward some theoretical or practical domain, rather than particular facts within that domain, which we would grasp in isolation from each other. To understand something, for Aristotle as for Plato, is to know something about its place within some explanatory structure.

---

[31] Strictly speaking this would have to be qualified: an expert understands, but would not be disposed to demonstrate, definitional principles. Still, an expert's understanding of her principles is informed by her knowledge of their explanatory status—that is, of the fact that we can demonstrate (and thus explain) everything on their basis, and that they are not themselves demonstrable (and are thus unexplainable). I take it there is an analogue in the moral case, where the virtuous have νοῦς of some of their deliberative premises, and know not to further deliberate about these premises before deciding on some course of action (cf. EN VI.11 1143a35–b5).

Exegetical considerations aside, this seems to me the right thing to say about theoretical understanding. A geometer's expertise doesn't lie in her knowledge of geometrical axioms and theorems, or even in her knowing a list of proofs connecting the two, but rather in her knowing in general *how to prove geometrical theorems*, and perhaps also in her appreciating certain theoretical connections between geometrical results that aren't obviously related. Theoretical expertise is thus synoptic—it requires a global understanding how certain truths depend on one another. It's also reflective—an expert understands her field, and also knows what it is she understands, and how it differs from what she doesn't.[32] Naturally an expert geometer will know all sorts of propositions and their corresponding proofs. But specifying the propositions and proofs she knows is a poor way to describe her geometrical expertise: her expertise lies primarily in her reflective, synoptic understanding of the contours and internal explanatory and inferential structure of the domain of geometrical truths.

So here are the main points so far. Aristotle's cognitive ideal is ἐπιστήμη, or scientific understanding. In *APo* I.2 Aristotle tells us that we understand something when we know why it must be the case, and explains that a certain kind of explanatory demonstration can yield such understanding. To grasp a demonstration in a way that will yield understanding, we must recognize the theoretical role played by the demonstration's premises—something that depends on our having a reflective and synoptic appreciation of the broader explanatory structure of the domain to which they belong. Scientific understanding is thus best interpreted as a systematic understanding of some domain of explanatorily connected facts—an understanding that manifests itself whenever an expert proves why some particular truth must hold through the kind of demonstrative argument Aristotle describes in the opening chapters of *APo*.

---

[32] Another Platonic insight I take Aristotle to endorse. For demonstrations begin from definitional principles, and taken together these principles demarcate the subject matter being treated by some science. An expert recognizes such principles as principles, and thereby knows the limits of her understanding. Thus an expert geometer will not only have the methodological knowledge necessary to prove geometrical results. She will also be able recognize when some proposition doesn't admit of geometrical proof: a disposition to demonstrate is also a disposition to not demonstrate when demonstration is inapt—because the target proposition is a principle, or belongs to some other domain.

1.3 Rationalism and First Principles

Aristotle's account of ἐπιστήμη, as I've presented it, doesn't explicitly tell us anything about how our grasp of demonstrative conclusions would be justified. But it's not unreasonable to read a concern for justification into his account. After all, Aristotle tells us that an expert's understanding of her demonstrated conclusions is grounded in her intuition of certain principles, which intuition is not itself grounded in any of its demonstrative consequences. He takes the structure of our understanding of some domain to be given by an asymmetric and transitive priority relation—our knowledge of demonstrative premises must somehow be *prior* to our knowledge of the conclusions we infer on their basis. And he tells us, in passages I will consider in more detail below, that an expert will be unshakably *convinced* of the truths she can demonstrate, and more convinced of the truth of her premises than she is of their consequences, and thus convinced of the truth of her principles most of all.

In light of these claims, a number of commentators have taken the view that first principles are not just explanatory primitives, but justificatory ones, too—that an expert invokes them to justify whatever she can demonstrate on their basis, and takes the principles themselves to be justified only by some brute, non-inferential form of rational intuition (which is either identical to or provided by νοῦς, as the view is usually developed). I will be referring to readings along these lines as *rationalist* readings, and to those who endorse them as *rationalists*, where this should be understood as a form of rational foundationalism about justification—all justification must ultimately issue from our rational intuition of certain principles, and this intuition is not itself justified by other means.[33]

---

[33] Frede (1996, 172) and Irwin (1988, 132–36) provide characteristic examples of this kind of take on Aristotle's epistemology—but see also Anagnostopoulos (2009, 105–11) and Fine (2010, 136–55) for more recent arguments in its defense. Views in a similar spirit can be found in Ferejohn (2009, 66, 75), Le Blond (1939, 127, 136–39), Ross (1949, 49–50), and Tuominen (2007, 182–83). Opposition to rationalist readings comes in many forms. Some argue that justification ultimately issues from perception, and so take Aristotle to be an empirically minded foundationalist (I take it views of this sort are expressed in Bolton (1987, 151ff), Bolton (1991, 16–17), Gotthelf (1987, 229–30), and McKirahan (1992, 257ff)). Others think that Aristotle is not a foundationalist at

It should be noted up front that the notion of justification invoked by rationalists is a highly restrictive one. After all, there is surely some everyday sense in which we can justify our beliefs in demonstrable conclusions without the sophisticated sort of demonstration described above. For example, we might be justified in believing that planets don't twinkle simply because we've observed this to be the case— even if we aren't able to supply a demonstration of this fact from astronomical principles, as an expert astronomer would. Or we might have justified beliefs whose contents match those of definitional principles, despite not having an expert's intuition of the principles in question.[34] So our intuition of principles could not be our ultimate source of justification in any humdrum, everyday sense.

The rationalist thought, rather, is that justification *in the strict sense* is expert justification, and found only in the demonstrative context— and must therefore ultimately derive from an intuition of principles. Everyday justification would then either not count as justification at all, or else count as justification only in an extended sense, insofar as it approximates the sort of justification supplied by demonstration.[35] Now, to claim that there is no justification (strictly speaking) outside the demonstrative context is not to deny that perception plays a critical role for Aristotle. Nor do rationalists need to dismiss Aristotle's account of the cognitive development leading from perception and memory to practical experience and, ultimately, νοῦς of scientific principles, as he presents it in *APo* II.19. On their view, the path from

all—that he conceives of justification as a matter of coherence between our beliefs, and even allows for a kind of justificatory circle between our perceptions and our intuition of principles (see Goldin (2013) for a recent expression of this view). Others yet think Aristotle takes the establishment of principles to be achieved dialectically, and to be a matter of coherence with ἔνδοξα which need not be empirically grounded (a view that goes back at least as far as Owen (1961)). In many cases these views stem from broader debates about the role of dialectic and the nature of ἔνδοξα in Aristotle, and whether or not they could be a source of justification for scientific principles—a helpful review and critique of which can be found in Frede (2012).

[34] We might justifiably believe, for instance, that triangles are three-sided rectilinear figures, even though we do not recognize this as an explanatorily primitive, indemonstrable geometrical principle, as an expert geometer would (cf. *APo* I.33 89a23–b6).

[35] Rationalists tend to endorse the more stringent version of their view, on which there is no justification at all that is not supplied by demonstration or the intuition of demonstrative principles (see below for some clear examples). For now I will focus on these more stringent views, but I will also consider the possibility of rationalist views that allow for inexpert forms of justification in 1.6.

perception to νοῦς would still be of genealogical or psychological interest, as a record of the *causes* of our coming to form some intuition. Here is how two prominent rationalists put the point:

> Experience and familiarity with appearances are useful to us as a way of approaching first principles; they may be psychologically indispensable as ways to form the right intuitions. But they form no part of the justification of first principles. When we come to have the right intuition we are aware of the principle as self-evident, with no external justification. That is its real nature, and that is what we grasp after we have used ordinary methods of inquiry. The acquisition of *nous* is not meant to be magical, entirely independent of inquiry. Nor, however, is it simply a summary of the inquiry, or a conclusion that depends on the inquiry for its warrant.[36]

> [T]o the extent that [Aristotle's account of our cognitive development] is a natural process based on perception, the relation between our perceptions and our knowledge of first principles, or whatever knowledge we have by reason, is a natural, a causal, rather than an epistemic relation. Our knowledge of first principles is not epistemically, but only causally, based on perception. And this is how Aristotle can be an extreme rationalist and still constantly insist on the fundamental importance of perception for knowledge.[37]

Thus on this sort of view perception and experience, necessary though they may be to bring about our cognitive development, are not states that provide the specific sort of justification or epistemic support first principles require. It's only when we intuit these principles— and thereby appreciate their role as justificatory primitives—that they provide the proper sort of grounding for our demonstrative conclusions.

Now, rationalists do not say much about the notion of justification they invoke when making claims of this sort. This makes their view

---

[36] Irwin (1988, 136).
[37] Frede (1996, 172).

somewhat elusive. But we can see, at a minimum, that they rely on a distinction between the "causal" or "psychological" contributions of various states, on the one hand, and their "epistemic" or "justificatory" role, on the other—a distinction which can be understood on the model of our contemporary distinction between the context of discovery and the context of justification. Here is Popper on the topic:

> The initial stage, the act of conceiving or inventing a theory, seems to me neither to call for logical analysis nor to be susceptible of it. The question how it happens that a new idea occurs to a man—whether it is a musical theme, a dramatic conflict, or a scientific theory—may be of great interest to empirical psychology; but it is irrelevant to the logical analysis of scientific knowledge. This latter is concerned not with questions of fact (Kant's *quid facti?*), but only with questions of justification or validity (Kant's *quid juris?*). Its questions are of the following kind. Can a statement be justified? And if so, how? [...] Accordingly I shall distinguish sharply between the process of conceiving a new idea, and the methods and results of examining it logically.[38]

So as Popper sees things, the psychological or cognitive underpinnings of our learning are matters of fact, and on their own these could not tell us anything about why we should believe certain claims, or how we should conceive of their justification, which are inherently normative questions. On this model, stories about our cognitive development might describe how we come to form some thought or articulate some idea, but epistemic norms like justification simply would not apply in this context.

The rationalist reading of Aristotle, then, is that justification only occurs in the context of a demonstrative science. Anyone might look at the sky and observe that planets don't twinkle. But this would

---

[38] Popper (1959, 7–8). In a similar vein, here is Frege on discovery and justification in mathematics: "the question of how we arrive at the content of a judgement should be kept distinct from the other question, Whence do we derive the justification for its assertion?" (1884, 3). For a similar take on rationalist readings of Aristotle, see Lennox (2011, 27).

tell us how our beliefs about planets are formed, and nothing more. Only through a demonstration can such a belief be justified (in the strict sense) and thus become a piece of scientific understanding. And that sort of justification—the justification had by someone with understanding—must ultimately be grounded in an intuition of demonstrative principles. So there are really two claims here: first, that Aristotle conceives of justification in this highly restrictive sense—a sense on which you cannot be justified in believing something you haven't intuited or demonstrated—and second, that Aristotle thinks an expert's rational intuition of her principles must be the ultimate foundation for any such justification.

Direct and indirect arguments have been made for these claims. The direct arguments aim to show that there is some part of Aristotle's account of scientific understanding that is well understood in terms of justification, conceived of as a norm that applies exclusively in the scientific context, after a grasp of principles has been achieved— and that Aristotle is a rational foundationalist about this sort of justification. The indirect arguments begin by noting that Aristotle never spells out any norms that would govern nondemonstrative inquiry, and infer from this, on principles of charity, that he must have intended his account of our cognitive development as a psychological description only. I think rationalist arguments fall short in both cases. In the rest of this chapter I will focus on the direct evidence. I'll address the indirect motivation in the next.

1.4 Understanding and Priority

Recall that Aristotle's principles are *primitives*; that is, *prior* to whatever we demonstrate on their basis. It's agreed by all that principles are *explanatory* primitives. But on the rationalist view principles are also justificatory primitives: they serve both as our ultimate explanations and, when properly understood, as our ultimate source of justification. This is supposed to follow from the use to which Aristotle puts his notion of priority when discussing our knowledge of principles and their demonstrative consequences—which he does most clearly in the following passage:

[8] they [=the premises in our demonstrations; first principles most of all] must be explanations and better known and prior [relative to our demonstrated conclusions]—explanations because we only understand something when we know its explanation, prior since they are explanations, and known beforehand not only in the sense that we comprehend what they mean, but also that we know them to be the case. (*APo* I.2 71b29–33)

Aristotle is elaborating here on three of the requirements on demonstrative premises presented in [7]. The first requirement is that these premises serve (via their shared middle term) as *explanations* for the conclusion being demonstrated. This follows straightforwardly from the requirement that demonstrations yield understanding, together with the definition of understanding in [6]. The second requirement is that these premises be *prior to* the conclusion derived on their basis: Aristotle simply states that this must be the case since the premises are explanations. The third requirement is that these premises be *better known than* the conclusion derived on their basis. Aristotle's discussion here is hard to follow: in his explanation "known beforehand" (προγινωσκόμενα) has replaced "better known" (γνωριμώτερα), but it's not immediately clear why these two relations would correspond, or why we would have to know the premises of our demonstrations before their conclusions.

Before addressing this difficulty, it'll be important to consider the next few lines, where Aristotle elaborates on these last two relations:

[9] Things are prior and better known in two ways; for it isn't the same to be prior by nature and prior in relation to us, nor to be better known and better known to us. I call prior and better known in relation to us items which are nearer to perception, prior and better known *simpliciter* items which are further away. What is most universal is furthest away, and the particulars are nearest—these are opposite to each other. (*APo* I.2 71b33–72a5)

Things can thus be prior and better known in two ways: according to an objective, "natural" order of explanation, on the one hand, and according to the order in which *we*, as non-experts, might go about learning things—i.e. typically starting from what we perceive.[39] In passage [8], Aristotle clearly means to tell us that principles are prior and better known *by nature*: he often emphasizes that scientific principles are the things farthest from perception and most universal.[40] And this natural order is precisely the order explanatory demonstrations are meant to preserve. So the kind of priority proper to first principles must track explanatory priority—things are prior and better known by nature when they're closer to the fundamental explanatory grounds for some scientific domain (so that principles are primitive and best known by nature).

Now, Aristotle also tells us, in [8], that principles will have to be known before their conclusions—that we will have to comprehend what they mean but also know that what they express is true (εἰδέναι ὅτι ἔστιν; cf. *APo* I.1 71a11–16). What he means by this is not that we would have to know principles before *learning* their demonstrative consequences. Indeed Aristotle often tells us the opposite—he tells us that principles are the last things we would learn, and that their discovery requires our already having gathered the facts pertinent to the scientific domain in question.[41] Thus it might be definitional that planets are heavenly bodies near the earth, but on his view we would learn this *after* gathering a range of observations about planets (e.g. that they do not twinkle, that they move only within the zodiac, and so on), even though the planets' proximity to the earth explains what we observe. So what Aristotle has in mind here is that we must have a certain kind of knowledge of principles before developing a certain kind of knowledge of their demonstrative consequences—we come to appreciate facts differently once we can demonstrate them,

---

[39] Unlike what's better known "by nature," what's better known "to us" depends on the subject—as Aristotle makes clear at *Top* VI.4 141b36ff and in passage [15], below. As I understand the claim here, perceptual knowledge is the knowledge that is (typically) better known to us *early on*, before we have made any progress in our inquiry. Different things can become better known to us as our inquiry progresses. We count as experts (i.e. have understanding) when what's better known to us just is what's better known by nature. But since Aristotle is *contrasting* what's better known to us with what's better known by nature, he presumably does not take "us" to be experts in this passage.

[40] See for instance *Top* VI.4 141b36ff, *Met* A9 992b24ff, or *Met* Z3 1029b3ff.

[41] See for instance *APr* I.30 46a17–27, *APo* II.1 89b29–31, *HA* I.6 491a7–14, or *PA* II.1 646a8–12.

and thereby come to understand things we already knew in some ordinary way, but we do not go from ignorance to knowledge by demonstration.[42]

Rationalist interpreters take Aristotle to be telling us two distinct things in passages [8] and [9]. First, that an expert's principles serve as *explanatory* primitives, and second, that they serve, when intuited, as basic sources of justification (as *epistemic* primitives).[43] Since the priority at play in [8] is priority "by nature," this would mean that an expert's intuition of first principles is objectively the right basis for justifying demonstrated claims, in addition to being (objectively) the right basis for explaining them. Thus on the rationalist reading, the claim that principles must be "known before" their conclusions is meant to guarantee that an expert's scientific understanding be *justified* in the right sort of way—and the characterization of these principles as "prior" to their demonstrative consequences is simply an expression of this justificatory precedence.

But what Aristotle actually says about epistemic priority (or "priority in knowledge") doesn't support interpretations of this sort. Here is the relevant passage in Aristotle's lexicon—the only place the notion is clearly spelled out:

[10] Things are called prior in another sense, on which what's prior in knowledge is [treated] as if it were also prior *simpliciter*. Of these the things prior in account are different from those prior in perception,

---

[42] Arguably coming to understand what we already know also counts as a form of learning for Aristotle—on which point see Bronstein (2016a, 31–42). We do learn the conclusions of our demonstrations in that sense, even if we do not *discover* them by demonstration.

[43] The second point need not follow from the first: in some cases we might initially know p without knowing anything about what might explain it, and then infer q as an explanation for p. The explanatory and epistemic orders would thus be opposite: p would be epistemically prior, but explanatorily posterior, to q. (In our example above, the planets' non-twinkling would be epistemically prior, but explanatorily posterior, to their being near the earth—our observation that planets don't twinkle helps justify our belief that they are near the earth, but their being near the earth explains why they don't twinkle.) On the rationalist reading, then, Aristotle is taking a stance in affirming that for an expert these two orders coincide—though there is of course a difficulty in stating things this way since rationalists think there is strictly speaking no justification for anyone but an expert. See Irwin (1988, 124–25, 134–36) for a more elaborate defense of these points.

for in account universals are prior, and in perception particulars.
(*Met* Δ11 1018b30–34)

Aristotle distinguishes two senses of epistemic priority here: epistemic priority "in account" (κατὰ τὸν λόγον) and epistemic priority "in perception" (κατὰ τὴν αἴσθησιν). This distinction is plainly meant to mirror the distinction (in [9]) between things prior by nature and things prior to us: in both cases, universals are prior in one sense (in account, by nature), and particulars in another (in perception, to us).

Both forms of priority fall under a general definition: to say that p is epistemically prior to q is to say that our knowledge of p doesn't depend on our knowledge of q.[44] In this definition "knowledge" is invoked in a *generic* sense, and the two species of epistemic priority in [10] correspond to the species of knowledge involved.[45] If the knowledge in question is understanding, then epistemic priority tracks explanatory priority: p can't be prior to q if q is part of the explanation why p, for then our understanding p would depend on our understanding q. This species of epistemic priority (epistemic priority "in account") is just a correlate of priority "by nature." However if the knowledge in question is knowledge of a different sort, then epistemic priority need not track explanatory priority: our knowing p might depend on our perceiving q, even if it turns out that p explains q. This species of epistemic priority (epistemic priority "in perception") is a correlate of priority "to us," or at least priority "to us" as we typically stand at the beginning of our inquiry, when we are not yet experts in the relevant domain. To keep this distinction straight I will use

---

[44] It's a bit later, at *Met* Δ11 1019a1ff, that Aristotle indicates that all senses of priority are cases in which certain things can exist without others, but not vice versa; so that, in the epistemic case presented here, it would be possible for some knowledge to exist in a subject without some other knowledge existing in that subject, but not vice versa. So "depends" in this formulation is shorthand for "depends *for its existence.*"

[45] I thus agree, on the surface, with Barnes' analysis: "there is an obvious analysis of '*P* is primitive,' viz. 'there is no *Q* prior to *P*,' i.e. 'there is no *Q* from which knowledge of *P* must be derived'" (1993, 94). However Barnes seems to take the "knowledge" in his formulation to denote *ordinary* knowledge. I think this is a mistake: "knowledge" is used in a generic sense, and only one species of priority involves ordinary knowledge.

"prior$_e$" for the former kind of epistemic priority, and "prior$_t$" for the latter.[46]

It's plain that principles are primitives in the sense that they are most prior$_e$. This leaves it open that principles would *not* be primitives in the sense that they are most prior$_t$ (i.e. primitive "to us," where "we" are beginners). Indeed, we should expect them not to be. For on Aristotle's definition, as reconstructed above, the knowledge that is most prior$_t$ is a form of knowledge that does not depend for its existence on our already having knowledge *of any sort*—and Aristotle explicitly tells us that this form of knowledge is provided by perception (*APo* II.19 99b32–35, on which more below). What Aristotle is saying in [8], then, is only that principles are most prior$_e$, which is just to say that our understanding of these principles does not depend on our understanding of anything else. And this simply follows from the fact that principles are explanatory primitives: our understanding of them could not depend on any further piece of understanding, for *that* understanding would then serve as part of an explanation for principles that are, by definition, unexplainable.[47]

So it's no surprise that Aristotle, in [8], tersely invokes our principles' explanatory role to support the claim that these principles must be prior to demonstrated conclusions ($\pi\rho\acute{o}\tau\epsilon\rho\alpha$, $\epsilon\emph{ἴ}\pi\epsilon\rho$ $\alpha\emph{ἴ}\tau\iota\alpha$, 71b31). Nor is it surprising that Aristotle often uses "immediate" (i.e. unexplainable) and "primitive" interchangeably.[48] This is not just a loose manner of putting things: the fact that our principles are explanatory primitives directly entails their status as epistemic primitives in account—i.e. as most prior$_e$. It does not entail, however, that they are most prior$_t$. In fact it suggests the opposite, since Aristotle

---

[46] The choice of subscripts here is meant to reflect Aristotle's own labels ("in account," "in perception"). As I understand him, Aristotle has in mind *explanatory* accounts, specifically, and is invoking perception as a source of knowledge that would *temporally* precede the development of any other, more sophisticated kind of knowledge—in inexpert subjects, that is.

[47] Of course it's consistent with this reading of [8] that Aristotle would *also* be concerned with justification. My claim is not that [8] disproves rationalist views—only that it does not count as evidence in their favor.

[48] This is true throughout *APo*, but for some clear examples see I.2 71b27, I.2 72a7, I.3 72b20, or I.9 75b39.

thinks we learn explanations after learning what they explain, and so learn principles last of all.

Aristotle's claim in [8], then, is only that the sort of explanatorily sensitive knowledge that constitutes an *understanding* of some demonstrated conclusion (as Aristotle describes it in [6]) will depend on an explanatorily sensitive understanding of the premises from which that conclusion is derived: to recognize the explanations for certain conclusions as explanations will require recognizing certain premises as explanatory primitives. Thus the sense in which an expert must "know" principles before knowing her conclusions is, specifically, that she must *understand* her principles before *understanding* her conclusions—which is just to say (on my reading of [10]) that principles are prior$_e$ and better known by nature, in the sense at play in [9]. Intuition, on this view, is just an understanding of principles as explanatory primitives, not something that supplies our demonstrative conclusions with a special sort of justification.

If this is right, Aristotle's discussion of priority does not itself indicate any concern with the justificatory structure of scientific understanding. Principles are indeed epistemic primitives (most prior$_e$), but this is just a reflection of their status as *explanatory* primitives. Since Aristotle is a foundationalist about explanation, he is a foundationalist about this sort of epistemic priority. But nowhere does he suggest that the principles that serve as ultimate explanations for an expert's demonstrative conclusions would *also* have to serve as the ultimate reasons an expert invokes as justification for her various demonstrative conclusions, as rationalists would have it. For all Aristotle says here, an expert might be justified in believing that planets don't twinkle because she has observed it, even if her observations do not explain their non-twinkling. Indeed his emphasis on perception's supplying our most prior$_t$ knowledge suggests such a view.[49]

---

[49] Suggests but does not establish—for the dependence between temporally prior and posterior knowledge is not explicitly spelled out. Rationalists might thus insist that perception is indeed most prior$_t$, but that this is because it serves as a causal precursor the rest of our learning, not because it serves to justify anything. I will be addressing this sort of response in our next chapter.

1.5 Understanding and Conviction

Aside from Aristotle's discussion of priority, the main place he may seem to exhibit rationalist tendencies is in his description of an expert's conviction about her principles and their consequences. Here is the key passage:[50]

> [11] Since you must know and be convinced of something [you demonstrate] by having the sort of deduction we call a demonstration, and there is such a deduction in virtue of those things being true—the things from which [the deduction] proceeds—you must not only know the primitives beforehand (all or some of them) but also know them *better*. For something always holds better of that because of which it holds, for instance, that because of which we love is better loved. So since we know and are convinced of [some conclusion] because of the primitives, we know better and are better convinced of these [primitives], because it's because of them that we know and are convinced of posterior things. (*APo* I.2 72a25–32) [...]
>
> Anyone who's going to have understanding through demonstration must not only know the principles better and be better convinced of them than what's demonstrated—there must also be nothing more convincing or better known for him among the opposites of the principles (from which there will be a deduction of the contrary mistake), since anyone with *simpliciter* understanding cannot be convinced otherwise [is ἀμετάπειστος]. (*APo* I.2 72a37–b4)

Thus first principles are not just explanatory primitives, and grasped by an expert as such—they are also, it seems, the things an expert is most *certain* about, to the point where nothing could convince her of their falsity. The level of conviction an expert displays toward various propositions will moreover correspond to their demonstrative priority: her conviction will be strongest in the case of first principles,

---

[50] On this passage see for instance Anagnostopoulos (2009, 107), Irwin (1988, 132), or Salmieri (2014, 5). I elide a small portion of it that does not affect the main conclusions.

and less and less strong as we move down the explanatory tree formed by their demonstrative consequences. For, as Aristotle explains, an expert will be more convinced of the causes of the things she's convinced about—and ultimately all her demonstrative conclusions hold *because* of certain principles, and so an expert will be convinced of these most of all.

The sort of "conviction" or "trust" (πίστις) at play here is not something that merely describes the confidence an expert might subjectively display toward her principles and their consequences.[51] When Aristotle says that an expert is most convinced of her principles, he means that an expert is most convinced of her principles *qua expert*: an expert's expertise is manifested in her taking her principles to be more secure than their demonstrative consequences. And part of what it is to be an expert is to be convinced of things that are, objectively, the things of which one ought to be convinced—an expert trusts the things that are objectively trustworthy. So to say that an expert will πιστεύειν X "more" or "better" than Y (or that for an expert X will be πιστότερον than Y) is to say that her belief in X will be held more strongly than her belief in Y because X and Y should be believed to just that degree.[52]

Now, rationalists may seem to have a plausible explanation for this claim: an expert will trust her demonstrative principles more than their consequences because she takes her intuition of these principles to *justify* whatever she derives on their basis. On this sort of view the justificatory role played by an expert's intuition of principles explains the confidence she displays toward these principles and their

---

[51] Aristotle uses πίστις to refer both to a cognitive state (a conviction, or a strongly held belief), and to the factors that contribute or ought to contribute to the development of such a state—so that, for instance, an argument or a speaker's character might count as types of πίστις. For the first sense, see e.g. *APo* II.3 90b14 and *An* III.3 428a20, or, in its more common verbal form (as in [11]), *Rhet* I.2 1356a6 or *Rhet* I.2 1366a11. For the second, see e.g. *Rhet* I.1 1354a15 or *Rhet* I.1 1355a4–5. For more on Aristotle's usage, see Grimaldi (1957).

[52] I remain neutral on whether we should identify πίστις with belief, and also on the relationship between πίστις and cognitive states like δόξα or ὑπόληψις. What matters here is that we can πιστεύειν things to various degrees, and that there is no restriction on the object of our πίστις (so that we can πιστεύειν demonstrative premises and conclusions, but we can also πιστεύειν any everyday fact). See Moss and Schwab (2019) for an account of the relationship between πίστις, δόξα, ὑπόληψις, and belief.

consequences. And the fact that first principles serve as justificatory primitives explains why an expert would never be convinced of competing alternatives, or seek to ground her conviction about principles in anything else: the expert is ἀμετάπειστος simply because there is no source of justification more basic than her intuition of principles.[53]

But Aristotle's views on conviction are more nuanced than what passage [11] suggests on its own. Consider, for instance, his remarks about principles and observation in the following methodological passages:[54]

[12] [The followers of Empedocles and Democritus], because of their love of these [principles], fall into the attitude of men who undertake the defense of a position in argument. For holding their principles as truth, they submit to everything that follows, as though some principles did not require to be judged from their results, and above all from their end. And that end, which in the case of productive understanding is the product, in the case of our understanding of nature is the phenomena, which are always authoritatively given by perception. (*Cael* III.7 306a11–17)

It's a strike against the followers of Empedocles and Democritus, then, that they fail to abandon their principles in the face of conflicting phenomena. In a similar vein, Aristotle tells us in *GA* that

---

[53] Of course this is not the only possible explanation for Aristotle's remarks. Some critics of rationalism argue that we should take the conviction at play here to reflect an expert's confidence *that her principles are explanatorily basic*, and *that demonstrations explain their conclusions*, rather than her confidence in the principles themselves (cf. Bronstein (2016a, 128) and Goldin (2013, 211–13)). Others have sought to draw a close conceptual connection between the claim that certain things are "better known by nature" and the claim that an expert will be "more" or "better" convinced of these things, and to distinguish demonstrative conviction and conviction based on experience (cf. Burnyeat (1981, 128) and McKirahan (1992, 35)). Though I sympathize with these views, it's important that Aristotle claims that an expert trusts her principles most of all, not that she trusts the status of her principles, or the fact that her principles are principles. And if there are indeed two forms of conviction, more would have to be said about the difference between the two, and about cases where they conflict—points I will consider in more detail below.

[54] The translation here is adapted from Stocks'.

[13] This is what seems to hold for the generation of bees, both from argument and from the things that are thought to be their characteristics. These characteristics haven't yet been sufficiently grasped, and if some day they are, we should then be more convinced by perception than arguments, and by arguments only if what they show agrees with the phenomena. (*GA* III.10 760b27–33)

Or again, in *GC*, that

[14] Lack of experience makes you less able to take a comprehensive view of the agreed upon [facts]. That's why those who are at home with natural [phenomena] are more able to lay down the sorts of principles that are [systematically] connected; while those who, from much [abstract] reasoning, have become unobservant of the [underlying] subject matter, are too quick to "prove" things with an eye toward [just] a few observations. (*GC* I.2 316a5–10)

These sorts of remarks are typical—Aristotle makes them often.[55] And they seem to indicate that principles are not premises we should be absolutely certain about, in the sense that we would believe them whatever their consequences. Demonstrations and their principles, these passages suggest, are worth believing only to the extent that they appropriately recover and explain our observations. If this is right, the claim that an expert must be ἀμετάπειστος and convinced of her principles more than their consequences should not rule out her giving up these principles were it discovered that they conflict with what we can observe.

Implicit in Aristotle's treatment of conviction, then, lies a separation between two distinct *sources* of conviction: conviction that stems from *argument*, on the one hand, and conviction that stems from *perception* or *observation* (broadly construed) on the other. There's good

---

[55] Earlier in *Cael* a similar charge is leveled at the Pythagoreans: "they are not seeking for theories and causes to account for the phenomena, but rather forcing the phenomena and trying to accommodate them to certain theories and opinions of their own" (II.13 293a25–27). See also *MA* I.1 698a11–14, where Aristotle emphasizes that universal explanations must always accommodate (or "fit," ἐφαρμόττειν) the particular phenomena they explain, and *EN* X.8 1179a16–22, where the same sentiment is voiced about general ethical claims.

independent evidence for separating these two sources of conviction when reading [11]: in the *Topics* Aristotle often affirms that someone with understanding cannot be convinced out of her conclusions, but always qualifies the claim by saying that an understander cannot be so convinced *by argument* (ὑπὸ λόγου).[56] This qualification is significant: not all our forms of knowledge are arrived at by argument, and *perceptual* knowledge in particular is often distinguished by Aristotle from λόγος-involving cognitive states.[57] So one way to understand passage [11] in light of Aristotle's methodological remarks is to take it to be concerned with just one source of conviction: conviction by *pure* argument, that is, by forms of argument that do not invoke as evidence our observations, or the fit between our observations and certain general principles. An expert might thus be convinced to give up certain principles on broadly empirical grounds, either because her principles directly conflict with observed phenomena, or (less directly) because they fail to explain some of our observations which other principles do explain. She will not be so moved, however, by arguments that would aim to undermine her principles some other way—purely verbal or sophistical arguments, say, or arguments relying on dialectical modes of reasoning, or invoking general theoretical considerations extending beyond her domain of expertise.[58]

Being an expert, then, does not require fanaticism about your principles. It doesn't even require that your overall conviction in some specific fact increase from your having a demonstration of it—you

[56] This is true of all but one occurrence of the term, which appears eleven times, and always in connection with the state of understanding (that the ἐπιστήμων is ἀμετάπειστος seems to be idiomatic—see *Top* V.2 130b16, V.4 133b29ff, V.4 134a1ff, V.5 134a35ff, V.5 134b16). Apart from these occurrences, the term only appears three times in the Aristotelian corpus: in passage [11], in the *Metaphysics* (where necessity is said to be ἀμετάπειστόν τι, because it's contrary to the movement that follows choice and reasoning, Δ5 1015a32–33), and in the *Magna Moralia* (where it's suggested that an *opinion* might resemble understanding if it's very firmly held and ἀμετάπειστον, II.6 1201b6). The association of understanding with unpersuadability goes back at least as far as *Timaeus* 51e1–4.

[57] As the passages in the main text already suggest—but see also Karbowski (2016, 120) and the discussion of Aristotle's prior knowledge requirement and its limits in our next chapter.

[58] On this point see *SE* 11 171b38–172a21 and *EE* I.6 1216b26–1217a10, and also Hasper (2013, 307–12) and Karbowski (2016, 126–32). Perceptual conviction, as I see it, is something achieved either by perception alone, or else by perception and induction—in the sense of "induction" I will be defending in chapter 3.

need not become more confident that planets don't twinkle when you learn to demonstrate it. What a demonstration needs to do is only increase a certain *kind* of conviction: conviction that is commensurate with our resistance to refutation by purely argumentative means—that is, by arguments that do not invoke our observations or the fit between principles and the observations they are meant to explain. Understood this way, passage [11] is telling us that an expert would be less likely to give up, when faced with a presumed counterargument, the claims that play a more significant explanatory role in her demonstrative system: it would take a stronger argument to make an expert give up on her explanantia than it would to make her give up what they explain. This is a sensible point, and a point that is quite compatible with her being open to giving up her principles under certain circumstances (in particular when they conflict with or fail to explain our observations).

Now, one might object here that a true expert should in fact never give up her principles. For while she would indeed be impervious to persuasion by pure argument, she would *also* have all the observable facts relevant to her domain of expertise at her disposal, and thus be impervious to persuasion on the basis of new empirical evidence. That is, new empirical evidence could, in principle, force an expert to give up her principles—but no such evidence is forthcoming, since an expert by definition knows everything there is to know about her domain. Thus one might object that the followers of Empedocles Aristotle criticizes in [12] are simply not experts, or that what they take to be principles are simply not principles. And if they were experts, absolute devotion to their principles would indeed be appropriate.

But while it may be true that on Aristotle's view experts (experts in the fullest sense, who know all there is to know about some domain) never give up their principles, this need not be taken to reflect any kind of fanaticism on their part. For these experts would not change their minds as a matter of fact, not as a matter of policy. In other words, they would be open to revising their principles if empirical evidence were brought to their attention that conflicted with these principles. It's only that, as a matter of fact, no such evidence exists. This, at any rate, seems to me the most plausible way to reconcile the claims made in [12]–[14] with the requirement that an expert be ἀμετάπειστος.

What all this shows, I think, is that passage [11] should not be taken to suggest that an expert's intuition of her principles provides a justificatory bedrock for her demonstrations. It is reasonable to think that an expert would be more convinced of explanatorily prior premises: these premises explain a broader range of phenomena, and giving them up means abandoning a broader portion of our demonstrative understanding—something that *should* require a stronger argument. But it remains clear that, as a matter of policy, principles should be given up when they lead to conclusions that conflict with observed phenomena: pure arguments could not sway an expert, but new observations could (even if they don't). Aristotle couldn't allow this if an expert's intuition of her principles served as her most basic source of justification. For that would rule out any scenario in which it would be reasonable for her to give up on these principles.

This already establishes, to my mind, that perception must play more than the "purely causal" role rationalists assign it—even setting aside the details of Aristotle's account of our cognitive development. For perception here is meant to provide a criterion for the adequacy of our principles: our demonstrative theories are based on principles whose status as principles depends on their ability to recover and explain our observations. I don't see how this could be squared with readings on which the contributions of perception are to be understood in merely psychological, descriptive terms, and excluded from playing any justificatory role.

So far, then, I've argued we should reject the direct motivation for rationalism: what Aristotle says about priority and expert conviction does not support rationalist theses, and even seems to provide some evidence against them. That leaves us with the indirect motivation for the view, according to which Aristotle's official account of our learning, as he presents it in *APo* II.19, only tells us about the causal origins of our inquiry into principles, and that he must therefore have intended our intuition of them to play the sort of justificatory role a purely causal story could not. Fully addressing this argument will be my focus in our next chapter. For now, I want to raise some broader concerns about using the notion of justification to interpret Aristotle's epistemology, and suggest an alternative way of making sense of the many different cognitive states he mentions in his account of our learning.

1.6 Justification and Epistemic Value in Aristotle

On rationalist readings of Aristotle's epistemology, an expert's noetic intuition of first principles justifies her understanding of the conclusions demonstrated on their basis—and nothing else justifies this noetic intuition. It follows that questions of justification are simply out of place outside the context of a demonstrative science. So far my argument against these readings has focused on Aristotle's discussions of epistemic priority and conviction, which rationalists (mistakenly, I submit) invoke in support of their view. But there's a broader conclusion I wish to defend here, which is that the terms in which rationalists cast their view often fail to correspond to the terms in which Aristotle presents his epistemology, and that in accepting these terms we run the risk of obfuscating some of his concerns.

The main issue, as I see it, is the assumption that there is some singular justificatory norm against which all forms of epistemic progress would be measured. Recall that, for rationalists, epistemic value is either identical with justification, or else derived from it. Typically, rationalists present their view as though states are epistemically valuable just in case they are justified, and everything that is not justified is of mere psychological interest (cf. p. 24). But they might also hold a slightly less stringent view, on which there is some sort of epistemic value to be found outside the demonstrative context, which would fall short of justification but approximate it to a sufficient degree.[59] Yet even then, to the extent that states do have epistemic value, it's assumed this value is to be understood only in relation to the ideal that is scientific understanding, and the sort of justification demonstrations might provide. And this is an assumption that I think we should reject.

---

[59] As is suggested, I think, by the discussion at Fine (2010, 152–55).

Admittedly, Aristotle's frequent portrayals of our epistemic progress as an advance toward what is "better known by nature" might seem to support such a view. Here is how he puts the point in the *Metaphysics*:

[15] Learning proceeds in this way for all, namely, through that which is less known by nature to that which is more known [by nature]: and just as in practical matters our function is to make what's actually good good for each, [proceeding] from what's good for each, so too [in theoretical matters our function is] to make things better known by nature better known to ourselves, [proceeding] from what's better known to ourselves. (*Met* Z3 1029b3–8)

Thus our function as learners of some theoretical domain is to make what's better known and prior by nature better known and prior to us. To realize this function we begin from what's best known to us before any learning has occurred—that is, from the things that are most prior$_t$, which are those closest to perception (cf. [9] and [10]). We make epistemic progress by moving from this initial knowledge to what is better known by nature—that is, toward the most prior$_e$ objective explanatory grounds for what any beginner might observe. Someone with scientific understanding just is someone who has fully succeeded in making prior to herself what is objectively prior. And so it may be tempting to think that any form of epistemic value would have to be understood as an approximation of this ideal scientific understanding.

But in fact it's doubtful any unique epistemic norm could be derived from this picture. First off, note that in [15] Aristotle draws a contrast between practical and theoretical forms of learning: the primary goal of the former is not to make better known to ourselves what's objectively better known, but rather to make *good* to ourselves what's objectively *good*. This is because, as Aristotle explains elsewhere, the end of theoretical understanding is an appreciation of the truth, while the end of practical forms of knowledge is action (cf. *MA* 7 701a10–13, *Met* α1 993b20–21, *EN* II.2 1103b27–28). So the norms that would govern practical and theoretical inquiries are quite different. A carpenter does not primarily seek to understand the full causal structure underlying her craft, or appreciate the nature of the right angle, as a geometer would—she primarily seeks to make good chairs. Nor does a virtuous agent primarily seek out an exact, demonstrative understanding of the nature of the human good—she primarily seeks to act virtuously, responding to her situation in the right way, and with the right motivation. Though craft knowledge and practical wisdom do involve some grasp of explanations, they do not require demonstrative expertise, and do not have such expertise as their ultimate goal.[60]

Even if we restrict ourselves to theoretical domains, what it takes to make better known to oneself what's objectively better known will depend on the sorts of objects under investigation. Thus while there may be norms that govern some specific kind of zoological or geometrical inquiry, Aristotle doesn't seem to think there is much to say about global norms that would apply to learning in general, whatever the discipline. For different disciplines have different principles, and it's not clear any singular method would allow us to secure principles in general, or be well-suited to learning of any sort (cf. *An* I.1 402a10–22, *PA* I.1 639a1ff).[61] So striving to make better known to ourselves what's objectively better known doesn't yield any unique set of norms we might use to direct our inquiry, even if we focus only on theoretical disciplines.

Finally, quite apart from the domain-specificity of our methods and the distinction between practical and theoretical forms of knowledge, Aristotle seems to allow for certain forms of epistemic progress which do not embody or approximate any the key characteristics of scientific understanding. This is brought out most clearly in his description of experience and craft at the beginning of the *Metaphysics*:[62]

---

[60] On these points see [53] and [54], and the discussion in 6.2. I will be arguing in 5.3 that there are important parallels between practical and theoretical understanding—but I do not think the former can plausibly be understood as an approximation or lesser version of the latter.

[61] I take the treatment of these key texts in Lennox (2011) and Lennox (2021) to be convincing. Below (p. 79) I will discuss how this bears on Aristotle's claim that we learn principles by induction. (But let's alleviate the suspense: I do not take this to be a methodological claim.)

[62] Here I adapt Ross' translation. See also *Met* A1 981a30ff, and *Met* A2 982a10ff.

[16] Concerning action, craft does not seem to differ in any way from experience—in fact we even see the experienced succeed more than those who have an account without experience. (*Met* A1 981a13–15)

[17] We think that knowledge and expertise belong to craft rather than to experience, and we suppose those with craft knowledge to be wiser than those with mere experience [...] because the former know the cause, but the latter do not. (*Met* A1 981a24–28)

Craft is portrayed here as superior to mere experience, but experience does remain sufficient to guarantee (as much as one could) our practical success: "concerning action" experience and craft are the same, and we do not succeed more for having the causal knowledge that makes those with craft knowledge "wiser" than those without.[63] This is because experience, like perception, deals with particulars, and acting the right way requires a grasp of particulars that cannot be achieved purely by thinking about causes and their explanatory consequences (cf. [2] and also [60], below). Thus *pure* causal knowledge (i.e. causal knowledge without experience) would not itself lead to practical success—textbooks don't make physicians, as Aristotle puts it elsewhere (*EN* X.9 1181b2–3). And *pure* experience allows us to succeed in various practical endeavors without any causal knowledge.

I will be discussing the relationship between experience and craft knowledge in more detail below (see in particular 5.3). What's important for now is that experience makes a critical contribution to our practical success, and that this contribution does not depend on its supplying us with any causal knowledge—and is indeed contrasted with the sort of wisdom such knowledge would exemplify. Because experience is contrasted with causal knowledge, it's hard to see how it would "approximate" scientific understanding, which, as I've argued, is a form of mastery over some domain's causal structure. And so it's hard to see how we should understand its contributions to our learning, if approximating such understanding is the only way to measure epistemic progress.

---

[63] For some qualifications on this claim, see 5.3 n56.

Of course rationalists are free to stipulate that reliable success does not imply justification—so that an experienced carpenter, despite her success at making chairs, would not be *justified* in believing she should join the feet this way, and the back this other way, and so on, to build a chair from the materials at her disposal. But Aristotle, as I will argue in more detail in our next chapter, plainly thinks of experience as an achievement in itself. So whether or not the carpenter's judgments count as "justified," we need a way of distinguishing between epistemic achievements like experience, which do not require any grasp of explanations, and epistemic achievements like craft and understanding, which do. Their independence gives us reason to doubt that these achievements are both subject to some single, overarching epistemic norm—as rationalists take justification to be.

So instead of asking what does or does not count as justified, or approximates expert justification to a sufficient degree, I suggest we allow that Aristotle's epistemology might accommodate a range of different epistemic desiderata—only some of which will be met by the various forms of knowledge presented in his account of our learning.[64] For instance, I argued above that perception plays two key epistemic roles: it serves as a source of *conviction*, and serves as an *authority* against which these principles must be assessed.[65] I also noted that

[64] See Alston (1993) for a contemporary presentation of this sort of approach. There's another issue, I think, with the focus on justification: nowadays *beliefs* are typically taken to be the things we justify, and beliefs are attitudes we typically individuate by their propositional contents, and which we think we might justify in isolation from each other. Aristotle's epistemic ideal, by contrast, is a holistic one—as I argued above, it's a requirement on our understanding some proposition that this proposition be grasped as part of some broader domain. Now, it may of course be possible to recast Aristotle's holistic views using our contemporary notions of belief and justification, or stipulate that justification operates in some holistic manner. My claim is only that this is an unnatural thing to do: by default this isn't a feature of our contemporary notion of justification, according to which we can justify beliefs in a piecemeal way, without appreciating their broader explanatory role in some discipline. Better to reject this framework than to try and bend it into use.

[65] To say that perceptual knowledge serves as our ultimate authority is not to say that it serves as a foundational source of justification. One might, as in Quine (1961, 41), endorse a form of confirmation holism and nonetheless take the "tribunal of sense experience" to be the final test of our beliefs (taken as a "corporate body," without any unique linear justificatory ordering between them). Or one might consider perceptual experience an ultimate authority without taking any position on its etiological or foundational role, as in Gupta (2006, 3–5).

it is a reliable guide to the *truth*, and that it supplies us with the most prior$_t$ knowledge on which the rest of our learning depends. Below I will consider in more detail what this dependence amounts to, and the contributions perception and experience make to the development of explanatory forms of knowledge—and argue that perception serves as a *foundation* for this more advanced knowledge. Still, Aristotle is clear that this explanatory knowledge does not issue from perception alone. So there are certain epistemic achievements that will exceed anything we could learn perceptually: perceptual knowledge is never explanatory, and perception itself does not disclose anything about the essences or necessary features of the things we perceive. It reveals to us that things are some way, but not what makes them so, and so cannot afford us the sort of synoptic, reflective understanding of reality an expert demonstrator might achieve.

Thus perception meets certain epistemic desiderata, and not others: it serves as a guide to the truth, and as a source of conviction and evidence, and (I will argue) as a foundation for more advanced knowledge, but it does not yield any sort of explanatory knowledge, or any insight into the nature of the things we perceive. Purely causal forms of knowledge have their own limitations: they reflect a certain kind of wisdom, but do not serve as practical guides, or as an authority against which our principles might be assessed. Aristotle does take scientific understanding to be our *highest* epistemic achievement, but in doing so he should not be read as denying perception and other non-explanatory forms of knowledge any epistemic role whatsoever. Nor should he be read as stipulating that justification *stricto sensu* is only found in the demonstrative context, and that any other sort of epistemically valuable state should be understood as an approximation thereof, or as a means to our intuition of basic justificatory principles. Epistemic value comes in many forms.

Now, I've been arguing in this section that there is no single epistemic norm that would apply to all forms of epistemic progress. In his account of our path from perception to scientific understanding, however, Aristotle doesn't just fail to present some singular epistemic norm: he seems unconcerned with epistemic norms altogether. And so it might be tempting to conclude, with rationalists, that his account must be taken only as a descriptive record of the causes underlying our cognitive development. I will argue in our next chapter that this would be a mistake: Aristotle may not have a general theory about what we should believe, or any singular method that would lead us from perception to scientific understanding, but his account of our derivation of more advanced forms of knowledge from perception is not the "merely causal" story rationalists take it to be. Perception serves as a foundation for more advanced knowledge, rather than a prompt for its development by other means.

2

Plato and Aristotle on Our Perceptual Beginnings

As I argued in our last chapter, Aristotle's epistemic ideal can be thought of as a disposition to demonstrate the truths in some domain that admit of demonstration. Such a disposition is a manifestation of an expert's understanding: a synoptic, reflective grasp of the explanatory and inferential relations between the various truths that make up some domain of expertise. On Aristotle's view, this understanding depends on an intuition of certain indemonstrable principles. And this intuition, like any other form of knowledge, ultimately derives from perception. My aim in this chapter is shed some light on what it would mean for our intuition of principles to *derive* from perception. I will argue that perception does not merely serve as a causal prerequisite for the derivation in question: perception provides the content on which our intuition is based, and supplies a form of knowledge that is valuable both in itself and as a foundation for theoretical forms of understanding.

The main evidence that this is the case stems from the contrast Aristotle draws between his account of our learning and the sort of innatist view we find defended in some of Plato's middle dialogues. On innatist views, perception serves, at best, as an *inspiration* for other forms of learning: it might give our inquiries some general direction, but does not provide the content on which more advanced forms of knowledge would be based. The knowledge it provides, if any, is valuable only in an instrumental way, insofar as it awakens our intellect and prompts us to reflect on what we perceive. Aristotle's rejection of innatism, as I will argue, stems from his rejection of such a deflationary view of perception's contributions to our learning: for Aristotle, perception is valuable because it leads to the development

Aristotle's Empiricism. Marc Gasser-Wingate,
Oxford University Press (2021). © Oxford University Press.
DOI: 10.1093/oso/9780197567487.003.0002

of advanced knowledge, but also because it supplies us with a form of knowledge that is valuable in itself, whatever it might inspire besides.

I'll end by distinguishing perception's foundational role from its role as a source of conviction, and as an authority against which our principles might be assessed—and arguing that we should not take this foundational role to imply that perception would serve to ground epistemic value in all its forms, or that it, rather than our intuition of principles, would provide some ultimate justificatory bedrock for the knowledge we might derive from it.

2.1 Aristotle on Learning

Aristotle announces in the opening lines of *APo* that "all teaching and all intellectual learning proceed from preexisting knowledge" (I.1 71a1–2).[1] The sense in which the preexisting knowledge is "preexisting," or such that we can "proceed" from it to further knowledge is never explicitly spelled out. At times, Aristotle seems to think that we are proceeding from a *state* with certain contents to a state with different contents, or to a different state with the same contents.[2] At others, he seems to think that certain *propositions* (or subpropositional *terms*) proceed from others, regardless of whether or not this is grasped by anyone.[3] The Greek itself is open to a range of different interpretations, for all Aristotle is saying is that something (a state, or proposition, or term) is, or comes to be, from (ἐκ) something else.

Some of these ambiguities stem from broader features of Aristotle's discussion of our cognitive states and their contents. On Aristotle's view, the possession of certain *concepts* manifests itself in a grasp of

---

[1] When he speaks of *intellectual* (διανοητική) learning in these lines, Aristotle means to include all non-perceptual forms of learning—cf. Bronstein (2016a, 15–16) and Mignucci (1975, 2–3).

[2] For states with different contents, see for instance *APo* I.1 71a8–9 (induction proceeds *from* particular cases to something universal), or *APo* II.19 as a whole. For different states with the same content, see for instance *APo* I.1 71a24ff (understanding something *simpliciter* proceeds *from* understanding that same thing universally).

[3] For propositions, see for instance the requirements on demonstration presented in [7] (demonstrative conclusions follow *from* premises that are better known, explanatory, etc.). For terms, see for instance *APo* I.4 73a34ff (the essence of triangle is *from* line, and the essence of line *from* point).

propositions *involving* these concepts: there is no sharp difference between a grasp of some concept "coming from" a grasp of some other concept and a grasp of some proposition "coming from" a grasp of some other proposition. In fact, Aristotle often treats as identical the grasp of a concept and the grasp of propositions with constituent terms involving the concept in question: someone might be said to understand *human being*, or, equivalently, to understand the definitional principle "human beings are rational animals," where these are simply two different, succinct ways of saying that this person displays demonstrative expertise in the field of human zoology.[4] Moreover, if such a person is in fact an expert, and thus understands things correctly, her grasp of explanations will reflect an objective explanatory order—so the fact that her knowledge of propositions or terms "follows from" her knowledge of other propositions or terms entails the existence of an actual explanatory ordering between the facts or entities corresponding to the propositions or terms in question.[5]

Thus for someone with scientific understanding, the "from" relation between states like νοῦς and ἐπιστήμη is meant to correspond to the "from" relation between propositions grasped in these states—a relation that will mirror the objective explanatory relation between the facts corresponding to the propositions in question. But the distinction Aristotle draws in [9] between epistemic priority *to us* (what's prior$_t$) and epistemic priority *by nature* (what's prior$_e$) carries over in this context as well: the knowledge displayed by an expert proceeds *from* knowledge that is prior$_e$, and so corresponds to the

---

[4] See Barnes (1993, 271), Kahn (1981, 393–95), Modrak (1981, 69–72), Modrak (1987, 164), Sorabji (1996, 315–16), or Taylor (1990, 127–28) for more thorough expositions of his usage.

[5] The requirement (expressed in [7]) that middle terms explain a syllogism's conclusion is a good example of Aristotle's protean usage. The thought here is not that some linguistic items count as explanations—the explanation why planets don't twinkle is that they are *in fact* near the earth, and has nothing linguistic about it (as Barnes rightly emphasizes (1993, 89–90)). Note also that the explanatory relation is something that holds between two *facts* (planets are near, planets don't twinkle), and not just between two *properties* (proximity, non-twinkling), though Aristotle often uses the latter formulation. So, to be fully explicit, a syllogism's conclusion is "explained by a middle term" when the fact expressed by this conclusion is explained by the fact that the referent of its subject term possesses the property referred to by the syllogism's middle term. I'll spare you such formulations in what follows.

objective explanatory order, while for the rest of us what we know proceeds *from* what is prior$_t$—something that might vary from person to person, or for the same person from one stage of her learning to the next, but ultimately must begin from perception.

So when Aristotle says that all our intellectual learning is based on preexisting knowledge, he doesn't just mean that, within the context of an axiomatized demonstrative science, we will begin with first principles and proceed by inferring explanatorily posterior conclusions from these principles. The requirement holds quite generally, for scientific understanding and non-scientific knowledge alike. And for the non-expert, the sort of knowledge on which learning depends will generally *not* be the knowledge which is objectively prior—for as Aristotle explains in [15], the learning process involves *making* what's prior by nature prior to us.

The specifics of our learning process, then—what knowledge comes from what for us—will inevitably depend on who we are, and the specifics of our epistemic situation. Nonetheless, Aristotle thinks there are broadly speaking only three ways in which anything could ever be learned: by demonstration, by induction (ἐπαγωγή), and by perception. And he makes it clear that perception is the most basic of these three modes of learning—at least in the sense that learning by induction and demonstration both depend on our perceiving certain things:[6]

[18] It's also clear that if some perception is missing, some under-standing must be missing as well—the understanding it's impossible to get since we learn either by induction or by demonstration, and demonstration is from universals and induction from particulars, and it's impossible to think about universals except by induction (since even the things we talk about by abstraction will be made known to us by induction—that some things are said of each kind, even if they aren't separable, insofar as each is a such-and-such) and impossible to induce without perception. For it's perception that's of particulars—for it isn't possible to get understanding of these [particulars]. For [one can't get understanding] from universals

---

[6] See also, in a similar vein, *APo* I.31 87b39–88a5.

without induction nor from induction without perception. (*APo* I.18 81a38–b9)

Aristotle therefore thinks we learn about particulars *perceptually*, advance from these particulars to a grasp of universals *inductively*, and eventually find ourselves able to learn *by demonstration*—the sort of learning available to those with full scientific understanding of some domain, and manifested through the sort of demonstration presented in [7]. If we fail to perceive we will lack a grasp of certain particulars, and induction will consequently fail to yield the grasp of universals necessary to demonstrate scientific conclusions. Perception is therefore meant to supply the knowledge upon which any other form of learning depends.

It's worth emphasizing at the outset that Aristotle does not seek an analogue of his formal demonstrative theory for perceptual or inductive learning. In the case of perception this is simply because perceptual knowledge isn't derived from any preexisting knowledge. In the case of induction, it's presumably because many different sorts of arguments might contribute to our inductive progress: to say that we learn by induction isn't to say that we learn via some specific mode of argument, but rather that we learn in a way that takes us from a grasp of particulars to a grasp of some universal, whatever the argumentative means. So we should not take the claim that we learn first principles dialectically (*Top* I.2 101a37–b4) to conflict with the claim that we learn first principles by induction (*APo* II.19 100b4).[7] For induction is a form of cognitive development whose achievement may well involve

---

[7] *Contra* Bolton (1991, 15–17), Lee (1935, 122–23), and Ross (1995, 55), among others. Note also that (somewhat confusingly) *demonstrative* methods can be used to realize inductive forms of learning, as Aristotle explains in *APo* II.8. So demonstrative arguments, aside from their typical use in the sort of demonstrative learning possible for an expert scientist, can contribute to non-demonstrative forms of learning for those who do not yet have complete scientific understanding. This is less paradoxical than it might sound: it's just to say that demonstrative methods can be used to develop demonstrative expertise. When demonstrations are used in this context their role is similar to that of dialectic or the method of division: they serve as an argumentative tool which promotes the sort of cognitive development that constitutes inductive learning. As I read Aristotle's remarks at *Met* A9 992b30–33, *definition* is also method that would bring about inductive learning (a method that would itself rely on division and demonstration). See Bronstein (2016a) for an illuminating exposition of these different methodological tools and their role in our learning.

dialectical methods—inductive progress is something we can realize dialectically, or to which dialectical arguments can at least contribute in a significant manner.

I'll be considering inductive learning in more detail in our next chapter. What matters for now is that Aristotle tells us all our learning depends in some way on perception—and that this is just a consequence of his preexisting knowledge requirement, applied to demonstrative learning and extended to the sort of learning that must occur before demonstrative learning is possible. And it may seem natural, in light of passage [18], to think that this must mean, at a minimum, that perception supplies the *content* from which our understanding is ultimately derived: we perceive particulars, these particulars instantiate (as we might put it) certain universals, and we come to grasp the universals they instantiate inductively, before demonstrating things about them and coming to understand them as an expert would.

Now, I think this does in fact capture one important part of Aristotle's view. But it's worth emphasizing that he does not say any of this directly—at least not in [18], and arguably nowhere else in the corpus, either. What he claims in [18] is only that it's impossible to engage in the inductive learning process without perceiving certain particulars. And this is compatible with there not being any interesting connection between the *content* of our perceptions and the *content* of the sort of knowledge perception and induction enable us to achieve. For all Aristotle says here, the universals we learn about inductively might not be *inferred* on the basis of their perceived instances. We might perceive certain particulars and then go on to learn universals in some manner that does not directly depend on what we perceived about these particulars—that is, without *deriving* them from whatever it is we perceive.

I'm not just being overdelicate in entertaining this possibility. Aristotle was writing in a context where it was a live option to deny any straightforward connection between the contents of our perception and the contents of the more advanced forms of universal knowledge issuing "from" the things we perceive. In fact we find just such a view presented in Plato's middle dialogues, as part of a broader innatist account of our learning—to which I'll now turn.

2.2 Perceptual Beginnings: A Platonic View

In various middle dialogues Plato has Socrates suggest that some of our perceptions prompt us to *recollect* our innate knowledge of the Forms. Indeed, in some places perception is even said to be *necessary* to prompt any sort of recollection, and so to be necessary for any sort of advanced learning, as we'll see below. But this recollection process does not involve any straightforward inference of our innate knowledge from what we perceive. That is, while we come to acquire (or make manifest) knowledge by first perceiving certain things, what we learn from perception is not meant to serve as foundation for the knowledge we end up recollecting. Our perceptions lead us to recollect, but the recollected knowledge is not based on what we perceive.

This point is brought out most clearly in the discussion of recollection we find in the *Phaedo*:[8]

> SOCRATES: Don't we further agree that when knowledge comes about in this way, it is recollection? What way do I mean? Like this: when someone sees or hears or in some other way perceives one thing and not only knows that thing but also thinks of another thing, of which the knowledge is not the same but different, are we not right to say that he recollects that second thing, the thought of which he grasps?

---

[8] The translation here is adapted from Grube's, following Sedley (2006) in a few places. In this context I render ἐπιστήμη "knowledge," which fits the examples better and leaves open the question whether the knowledge in question is mundane knowledge (what ordinary rational beings would know about X) or something more sophisticated (philosophical knowledge of the Form of X). For the former view, see for instance Ackrill (1973) or Bostock (1986, 66–72); for the latter see Scott (1995, 53–85). I think the latter view is right, but nothing in my argument here hangs on this: my main concern is the connection between our perceptions and more advanced cognitive states we reach as a result of perceiving certain things—whether these more advanced states be philosophical knowledge of the Forms or something more mundane.

SIMMIAS: How do you mean?

Things of this sort: surely, to know a human being is different from knowing a lyre. —Of course.

Well, you know what happens to lovers: whenever they see a lyre, a garment or anything else that their beloved is accustomed to use, they know the lyre, and grasp in their mind the form of the boy to whom it belongs. This is recollection, just as someone, on seeing Simmias, often recollects Cebes, and there are thousands of other such occurrences. —Thousands indeed.

(*Phaedo* 73c4–d11)

Thus recollection, Socrates and Simmias agree, doesn't require any resemblance between what we perceive and what we're reminded of: we can see one person and recollect a different person, or even perceive a lyre or garment and recollect the person to whom they belong. So while we are often reminded of something by its likeness, this is not an essential feature of the recollection process—as Socrates puts the point a bit later, you might be reminded of Simmias by seeing a portrait of Simmias, but you might also be reminded of Cebes by that very same portrait (73e5–74a1). What we recollect might but need not be similar to whatever prompts our recollection.

Now, it's eventually agreed that when it comes to our recollection of the Forms, there *is*, in fact, a similarity between what we recollect and what prompts our recollection: our recollection of the Equal is said to be prompted by our seeing equal sticks, and these sticks are said to *resemble* the Equal, though the similarity is acknowledged to be a very deficient one (74b6–c3, 74d4–8). It's a controversial question exactly what the similarity relation is meant to be here, and what its deficiency consists in.[9] But it's significant that Socrates twice emphasizes that

[9] The issue turns on the difficult claim that "equal stones and sticks, while remaining the same, sometimes appear equal to one and unequal to another" while "the Equals themselves never appear to [Simmias] to be unequal, or Equality Inequality" (74b6–c3). I can't hope to give an account of the metaphysics underlying these claims here. What matters for my present purposes (and for this particular argument in the *Phaedo*) is only that perceptible Xs and the Form of X be different sorts of entities, and that the former fall short of the latter—in a way that is reflected in the sort of knowledge we might have of both Forms and their perceptible participants.

his argument for recollection does not depend on the specifics of our answer to this question.

Consider for instance what he says after distinguishing equal particulars from the Form of Equality:[10]

> These equals and the Equal itself are therefore not the same? —I don't think they're the same at all, Socrates.
>
> But it is from these equals, though they are different from that Equal, that you have thought of and acquired knowledge of the Equal? — Very true.
>
> Whether it be similar to them or dissimilar? —Certainly.
>
> It makes no difference. As long as the sight of one thing makes you think of another, whether it be similar or dissimilar, this must of necessity be recollection. —Quite so.
>
> (*Phaedo* 74c4–d3)

It makes no difference, then, whether equal sticks are taken to be dissimilar to the Equal or deficiently similar to it. What matters to Socrates' argument is only that our knowledge of equal sticks be different from our knowledge of the Equal—its objects, the equal sticks, being either dissimilar or deficiently similar to the Equal—and remind us of this latter knowledge. This would suffice to establish that we can *recollect* our knowledge of the Forms in our embodied state, starting from our experience perceiving everyday objects. If the objects we are reminded of are similar to those we perceive, we would be recollecting as we do when we recollect Simmias upon seeing his portrait. If the objects we are reminded of are dissimilar to those we perceive, we would be recollecting as we do when we recollect Cebes upon seeing Simmias' portrait.

---

[10] See also 76a1–6: "it was seen to be possible for someone to see or hear or otherwise perceive something, and from this to think of something else which he had forgotten and which is related to the first, being *either similar or dissimilar*." It's understandable that Socrates would not want his argument to depend on some particular conception of the relationship between particulars and Forms, since later on he admits to being rather unsure about the nature of this relationship: beautiful things are said to "participate" or "share" in the Beautiful, but Socrates avoids taking any stance on what exactly this participation relation would be (cf. 100c–d).

What *is* critical to this argument is that in cases where we perceive likenesses of the Forms, our perceptions also make us aware of the fact that these likenesses are *deficient*—so that in perceiving equal sticks, for instance, we are made aware of their *deficient* similarity to the Equal, just as we would perceive a portrait of Simmias as something that only deficiently resembles Simmias (presumably only Simmias himself non-deficiently resembles Simmias). Thus while the exact details of the relationship between particulars and Forms may not matter, Socrates insists that it must be clear to us from our experience with equal sticks that their perceived equality "falls short of" or "strives to be like" the Equal (74e1, 75a2). This is critical in the context of his argument, because it's our awareness of this shortfall that is meant to establish that we had knowledge of the Equal prior to our perceiving equal sticks: the thought is that we can't be aware of a *shortfall* or *deficiency* without prior knowledge of what our perceptions fall short of.

The point is best expressed in the following exchange:

> But from our perceptions we must think (ἐννοῆσαι) 'everything in our perceptions is striving to reach that thing, what Equal is, but falls short of it.' Or how do we put it? —Just so.
> Then before we began to see or hear or otherwise perceive, we must have possessed knowledge of what the Equal itself is, if we were about to refer the equals from our perceptions to it, thinking that all such things strive to be like it, but are inferior. —That's right.
>
> (*Phaedo* 75a11–b8)

On this sort of picture, then, we learn by recollecting, and everyday perceptions prompt our recollection. They do so in part by making us aware of their shortcomings: by perceiving equal sticks we are made aware that the sticks we perceive fall short of the Equal.[11] This serves as evidence that we had prior knowledge of the Equal—the latent

---

[11] We should allow here that we may not be able to *articulate* this, or at least that we may not be able to do so merely in virtue of our perceptual experience—it might still take some work on our part to make our awareness of this fact explicit, for it might not be transparent to us what we ἐννοεῖν. On the many possible meanings of this term and its cognates in this context, see Bedu-Addo (1991, 49) or Kelsey (2000, 95–97). I

knowledge our recollection would, if brought to completion, serve to make manifest.

And this is not just one of many possible ways we could learn about the Forms. Socrates and Simmias agree that perception is the *only* way we could begin the recollection process, and that perception is therefore a *necessary* prerequisite for any advanced knowledge of the Forms.[12] Here is how Plato has them put the point:

> What's more we agree to this: that we didn't come to think [that particulars strive to be like Forms], and can't come to think this, except from seeing, or from touching, or from some other one of the senses. I treat them all the same. —And they are the same, Socrates, at any rate in relation to what the argument is trying to make clear.
>
> (*Phaedo* 75a5–10)

It's a key part of this view, then, that we need perceptions to prompt our recollection of the Forms. So Socrates and Simmias, it seems, would happily agree with Aristotle (on the surface, at any rate) that advanced knowledge must come "from" perception. In fact they use the very same language to express this point in the *Phaedo* and *APo*

do think "think," as I've rendered it in main text, is the most plausible translation—keeping in mind that our thinking that equal sticks fall short of the Equal is something that is said to come *from* our perceptions, and so need not be taken to be simultaneous with our perceiving equal sticks. And keeping in mind, also, that this thought might not occur to just *anyone*: the sight of equal sticks might not prompt the thought of their deficiency to the lovers of sights and sounds, say (cf. *Republic* 476c), or those "twisted by bad company into lives of injustice" (*Phaedrus* 250a). Socrates and Simmias do agree that when recollecting from likenesses we *necessarily* think of these likenesses as falling short of what we recollect (74a5–8), but "we," in this context, might already be assumed to have been taught to attend to the intelligible features of the world, rather than its sensible ones only (cf. *Republic* 518d–519b, *Phaedo* 82d–83a). On who "we" might be, see Scott (1995, 55–59) or Sedley (2007, 74–76).

[12] Or at least, perception is a necessary prerequisite *for us humans*, given our embodied state. For as Socrates makes clear, it would be better to investigate reality unfettered by our bodily constraints—as lovers of learning our souls are "imprisoned" in our bodies, and forced to examine things "as through a cage," but in the ideal case we would proceed without attending to perceptible things (82d–83a). Or maybe rather by attending to them only to the extent that they enable intellectual forms of learning—on which point see also *Phaedo* 62b and 64e–67a. In their prenatal, discarnate condition our souls *did* apprehend the Forms directly—using not perception but φρόνησις (*Phaedo* 76c12, cf. *Meno* 81c).

respectively: it's ἐκ τῶν αἰσθήσεων that we are prompted to think of perceptual deficiency, and thereby refer our perceptions to the knowledge of Forms we go on to recollect (75a7, 75a11; cf. *APo* II.19 99b29, 100a3).

But on the Platonic view the knowledge of the Forms we recollect is different in kind from our perceptual grasp of sticks and stones, and not something we *infer* from what perception itself teaches us about these sticks and stones. For this knowledge is something we're already meant to possess, in some latent form, at birth—before we perceive anything at all. And perception contributes to our recovering this knowledge only by compelling us to reflect on its own deficiencies: our perceiving certain particulars causes us to think that what we perceive falls short of some other reality, and thereby puts us on the path toward recollecting our knowledge of this other reality. So perception does cause the rest of our learning, but it doesn't do so by supplying the content from which our knowledge of Forms would be derived. For it does not itself supply us with an independently valuable form of knowledge, or report anything coherent enough to serve as a basis for our learning: that we must begin from perception is a lamentable feature of our embodied existence, and what we learn from perception is valuable only because it enables us to reflect on its incoherence and thereby begin the process of recollection. Thus any valuable form of knowledge is really achieved by recollection, for which perception happens to be a necessary precondition—at least for embodied creatures like ourselves.

This is a point we find articulated in more detail in a parallel discussion of perception's role in our learning at *Republic* VII 523a–525a. In this part of the *Republic* Socrates is trying to impress on Glaucon the critical role arithmetic plays in the guardians' education. Arithmetic is said to be critical because it allows us to distinguish the one from the many, and in particular to think of something as one specific *sort* of thing, separate from others. One of the key ways in which such distinctions are useful, Socrates explains, is that they allow us to sort out the contents of certain confusing perceptions—the perceptions he calls *summoners*:

Some perceptions don't summon the intellect to look into them: things are already being adequately discerned by perception. But others do exhort it in every way to look into them, because perception isn't yielding anything sound.

(*Republic* VII 523a10–b4)

The ones that don't summon the intellect are those that don't wander off into an opposing perception at the same time. The ones that do wander off this way I call *summoners*—whenever perception doesn't reveal *this* any more than its opposite, whether the things impressed upon it be near or far away.

(*Republic* VII 523b9–c4)

So not *everything* we perceive is confusing—to borrow Socrates' example, when perceiving fingers our perceptions do not tell us they are also *non-fingers* (523c5–6). But some of the things we perceive do "go off into an opposing perception," so that for instance some finger might be perceived to be big but also small, or hard but also soft (523e), or, one presumes, two sticks equal but also not (cf. *Phaedo* 74b6–c3).[13] Because of their perplexing reports, such perceptions "summon our intellect" to further investigate them, using arithmetic to determine "whether each of the things announced are one or two" (524b4–5), and eventually recognize big and small as separate things, not "mixed up" the way perception reports them to be (524c6–8). In so doing perception leads us to use arithmetic, and thus prompts our intellect to "draw the soul away from the realm of becoming [i.e. what's perceptible] and toward the realm of being [i.e. what's intelligible]" (521d3–4).

Now, neither recollection nor innate knowledge are mentioned in these passages. But there are some clear structural similarities with the view presented in the *Phaedo*. For here too, perception's contribution to our learning stems from its deficiencies: some of our perceptions puzzle us, our puzzlement leads our soul to recruit its intellect, and

---

[13] And this is not because only one of these qualities is accurately perceived: Socrates is careful to specify that *even under ideal conditions* we might see a finger as both big and small, or feel something as both hard and soft (523b5–8).

our intellect helps us make sense of what we perceive, by sorting out its
conflicting reports. In doing so it helps turn us away from the realm of
becoming and toward the realm of being. But any knowledge we have
of this latter realm must have intellectual origins—perception does aid
our progress by summoning our intellectual resources, but is never
used as a source of evidence we might use to learn about the One and
the Many, say. For our knowledge of arithmetic is meant to be there for
perception to summon—when we confusedly perceive we are already
in a position to engage in the sort of "calculation and insight" that
would clear up our confusion (524b3–5).[14]

As in the *Phaedo*, anything we learn from perception would be
valuable only insofar as it turns the soul towards "the study of
what is" (525a1). Thus in the cases under consideration, we see one
thing and also see many (525a4–5), and this makes our perceptual
experiences well-suited to summon our intellect, and reflect on what
makes anything "one" or "many" in the first place. But the perceptions
that help us make progress in this way are precisely the ones whose
shortcomings are obvious to us—it's because what we perceive is so
puzzling that we are led to think of arithmetic. The perceptions that
don't puzzle us don't help us make progress in this way. So it's not
as though perception would generally provide a firm foundation for
our knowledge of arithmetic, or supply us with an imperfect but
practicable grasp of arithmetic that we might reflect upon and come to
understand more precisely. The whole point is to force the soul *away*
from what's perceptible, and to compel it "to speak of the numbers
themselves, never allowing anyone's suggestion that they be spoken
of as they pertain to visible or tangible bodies" (525d6–7). Here too,
perception's necessity is a concession to our embodied existence, from
which we seek to free ourselves as much as possible in our learning.[15]

---

[14] While it's not suggested in our passage that this knowledge of arithmetic would
be *innate* knowledge of the Forms of the One and Many, or that our intellect helps us
by helping us *recollect* this knowledge, this seems to me a natural suggestion, especially
given the parallels with the discussion of recollection in the *Phaedo*. But I won't insist
on this. What matters is the structural similarity in these two accounts of our learning,
and the respective contributions perception and the intellect make to our epistemic
development—which I will be further articulating below.

[15] As in the *Phaedo*, it should be acknowledge that some might not be puzzled by
summoning perceptions. The guardians discussed here have already undergone a good

And here too, our epistemic progress is measured strictly by how far we've left the perceptible realm behind.

All this indicates a rather deflationary take on perception's role in our learning: perception is a critical causal factor in our coming to know things, but its contribution is indirect, serving only as a means of summoning an intellectual faculty that helps us recollect. This makes perception a *sine qua non* for the development of our understanding, but not something that provides the basic content from which the content of this understanding would be derived. Of course this is not to say that there is no connection at all between the content of our perceptions and that of the advanced knowledge we recollect. Only some perceptions are summoners, after all, and those perceptions summon us to investigate certain things and not others—so that we perceive sticks to be equal and not equal, say, and go on to learn about Equality, and not something else. Elsewhere it is suggested that the *Beautiful* might play a special role in drawing our souls away from perceptible reality—a role other Forms might not (*Phaedrus* 249c–251a). Even so, perception is not a *foundation* for the more advanced knowledge it prompts us to recollect: its value lies only in its potential to inspire our intellect, and not in what, if anything, we learn from it directly. For we might well accept that what we perceive gives our intellectual inquiries some broad direction and nonetheless deny that our intellect relies, in its inquiries, on what perception itself reports.

Consider as an analogy the role an especially bad lecture might play in your learning. Suppose you leave this lecture so confused and irritated you decide you have to go back to study the material on your own. As a result of your studying you eventually sort out what the lecture so poorly presented, and learn something about the material the lecture was meant to explain. In this scenario the lecture acted as a stimulus: it started a causal chain that led to your learning something. It also gave your investigations some general direction: you focused on the material the lecture presented in an inadequate way. Still, what

you ended up learning was not *based* on the content of the lecture—
what you learned you learned on your own, as the result of your
independent study. Nor was the lecture itself serving as a valuable
source of information in your studying. If anything, the lecture in this
scenario contributed to your learning by being especially bad—just as
incoherent summoners are more useful than coherent perceptions.

I think we can distinguish two components to the Platonic account
I've been presenting in this section, as it pertains to perception's role
in our learning:

(a) the view that perception contributes to our learning only by
prompting the sort of intellectual work that aims at making manifest
some latent innate knowledge (i.e. the work that leads to recollection).[16]

(b) the view that perception, when it contributes to our learning,
does so in virtue of its deficiencies.

Of course these two points are related. Plausibly (b) is an important
motivation for (a): because perception is so deficient, any contribution
it makes to our learning must be understood in terms of the knowledge
it helps us recover by other (i.e. intellectual) means, and which would
serve to sort out what perception alone could not make clear. But
one could still hold (a) without holding (b): perception might not
be deficient, and still contribute to our learning only by summoning
our intellect—which it would do some other way. Likewise, one could
hold (b) without positing the latent innate knowledge mentioned
in (a): perception might be deficient and prompt some intellectual
work whose operation is not understood on the recollection model
(one would then need some alternative account of the nature and
origin of the sort of knowledge that is immune from perceptual
deficiency). One could also hold (b) without thinking that perception's

---

[16] Again, the *Republic* passages do not mention innate knowledge or recollection.
But to my mind, something like (a) must be in the background. For a key point in these
passages is that there is a certain kind of knowledge we could develop only by intellectual
means, once we turn away from incoherent "summoning" perceptions. So whether or
not we think there is latent innate knowledge and some recollection mechanism to make
it manifest, the *Republic* view does depend on their being *something* to be learned by
purely intellectual means, and on the thought that certain perceptions would serve only
to prompt our learning of it.

summoning powers are its *only* contribution to our learning, as posited in (a).[17]

As I understand it, however, the Platonic take on perceptual learning does indeed combine both (a) and (b): perception is deficient, and *therefore* valuable only insofar as it promotes purely intellectual forms of learning. This is significant because Aristotle's dismissal of Platonic innatism (especially in [19], below) centers on the positing of innate forms of advanced knowledge, and is thus more easily read as an attack on (a). But part of his argument against innatism—at least as I will reconstruct it in what follows—is more easily read as a rejection of (b): Aristotle emphasizes that perception leads to more advanced forms of knowledge not by being deficient, but by being itself a valuable (if nonrational, and thus limited) source of knowledge. What I want to emphasize here is that this argument would, if successful, undercut one of the key motivations for (a): if perception is *not* an inherently deficient mode of apprehension, it can contribute to our learning in a more than purely instrumental manner. And if this is right we can explain the development of advanced forms of knowledge without positing their innate existence. So if Aristotle can develop an account of perceptual learning on which perception would provide a plausible basis for the development of more advanced knowledge, he will be rejecting (b) in a way that undermines some of the more controversial parts of (a). He would thus be rejecting not only the recollection model (or some structural analogue) but also one of the key motivations for adopting that model in the first place.

So far, then, I've argued that Aristotle thinks all our knowledge comes "from" perception, but that (outside his demonstrative treatment of ἐπιστήμη) he does not say much about what one form of knowledge being "from" another might entail. And I've suggested we should take some care in approaching this question: though it may seem natural to read him as suggesting a straightforward inference from perceptible contents to more advanced forms of knowledge, the claims in passages like [18] do not say anything like this directly, and

---

[17] The non-summoning perceptions mentioned at *Republic* 523c5–6 might point in this direction—though it is not made clear how these are meant to contribute to our learning.

are indeed compatible with a range of different views, including the Platonic view that our learning would begin with perception only in the sense that perception acts as a "summoner" for our intellectual recollection of innate knowledge.[18] The more advanced cognitive states resulting from such summons could still be said to proceed *from* perception, in the sense that they would causally depend on our perceiving certain things—the things which inspire us and awaken our intellect. So the claim that all our learning begins from what we perceive does not yet distinguish Aristotle's view from the sort of position advanced in these dialogues.

I'll now consider Aristotle's attempt to position his views on perception against the sort of Platonic picture I've been presenting here, and what this tells us about his conception of our perceptual beginnings.

2.3 Perceptual Beginnings and Our Epistemic Ascent

At the end of *APo*, Aristotle explains how we learn the scientific principles from which demonstrations begin. He considers the possibility that our knowledge of these principles is *innate*, but quickly rejects this as absurd:

> [19] [One might wonder:] is it that the states [i.e. those whose objects are first principles], not being present in us, come to be in us, or is it rather that they are present in us without its being noticed? It'd be absurd if we did have such states [from birth]—for then we'd have pieces of knowledge more exact than demonstrations without its being noticed. But if we acquire them without having had them earlier, how would we come to know and learn except through some preexisting knowledge? For that's impossible, just as we said about

---

[18] I won't seek to argue here that Plato actually endorsed such a deflationary conception of our perceptual beginnings, or investigate how this conception coheres with the role perception is said to play in other dialogues, or even in other parts of the dialogues I've discussed. What matters for my purposes is only that Aristotle would have been familiar with these deflationary innatist views, whether they are Plato's or just Platonic. (For a more nuanced take of the contributions of perception and experience, see for instance *Philebus* 58a–d.)

demonstration. It's clear, then, both that we cannot possess these states and also that they cannot come about in us when we are ignorant and possess no state at all. (*APo* II.19 99b25–32)

The kind of view Aristotle calls absurd in this passage is one on which we would always know scientific principles, though we would not always *realize* that we do. On this view our knowledge of principles would always be present in our souls in a latent form, and some sort of recognition process would then serve to make this latent knowledge manifest. This is just the role played, for instance, by Platonic recollection—a case Aristotle surely had in mind.[19]

Aristotle, then, thinks it absurd that our understanding of principles would exist in some latent form—exact forms of knowledge must be manifest, and our understanding of principles is the most exact knowledge we can achieve.[20] If our understanding doesn't already exist in some latent form, it must be *derived* from some other (less exact) preexisting knowledge. And since, as we saw above, all non-perceptual knowledge must itself be based on further preexisting knowledge, Aristotle concludes that

[20] d we must possess some sort of capacity, but not one which will be more valuable than these states [which know first principles] in respect of exactness. And this certainly seems to be the case for all animals: they have an innate discriminatory capacity called perception. (*APo* II.19 99b32–35)

---

[19] Plato would not put the point in terms of scientific principles, but plainly the common thought is that some sort of *advanced knowledge* (knowledge of Forms, or of ultimate demonstrative principles) is innate.

[20] Or at least it must be manifest to us that we already knew exact things *at some point during our learning of them*—a more charitable reading defended in Bronstein (2016b). Aristotle doesn't say much about the notion of exactness (ἀκρίβεια) at play in this passage, nor does he ever defend the claim that exact states must be manifest. But exactness does at a minimum seem to track priority—a piece of knowledge is more exact than another if it's closer to first principles (so that an expert's knowledge of first principles is most exact). This is also the term used by Plato to characterize the geometrical knowledge Meno's slave might acquire after some practice on his own (*Meno* 85c–d).

Aristotle's argument here is somewhat condensed—presumably we would have wanted him to identify some preexisting *knowledge* or *state* rather than a preexisting capacity. Still, the general thought is clear: perception is a capacity that normally gives rise to certain states in a perceiving subject, and these states are meant to constitute the basic form of knowledge Aristotle's account requires.

Naturally perception itself doesn't yield an understanding of first principles—Aristotle thinks perception only tells us about particulars, and thus never yields the sort of universal explanatory knowledge scientific understanding requires. We therefore need some account of the cognitive development leading us from our perceptions to an intuition of the principles on which our understanding is based. This is the account Aristotle attempts in the rest of *APo* II.19, which describes the development he takes to be achieved by induction (100b4). So on Aristotle's account our ability to understand things scientifically isn't the result of some innate knowledge within us, but rather the result of our progressive inductive development from basic perceptual knowledge to a sophisticated grasp of the principles proper to some scientific domain.

It seems to me clear that, in this dialectical context, perceptual knowledge cannot be "basic" in a merely etiological sense—that is, merely in the sense that it would serve as an original *cause* occasioning the rest of our learning. For Aristotle thinks of his account as an *alternative* to Platonic innatism. And Platonic innatism, as I've been arguing, is compatible with (and indeed endorses) the view that the development of scientific understanding is prompted by some of our perceptions (cf. point (a), above). So if Aristotle's invocation of perception in his inductive account is going to challenge the sort of innatist he portrays in [19], perception must play more than the causal role Platonic innatists already took it to play. To insist on our perceptual beginnings would otherwise simply be missing the point.

Now, it might be objected here that a more deflationary reading of Aristotle's challenge is possible, on which his point in [20] would simply be that perception is a *sufficient* causal prerequisite for the rest of our learning: we do not need to posit, in addition, the existence of innate knowledge to explain how our learning might get started.

That would be enough to distinguish his view from those of Platonic innatists, even if we read Aristotle's account of our development in purely causal terms, as rationalist interpreters would have it—innatists think perception and innate knowledge are jointly sufficient to cause the rest of our learning, while Aristotle thinks perception can do the job alone.

But I think there are good reasons to resist readings of this sort. Consider, first, the emphasis the Platonic view places on the *inadequacy* of perception: perception is portrayed as something we should strive to turn away from—an inherently deficient mode of apprehension that promotes our learning only by awakening our intellect to make sense of its confusing reports (cf. point (b), above). On this picture innate knowledge is not just one of two causal prerequisites for our learning. It serves to *correct* or *sort out* what perception alone could not make clear. We should expect Aristotle's own account of our learning to be responsive to this concern. To insist that perception is sufficient as a starting point for our learning, in this context, is also to say (perhaps implicitly) that it provides a valuable form of knowledge even without the corrective assistance of the intellect.

And there is good evidence Aristotle held just such a view. He consistently portrays the practical experience we develop on perceptual, non-intellectual grounds as an epistemic *achievement*—as something that is not only prompted by perception but that is epistemically good *because* of its perceptual grounding. He tells us at *Met* A1 981a13–15 (=[16]) that those with experience might succeed more often than those with intellectual forms of wisdom only. He tells us at *EN* VI.11 1143b11–14 (=[62]) that we should attend to what older people say even if they cannot demonstrate anything because "they see things right, because experience has given them an eye." By way of contrast, here is what Socrates has to say about experience in the *Gorgias*:[21]

> I was saying, wasn't I, that I didn't think that pastry baking is a craft, but a knack (ἐμπειρία), whereas medicine is a craft. I said that the one, medicine, has investigated both the nature of the object it serves

---

[21] Following Zeyl's translation with slight adaptations.

and the cause of the things it does, and is able to give an account of each of these. The other, the one concerned with pleasure, to which the whole of its service is entirely devoted, proceeds toward its object in a quite uncraftlike way, without having at all considered either the nature of pleasure or its cause. It does so without any account whatsoever, and without enumerating things, so to speak. Through routine and knack it merely preserves the memory of what customarily happens, and that's how it also supplies its pleasures.

(Gorgias 500e4–501b1)

The rendering of ἐμπειρία as "knack" plainly fits the context: Socrates is seeking to distinguish oratory from justice, and claims it stands in the same relation as pastry baking stands to medicine—the former is directed at producing pleasurable sensations, or the *appearance* of goodness, while the latter is concerned with what is actually good. In doing so he paints pastry baking (and oratory) as shameful practices, which "wear the mask" of the crafts as which they appear (465b). And there's some evidence that Aristotle intends his positive stance on experience as an implicit rebuttal of views of this sort: after describing experience in *Met* A1, Aristotle approvingly cites Polus' dictum "experience made craft, inexperience luck" (981a4–5), no doubt alluding to the sort of view ridiculed earlier in the *Gorgias* ("experience causes our times to march down the path of craft, while inexperience causes them to march down the path of luck" 448c6–7).[22] In a similar vein, Aristotle characterizes perception, in [20], as a capacity to *discriminate* (99b35), which is just the sort of thing an innatist would deny: Socrates tells us in the *Republic* that "something [i.e. the intellect] is needed to discriminate (ἐπικρίνειν)" whenever perception tells us one thing as well as its opposite, and that this is precisely what perception recruits our intellect to do (524e4).[23]

---

[22] On this point see also Auffret (2011).

[23] This is qualified in a later passage, where it's claimed that philosophers can discriminate using both experience and reason (582a5), but even then it is added that reason remains the distinctively philosophical tool, to be relied on above anything else (582d). See also *Theaetetus* 186b8ff on the soul "rising up to discriminate (κρίνειν)" the deliverances of our senses.

Consider, finally, a broader dialectical point. In the *Phaedo* already we find a developmental story similar to the one Aristotle is advancing in *APo* II.19: in his autobiography, Socrates declares that he became dissatisfied with certain forms of causal explanation, and presents as an example the view according to which "the brain provides our senses of hearing and sight and smell, from which come memory and opinion, and from memory and opinion which has become stable, comes understanding" (96b5–8).[24] If Aristotle were simply reiterating a variant on this account as a record of the causal antecedents to scientific understanding, he would be somewhat blithely disregarding Socrates' concerns about causal explanations of our learning— concerns raised just a few moments after he articulates his own account of learning as recollection.[25] A charitable reading of Aristotle's response to Platonic innatism should not ascribe to him such neglect, and should therefore not be understood in purely causal terms. So while [20] might, in isolation, allow for the sort of "purely causal" reading rationalists endorse, the broader dialectical context makes this reading an implausible one.

I conclude that perception should be taken to play an epistemically significant role in Aristotle's account. If perception served only to stimulate our intellect or promote our learning by other means, Aristotle's account wouldn't constitute a plausible challenge to the sort of innatism he finds absurd. What's needed is a view on which perception is taken seriously—that is, a view on which perception contributes to our learning not by confusing us, but by yielding the sort of knowledge from which more advanced forms of understanding

---

[24] Of course this is not exactly Aristotle's account of our learning—but on the surface it is very similar to it, and the similarities would have been clear to his audience. For more on the parallels between the two, see Adamson (2010). (When I describe the sort of explanation Socrates rejects as "causal," I mean it in the sense of efficient causation, which is the sense relevant to the rationalist view. There are difficult questions about what sort of causal account Socrates did endorse, but what matters here is that he did not find records of efficient causes satisfactory.)

[25] To my mind this shows that recollection is not intended as a "purely causal" account of our learning: perception does cause the rest of our learning, but our innate knowledge of Forms is not posited as just another necessary cause to get our learning started (though it may be that as well). If the Platonic innatist account is not understood in purely causal terms, Aristotle's challenge to it should not be understood in such terms, either.

might be inferred. This is just the sort of view Aristotle's positive remarks about perception and the perceptually grounded state of experience would appear to suggest—a view we find confirmed in Aristotle's inductive account of our learning, and which is motivated by his generous conception of the role perception plays in guiding our various behaviors and practices without the assistance from the intellect. Or so I will be arguing below, after considering in more detail what perception's foundational role might tell us about its broader epistemic profile.

2.4 Perceptual Foundations and Perception's Epistemic Value

On the view I've defended, Aristotle is a certain sort of foundationalist about perception. He is a foundationalist in the sense that perception supplies us with our most prior$_t$ knowledge: the only knowledge the existence of which does not depend on the temporally prior existence of any other knowledge. I've argued that this dependence is not a merely causal matter: perceptual knowledge is itself a valuable source of knowledge about the world, from which we might infer (and not, say, be inspired to recollect) more advanced forms of understanding. Of course, perceptual knowledge is *also* valuable in an instrumental way, as a means to the development these more advanced forms of understanding. Just as Aristotle thinks certain ends are good for their own sake and for the sake of the highest human good (*EN* I.7 1097a25–34), so too is perceptual knowledge valuable in itself and as a prerequisite for the development of Aristotle's epistemic ideal. The important point is that perception's contributions to our learning are not valuable *only* because they lead to valuable forms of knowledge.[26]

---

[26] Rationalist readers might insist here that perceptual knowledge could only be "valuable" in a loose sense, since it doesn't yet allow us to justify things in the specific way they envision. But rationalists do not specify what it is they envision, except by contrasting norms like justification with a purely descriptive context of discovery. One thing I hope to have shown here is that this dichotomy does not give us the resources to make sense of everything Aristotle has to say about our learning. If we restrict talk of justification to the realm of demonstrative science, we will still need to account for the dependence relations that hold between the lesser forms of knowledge

To say that Aristotle is a foundationalist in this sense is not to say that perception serves as a *unique* source of epistemic value, as our intuition of principles would on the rationalist view. For some critical parts of our epistemic development will inevitably depend on considerations that do not derive from what we perceive. Recall, for instance, that Aristotle thinks we can develop conviction "by argument" in a manner that might conflict with what's perceptually convincing. And recall that even conviction "by perception" requires more than what perception teaches us on its own. In [12]–[14], Aristotle tells us that our principles are vindicated by their ability to explain some body of observational evidence—so it seems clear from these passages that he takes *explanatory power* to play some key role, or at least contribute to the conviction we have about our principles on perceptual grounds. But these considerations are not exhaustive, and so it's probably best, as I argued at the end of our last chapter, to resist the thought that any sort of epistemic assessment must be understood relative to some single epistemic norm. Thus I do not think we should take Aristotle to be committed to a view on which any sort of justification or epistemic value must ultimately issue from perception.

Aristotle's foundationalism does, however, add an additional dimension to perception's epistemic profile. For one might consider perception an authority and a source of conviction (and even a guide to some part of the truth) without yet taking any position on its role as a starting point for our cognitive development, or on the broader significance of Aristotle's account of this development. What I hope to have shown is that this account is not just a record of causal precursors to the development of scientific understanding—and that perception's role at the start of this account is therefore not merely of etiological interest. None of this is to deny that Aristotle thinks of our cognitive development in causal terms: his explanation how we come to know definitional first principles proceeds by describing how various concepts arise in our souls, and how the cognitive states

that precede our intuition of principles, which are neither merely causal relations nor the dependence relations that would obtain between demonstrative premises and conclusions. Justification, as rationalists understand it, is too blunt a norm to capture this aspect of Aristotle's account.

necessary for their acquisition are caused (under good circumstances) by other, more basic cognitive states. But one should keep distinct *causal* accounts of perception's role in our cognitive development from *merely causal* accounts of the sort Plato presents in some of his dialogues.[27] Properly understood, perception is both the causal origin *and* the foundation for the more advanced states featured in Aristotle's account of our cognitive development—in the sense that it provides a form of knowledge that is valuable in itself, and might be relied on, rather than turned away from, in our learning.

Whether this is a plausible response to Platonic innatism will of course depend on the details of Aristotle's account: his conception of perceptual contents, of the sort of knowledge perception affords us, and of our derivation of advanced forms of intellectual knowledge from what we perceive. One might, after all, agree with what was said so far yet still think perception too limited in its reach to yield the sort of foundation Aristotle's account would require. For the fact that perception plays a foundational role does not explain how exactly it would do so—an especially pressing concern given that perception is meant to be a cognitive power we share with lower animals, some of which barely exhibit any awareness of their surroundings. But I think Aristotle has the resources to address concerns of this sort, and to back up his optimistic take on perception. I'll be considering more closely his views on our cognitive development in the following three chapters, starting with his inductive account of our learning, and then focusing more closely on what it is perception contributes to this inductive process, and the nature of the discriminatory powers that make possible its contribution. For now, I hope to have shown that Aristotle's ambitions in providing such an account are not purely descriptive: he explicitly contrasts his view to certain innatist alternatives, and the only charitable way to read his emphasis on our perceptual beginnings, in this context, is to take perception to serve an epistemically significant role—as a capacity whose exercise would not only prompt the rest of our cognitive development, but also supply us with a valuable (if limited) form of knowledge, from which more advanced knowledge might be inferred.

---

[27] On this point, see also Tuominen (2014).

3

Understanding by Induction

I've argued above that Aristotle thinks that our understanding of some scientific domain can be organized in an axiomatic system that makes clear why the things we understand about that domain must hold. What makes this clear is a certain sort of explanatory demonstration, and one of the requirements on demonstrations is that they begin from the first principles proper to the scientific domain being studied. These principles are explanatory primitives, and so, since demonstrations explain their conclusions, they cannot themselves be demonstrated. But they are nonetheless grounded in other forms of knowledge: we learn first principles by *induction*, a form of cognitive development that begins with perception and progresses through a series of increasingly sophisticated cognitive states until it reaches the state Aristotle calls νοῦς—the knowledge of first principles on which our demonstrative understanding depends. Thus on Aristotle's view, though we can't develop a demonstrative understanding of first principles, we can come to grasp them in a nondemonstrative way. We do so by induction.

This, at any rate, is what Aristotle seems to tell us in the final chapter of his *Analytics*.[1] But few take him at his word. For νοῦς is an extremely demanding cognitive achievement: to have νοῦς of principles is not just to know certain premises, but also to recognize these premises as the necessary and explanatorily primitive truths from which all our scientific understanding is derived—to be poised to deploy them in demonstrations, and to appreciate their basic role in some science (cf. p. 20). And it might seem that even if Aristotle's account of our learning is successful in explaining how we grasp the *content* of first principles, it could not make it clear how we come to know first principles *as such*: one might grant that induction allows us to establish

---

[1] And also (perhaps less directly) in [18].

Aristotle's Empiricism. Marc Gasser-Wingate,
Oxford University Press (2021). © Oxford University Press.
DOI: 10.1093/oso/9780197567487.003.0003

certain key premises, but deny that it reveals anything about the explanatory role these premises play in an axiomatized science, and so deny that it delivers the sort of high-powered theoretical achievement a noetic grasp of principles would entail.

This difficulty has led a number of commentators to circumscribe the role induction would play in Aristotle's account of our learning. Some have argued that νοῦς should be understood both as the state we acquire when we know first principles *and* as the faculty which allows us to move from some inductive conclusion—knowledge that humans are rational animals, say—to the theoretically sensitive grasp we're supposed to reach in the last stage of our intellectual development— knowledge that "humans are rational animals" meets the requirements necessary to count as a biological or zoological first principle.[2] Others have urged a deflationary reading of the chapter, on which Aristotle would be offering a highly elliptical explanation of our acquisition of first principles, and omitting a number of key post-inductive stages from our complete epistemic ascent.[3] In both cases, the motivating thought is that induction alone could not explain how we come to grasp first principles in the right sort of way—and that Aristotle must therefore be relying on some additional faculties, or explaining something else.

I think this line of thought should be resisted: it fails to do justice to the subtle role induction plays in Aristotle's account, and rests on an overly narrow view of the sort of achievement inductive progress represents. My aim in this chapter is to defend a more expansive read-ing of Aristotelian induction, and argue that, properly understood, induction *is* a reasonable answer to the question how we grasp first principles. The argument will have two parts. I'll begin by describing the role induction plays in the developmental account provided in *APo* II.19. I'll argue that induction is the process responsible for (i) our cognitive advance from perceived particulars to certain universal conclusions we grasp as explanations for our perceptions, and (ii) our cognitive advance from a range of universal conclusions of this sort to a theoretically sensitive grasp of scientific first principles. I'll then

---

[2] See e.g. Bayer (1997, 136–41), Irwin (1988, 134–37), or Le Blond (1939, 136).

[3] See e.g. Bronstein (2012, 52–54), or Kahn (1981, 367–68).

spell out what both forms of progress have in common, and argue that their characterization as forms of induction makes good sense in the context of *APo*.

In doing so I hope to resist two-track readings of Aristotle's account of our learning, on which induction supplies a preliminary, low-grade form of knowledge, and νοῦς then operates on this knowledge and turns it into scientific understanding. But I also hope to shed some light on the structure of the sort of cognitive advance leading from perception to first principles, the early stages of which will be my focus in following chapters.

3.1 Demonstrative Understanding and νοῦς

Here is a natural challenge one might raise to the demonstrative account of scientific understanding Aristotle develops in his *Analytics* (a challenge Aristotle himself considers in *APo* I.3). If we only understand the things we demonstrate, we won't *understand* indemonstrable first principles. And if we don't understand them—if we only grasp them in some less robust manner, or don't grasp them at all—it's not clear how we could understand what's demonstrated on their basis. So it's natural to ask what kind of knowledge we have of first principles, and how, on Aristotle's view, that knowledge might be brought about.

Now, it's clear that Aristotle doesn't think this challenge really threatens the possibility of scientific understanding. Despite acknowledging that demanding demonstrations of first principles would yield an explanatory regress, and that such a regress would make scientific understanding impossible (*APo* I.3 72b5–15), his response is simply to insist that we do, in fact, possess scientific understanding, and that we must therefore have a nondemonstrative grasp of principles of some kind or another (72b18–22).

But such insistence doesn't answer the explanatory demand implicit in the challenge: if the concern was that Aristotle's account failed to *explain* the origins of our grasp of first principles, then insisting that we must have such a grasp is no help. What we want to know is how, on Aristotle's account, we could come to grasp them in the way that makes demonstrative understanding possible.[4] A satisfactory explanation, moreover, would have to make clear not only how we come to grasp the *content* of first principles, but also how we come to grasp the principles *as such*. That is, it wouldn't be enough to explain how we discover propositions which happen to express necessary, explanatorily basic facts; Aristotle's account requires an explanation how we recognize first principles *as* necessary and explanatorily primitive.[5] This isn't something Aristotle ever says directly, but there are good reasons to think he held such a view.

Recall, first, that Aristotle's conception of scientific understanding requires a grasp of explanations in their theoretical role: Aristotle thinks we understand things only when we know "of the explanation why something is the case that it is its explanation" (*APo* I.2 71b10–12), and a demonstration only yields understanding of this sort for someone who recognizes its middle term as an explanation for the demonstrated conclusion.[6] This is just a consequence of the synoptic and reflective character of demonstrative understanding (cf. p. 20). Though one could produce a demonstration without appreciating the theoretical role played by its premises, such an appreciation is necessary for anyone to actually understand the demonstrated conclusion—to not simply see that this conclusion is true, but to know why it must be so.

Demonstrations, then, only yield understanding when we grasp them in a theoretically sensitive way. It's natural to think that this

---

[4] Aristotle's other remarks in I.3 fail to address this concern ("we argue in this way; and we also assert that there is not only understanding but also some principle of understanding by which we know [definitional] first principles," 72b23–25). The "principle of understanding" in question is later identified as νοῦς (*APo* I.33 88b36, II.19 100b15), but aside from giving it a name Aristotle doesn't describe the state any further. We find a similar argument at *EN* VI.6, where after ruling out other candidates (ἐπιστήμη, φρόνησις, σοφία) Aristotle concludes by elimination that we must have νοῦς of first principles (1141a7).

[5] In what follows, I will exclusively concern myself with our recognition of principles in their explanatory role, setting aside our recognition of their necessity. Recall that on Aristotle's view, the necessity of definitional principles is closely linked to their role as explanatory primitives (cf. p. 17).

[6] Or, if the demonstration requires multiple explanatory syllogisms, for someone who grasps the explanatory role played by the middle terms of each of the syllogisms that make up the demonstration.

requirement for theoretical sensitivity would extend to the first principles from which demonstrations begin. To deny this is to claim that we could grasp the explanatory status of any demonstrated truth, yet somehow remain ignorant about the explanatory status of the premises from which our demonstrations begin. And this is implausible: an expert astronomer will surely recognize not only what astronomical first principles explain, but also that they are not themselves explained by further astronomical facts (cf. p. 18).

There are also more direct interpretive reasons to favor an ambitious interpretation of our noetic grasp of first principles. Indeed, some of Aristotle's arguments rest on the assumption that we grasp the theoretical role of first principles, and not just their content. Consider for instance the claim (appearing in [11]) that experts are convinced of first principles more than they are of the conclusions demonstrated on their basis. The reason adduced is that "something always holds better of that because of which it holds, for instance, that because of which we love is better loved" (*APo* I.2 72a29–30). Since an expert is ultimately convinced of all her demonstrated conclusions *because* of the principles from which she derives them, Aristotle argues, she will be convinced of these principles most of all. And it's clear her conviction here will depend on her grasping these principles *as explanatory* of their conclusions—that is, as the things because of which her conclusions hold. If she didn't, she wouldn't be better convinced of them—or at least not for the reason Aristotle gives here.

So Aristotle owes us an account of how a grasp of first principles might be brought about, and this account would have to make clear not only how we come to know the content of first principles, but also how we come to recognize their status as explanatory primitives.

3.2 Learning in *APo* II.19: Some Preliminaries

Such an account is precisely what Aristotle presents in *APo* II.19. The chapter is set up as an answer to two questions: how first principles come to be known, and what the state is which knows them. The second question is set aside until the last few lines of the chapter (100b5–17), where Aristotle argues that νοῦς must know first principles because it's the only state truer and more exact than scientific understanding. The point here is merely terminological, and isn't intended to shed any light on the nature or origin of the state: to say that νοῦς is the state that knows principles is not to say that knowledge of principles was acquired through the use of νοῦς; it's only to say that νοῦς is the state a subject is in when she does grasp them (whatever the process of her coming to grasp them might be).[7] Aristotle's main concern is the first question, about how definitional first principles come to be known, and his response to it ("by induction") will be my focus here.

Before turning to this response I want to make a few preliminary points about its scope. I argued above that Aristotle's account will have to be ambitious: it must not only explain how we come to know certain propositions, but also how we come to recognize their theoretical status. But it's important to consider the sort of explanation Aristotle is attempting here. Aristotle is plainly not attempting to describe an inferential procedure or method which, if carefully followed, would reliably establish the first principles proper to some scientific domain, and show that these principles are explanatory primitives. His aim is, rather, to describe the kind of cognitive development necessary to acquire the state required for a proper grasp of first principles— where it would be a separate question what sort of method (or set of methods) is best suited to bring about the development in question.

Nor is Aristotle describing a development anyone must necessarily undergo, at an individual level, in order to understand some domain scientifically. Indeed, it's central to his conception of scientific understanding that those who understand be able to teach.[8] A beginner could thus presumably learn geometrical principles (and their theoretical role) from an expert geometer, and perhaps even come to have

---

[7] I take Barnes' arguments to this effect to be decisive (1993, 267–70). In what follows I'll be speaking of νοῦς of principles as a grasp of propositions, but recall that this is one of the places where Aristotle elides the distinction between our understanding x and our understanding *that x is F* (cf. pp. 48–49). So to explain how νοῦς of *human being* is developed is also to explain how νοῦς of the definition of *human being* is developed— where this would require the sort of theoretically sensitive grasp of such a definition described in our previous section.

[8] This is something Aristotle frequently emphasizes, but for some clear examples see *Met* A1 981b7–10, *Met* A2 982a12–14, *Met* E2 1027a20–22, or *EE* I.1 1014a18–19.

νοῦς of these principles as a result of her lessons: the expert would simply present it as a principle that triangles are three-sided rectilinear figures, and show what can be derived from this and various other geometrical definitions. Of course this sort of teaching might involve guiding a student through various proofs, as Socrates guides Meno's slave—but it would not require that the student derive geometrical definitions through her own use of induction, starting from what she herself perceives. What Aristotle is attempting to describe is the development necessary for the *initial* discovery of principles—that is, the development that made it possible for scientific understanding of some domain to come about in the first place, before anyone was around to teach it.[9]

So when Aristotle tells us that we learn first principles by induction, he doesn't mean that there is some sort of inductive method all aspiring scientists should be following, which would begin from what each of them observes individually, and end with the highest form of scientific expertise. What he means is that a certain form of cognitive development (an *inductive* form of development) explains how the state required for a grasp of principles could have been developed in the first place.[10] Thus *APo* II.19 should not be read as a practical guide that would lead a student of nature toward scientific expertise. It should be read as a high-level account of the learning of first principles, which seeks to describe how universal knowledge could possibly be developed, and which of our cognitive capacities are involved in its development.

One final preliminary. It's important to keep in mind that Aristotle presents his account as an alternative to Platonic innatism—a view

---

[9] Note that one can hold this sort of line about scientific understanding and nonetheless insist that *practical* forms of knowledge do require first-hand, perceptually-grounded experience, as Aristotle often indicates—e.g. at *EN* VI.8 1142a11–20 (=[61]) and X.9 1181b1–12, which passages will be considered in more detail in chapter 6.

[10] This way of understanding Aristotle's ambitions will be defended more fully below. For now, note that thinking of induction as the sole *method* by which we learn scientific principles seems to contradict Aristotle's methodological remarks in *APo* II.8–10 and II.13. It also conflicts with the concern Aristotle voices in *An* I.1, namely that there may be no single method we could apply to discover the definitions proper to any domain (402a16–17).

on which we would be born already knowing principles (or their Platonic equivalents) in some latent manner, and our learning of these principles would be a matter of making our latent knowledge manifest (by recollecting it, say). As we saw in our last chapter, Aristotle intends his invocation of our perceptual beginnings as a rejection of such innatist views. But of course perception alone doesn't yield knowledge of first principles: as Aristotle often reminds us, we perceive particulars, while scientific understanding deals with universals (*APo* I.31 87b33–35), and we never perceive anything *as* necessary, or *as* explanatory of some given phenomenon (*APo* II.7 92b2–3). So to account for our learning of principles, we need some process to take us from our perceptions to νοῦς of first principles; the process Aristotle goes on to describe in the rest of the chapter, and which he eventually identifies as induction (100b4, on which see our next section). Instead of beginning with advanced latent knowledge and achieving understanding by recollection, we begin with basic perceptual knowledge and achieve understanding by induction.

To my mind, this framing already rules out any deflationary reading of Aristotle's inductive account. For Aristotle's target here is a view that seeks to explain how advanced forms of knowledge might come about—recollection is meant to explain how we achieve sophisticated forms of understanding, not how we come to know general facts on the basis of which we might, by other means, achieve more advanced forms of theoretical understanding.[11] So what we would expect from Aristotle, in the rest of this chapter, is precisely this sort of account, and not an explanation of how one comes to learn certain basic generalizations. A partial account of our learning simply wouldn't

---

[11] Not everyone would agree that recollection always plays this role for Plato. (See for instance Bostock (1986, 67–68), though he distinguishes recollection's role in the *Phaedo* from its role in the *Meno*. Fine (2003, 61–65), Nehamas (1985, 20–24) and Scott (1995, chs. 1–2) all take recollection to result in advanced knowledge.) For my purposes, however, it's sufficient that *Aristotle* considers the kind of knowledge being retrieved to be knowledge of a sophisticated sort. And I think his emphasis on the exactness of this knowledge is good evidence that he does—recall that Plato also emphasizes exactness when describing the kind of knowledge Meno's slave might acquire after rehearsing his geometry lesson on his own (cf. 2.3 n20).

constitute a proper response to the kind of innatist portrayed in *APo* II.19.[12]

Further evidence that Aristotle intends his account as a complete one is provided by the range of cognitive capacities he thinks it must involve:

> [21] Given that perception is present in them, some animals retain what they've perceived, and others don't—and those that don't have no knowledge except what they perceive (either none at all, or none concerning the things they don't retain). But some can still hold [what they perceive] in their soul even after perceiving. When many such things are [retained] there's a further difference: in some reason [λόγος] comes about from the retention of such things, while in others it doesn't. (*APo* II.19 99b36–100a3)

As I read it, this passage offers a classification of animals according to the capacities they're endowed with or which they naturally develop: all animals can perceive, only some of these can remember what they perceive, and fewer still come to reason based on what they remember.[13] In the rest of the chapter Aristotle will explain how these

---

[12] It's true, as Bronstein (2012, 36) notes, that Aristotle distinguishes himself from the innatist already by positing perception, rather than some latent innate knowledge, as the source of advanced forms of knowledge. But "perception" is a satisfactory answer to the question how first principles come to be known only if that answer is accompanied by an account of our development from perception to νοῦς of first principles. In other words, pointing to the origin of our knowledge of first principles might be enough to *distinguish* one's view from an innatist one, but it isn't enough to provide a plausible alternative to innatism if the view is conceived of as an explanation for a sophisticated sort of learning—which I think is the natural way to think of it here. Nor would it be sufficient to posit perception as our starting point and go on to describe the preliminary steps of our development: the innatist could happily grant that this preliminary learning happens as Aristotle describes, yet insist that *advanced* learning, which yields a much more robust form of knowledge, requires us to posit some sort of latent innate knowledge, and a recollection mechanism to make it manifest.

[13] Some commentators translate the λόγος at 100a2 as "account" rather than "reason," and interpret the last sentence in this passage as a rather condensed description of our cognitive development, where grasping an account is assimilated with grasping a definitional first principle (see for instance Barnes (1993, 262), Bayer (1997, 120), Frede (1996, 169), Hankinson (2011, 46), Modrak (1987, 162), or Tuominen (2010, 123)). An interpretation closer to my own is defended in Bronstein (2012, 40–41), Gregorić and Grgić (2006, 21–23), and Hamlyn (1976, 176–77). Barnes (1993, 262) argues that such an interpretation "cannot be squared with the developmental language of 100a2-3" (i.e. γίνεσθαι λόγον ἐκ τῆς τῶν τοιούτων μονῆς). But I find this

capacities make possible certain forms of knowledge—in particular how they make possible νοῦς of first principles in animals who can develop an ability to reason. If such an explanation makes clear why the resulting knowledge would be sensitive to the theoretical status of these principles, it will constitute a good response to the challenge raised in *APo* I.3. I'll now turn to Aristotle's account, paying special attention to the role played by induction.

3.3 Learning in *APo* II.19: Induction

Here is Aristotle's initial description of our epistemic ascent from perception to νοῦς:

> [22] So from perception there comes memory, as we say, and from repeated memories of the same thing [there comes] experience (ἐμπειρία); for many memories constitute a single experience. And from experience, or rather from the whole universal which has come to rest in the soul, the one apart from the many, that which is one and the same in all these things, [comes] a principle of craft or understanding [i.e. νοῦς]—of craft if it concerns coming-to-be, of understanding if it concerns what is. (*APo* II.19 100a3–9)

The main interpretive difficulty here concerns the ἤ at 100a6. I've rendered it as progressive ("or *rather*") rather than epexegetic or disjunctive; that is, I think Aristotle doesn't *assimilate* experience with the stage at which "the whole universal has come to rest in the

unconvincing: animals can be classified according to whether or not they *develop* certain capacities as much as whether or not they're born with them (in fact similar language is used at *Met* A1 980a27–29, in a passage which is clearly not meant to summarize our cognitive development). In any case, if Aristotle *were* offering a condensed version of our cognitive development, he'd be omitting some of the intermediate stages he seems keen on emphasizing in other texts, most notably experience. For a parallel passage that supports my favored interpretation, see *Met* A1 980a28–b28, which ends by drawing a contrast between nonhuman animals, who live "by appearances and memories" and human beings, who live "also by craft and by reasonings (λογισμοῖς)." The contrast doesn't exactly match the classification here, but it does lend some support to the thought that λόγος should be taken here as a nonspecific kind of reasoning ability. See also *An* III.3 427b11–16, where animals are being classified according to their capacities, and those able to think (διανοεῖσθαι, in a quite general sense) are said to have λόγος.

soul," but rather thinks of these as two different stages on the path to first principles.[14] Such a reading seems to me well supported by *Met* A1, where Aristotle associates the grasp of universals with a certain kind of craft knowledge, and distinguishes this knowledge from that possessed at the stage of experience—as he puts it, "experience is knowledge of particulars, and craft of universals" (981a15–16). I'll be discussing this passage in more detail below—for now I only want to note that such remarks are hard to square with the view that experience would itself be the state in which some universal has come to rest in our soul. If this is right, it gives us some reason to think that Aristotle is distinguishing *four* stages prior to νοῦς of first principles:[15] perception, memory, experience, and an unnamed stage beyond experience in which the inquiring subject grasps "the whole universal."

How do we progress from one cognitive stage to the next? Aristotle starts with a somewhat unhelpful analogy:

[23] Thus the states [which know first principles] neither inhere [in us] in a determinate form, nor come about from more knowing states, but rather from perception—just as in battle when a rout has occurred, one [soldier] makes a stand, then another does, then another, until a starting point is reached (ἕως ἐπὶ ἀρχὴν ἦλθεν).[16] And the soul is the sort of thing that can undergo this. (*APo* II.19 100a10–14)

---

[14] I don't know of anyone committed to a disjunctive reading (but see Tuominen (2010, 126–27)). Defenders of the epexegetic reading include Barnes (1993, 264), Hasper and Yurdin (2014, 122–23), Le Blond (1939, 129–30), and Ross (1949, 674). Recent proponents of the progressive reading include Bronstein (2012, 44), Charles (2000, 150), Lesher (1973, 59), and McKirahan (1992, 243). I call this reading "progressive" rather than "corrective" to underline that it wouldn't be *false* to claim that a principle of craft or understanding comes from experience—it is simply more *accurate* to say that it comes from the proximate state following experience.

[15] In this passage νοῦς is identified as a "principle of craft or understanding," which is in line with the terminology Aristotle uses elsewhere in *APo* (see *APo* I.3 72b24, I.33 88b36, and II.19 100b15).

[16] Taking the ἦλθεν at 100a13 in an impersonal sense. For a survey of the many possible interpretations of this simile, see Lesher (2010).

Without reading too much into the details of the battle scene, Aristotle seems to be suggesting here that our progress from perception to first principles resembles a rout in which soldiers make successive stands. It's hard to determine what these stands might represent on the basis of this passage alone, but Aristotle elaborates in the next few lines:[17]

> [24] Let's repeat what we've just said, though not clearly. [24a] When one of the undifferentiated things (τῶν ἀδιαφόρων ἑνός) makes a stand, there is for the first time a universal in the soul; for although you perceive particulars, perception is of universals—e.g. of human being, not of Callias the human being. [24b] And again a stand is made among these, until something partless and universal makes a stand—for instance 'such-and-such an animal' makes a stand, until 'animal' does; and likewise with 'animal.' [24c] Thus it's clear that we must get to know the primitives (τὰ πρῶτα) by induction; for this is how perception creates universals in us (τὸ καθόλου ἐμποιεῖ). (APo II.19 100a14–b5)

In broad terms, the structure of this passage is this: a first stand occurs when [24a] a universal is first brought about from perception, after which [24b] higher and higher universals successively make their own stands until we reach a universal which is "partless and universal." Aristotle concludes [24c] that we must grasp first principles (which he calls "primitives" here) inductively, because (γάρ) it's through induction that perception creates universals in us.

A natural thought here would be that the universals perception creates in us just *are* first principles. On this reading Aristotle would be claiming that a single inductive process takes us straight from perception to νοῦς of principles, and that this is why we grasp principles inductively. But there are good reasons to reject such an interpretation. For one thing, it wouldn't tell us anything about how induction relates to the various cognitive states Aristotle identified as key steps in our cognitive ascent. It also seems hard to square this kind of reading with Aristotle's description of various interrelated

---

[17] I take the "just" (πάλαι) at 100a14 to refer to 100a3–9, rather than anything farther back (cf. Barnes (1993, 265)).

universals making *successive* stands in our soul—unless all these universal stands are somehow meant to be part of a single inductive process.[18]

In fact Aristotle's argument is more subtle than this. He begins (in [24a]) by identifying a first "stand" with the development of a first universal in our soul. When he proceeds (in [24b]) to describe the development of higher universals in terms of "stands," his point is that the *kind* of process responsible for the first stand is also responsible for subsequent ones. And when he concludes from this ($\delta\tilde{\eta}\lambda ov\ \delta\acute{\eta}$, in [24c]) that *induction* must be responsible for our grasp of first principles, he's leaving out the key premise that induction is the process responsible for the first stand in our soul—which is precisely the premise he supplies to support ($\gamma\acute{\alpha}\rho$) his conclusion at the very end of our passage.[19] In short, then, his argument has the following form: some sort of process is responsible for our first grasp of a universal, the same sort of process leads us to grasp higher and higher universals until we reach first principles, so *induction* must lead us to first principles, since induction is the process responsible for our first grasp of a universal.

What we should take away from this is that Aristotle isn't claiming that a *single* induction takes us from perception to first principles. Nor is he inferring, as commentators often assume, that we know first principles inductively merely from the fact that we come to grasp increasingly *general* universals. His claim is rather that the processes responsible for the first and subsequent universal stands in our soul are all *instances* of a certain kind of induction—namely, the kind of

[18] There's also some evidence against this view at *APo* II.7 92a34–b1, where Aristotle tells us that we can't learn definitions just by moving from particulars to universals, as we do when progressing inductively. Of course I am arguing here that he does in fact think we learn definitions inductively. As I understand his claim he is denying only that any *single* induction would yield an understanding of principles. (See p. 96 for the view that repeated inductions could serve to establish definitions.)

[19] I disagree with Hamlyn, who denies that the $o\H{v}\tau\omega$ at 100b5 refers to induction on the grounds that universals are already said to be present in the soul at the perceptual level, before any induction has taken place (1976, 180–81). Hamlyn fails to consider that one might grasp universals in quite different ways: a universal might be in the perceiver's soul even if she doesn't recognize it as such, and induction might therefore produce a certain *kind* of grasp universals which perception does not. I'll be discussing the grasp in question in more detail below.

induction at play when we first grasp a universal on the basis of our perceptions. We grasp first principles through repeated inductions of this sort, rather than relying on a single inductive step, and this regardless of the relative generality of the universals in question.

One difficulty with the reading I'm suggesting is that these inductive processes don't seem to have much in common: the first takes us from a grasp of one or more perceived individuals to a grasp of some universal, while subsequent inductions begin already at the level of universals, and take us to further universals. Moreover, the two processes may seem to reflect different sorts of cognitive achievements. For (one might think) the development from perception to our very first grasp of some universal happens at a rather basic conceptual level, while progressing through higher universals involves serious intellectual work—especially if the advance involves a theoretically sensitive grasp of the relevant universals. So it's not clear at all how these two forms of progress could be of the same type.

I think we face an interpretive dilemma. If "induction" is just understood as a placeholder for "any cognitive progress from the less to the more general" (cf. Barnes (1993, 267)), then it's clear enough how it might account for both our advance from particular perceptions to certain universal conclusions and our later ascent to further, more general universals. But it's hard to see how "progressing to the more general," on its own, would ever yield a *theoretically sensitive* grasp of definitional principles. Assuming we've encountered a number of human beings and come to grasp that human beings are rational animals, for instance, how are we supposed to *induce* that we shouldn't look for a further explanation of this fact, or *induce* that it expresses what it is, essentially, to be a human being? If induction is just a form of progress to the more general, it would never tell us anything about any proposition's explanatory role—which is precisely what (I've argued) Aristotle seeks to explain in this chapter.

If, on the other hand, "induction" is taken to be a more robust sort of process—the sort of process which might actually yield a theoretically sensitive grasp of first principles—then our interpretive challenge is to explain what *sort* of cognitive progress it's meant to represent. For it isn't clear what unifies our progress from perception to universals and our later progress to first principles, or, in Aristotle's terminology, what unifies the first and subsequent universal stands in our souls. And even if these two forms of progress do have something in common, it may seem doubtful that they could count as cases of Aristotelian induction—for induction, one might think, never affords us the grasp of *explanatory priority* required for our epistemic ascent.

I think we should opt for the second horn of this dilemma: the more robust notion of induction can be given a unified account, and some of Aristotle's remarks elsewhere in *APo* suggest that ἐπαγωγή can encompass quite sophisticated forms of cognitive progress. Before offering a defense of these claims, however, I want to clarify one last point about the (quite difficult) passage [24].

Aristotle claims in [24a] that "undifferentiated things" (ἀδιάφορα) make a stand in our souls. I'll be interpreting these as *infimae species*, which are "undifferentiated things" because one can't differentiate them into further species.[20] A worry that's often raised with this interpretation is that it seems to make Aristotle's account incomplete, assuming from the start that we can grasp universals like "human being" without explaining their development on the basis of what we perceive—for simply stating that perception is somehow "of the universal" isn't saying much. My response to this worry is twofold. First, our perceptual grasp of universals should not be *assimilated* with our grasp of undifferentiated things: the fact that perception is "of universals" features in Aristotle's *explanation* how a grasp of *infimae species* might possibly come about, but it doesn't yield that grasp itself. Second, nothing in II.19 prevents the "first stand" from occurring at a

---

[20] Some commentators (e.g. Bronstein (2012, 55)) suggest taking the ἀδιάφορα as *individual members* of some species, undifferentiated because they belong to the same species, while others (e.g. Bolton (1991, 6)) identify them with the "confused" (συγκεχυμένα) universals of *Phys* I.1 184a22, undifferentiated because their features haven't yet been spelled out in detail. One difficulty with the first kind of reading is that it isn't clear how the *next* stand—that by which we reach a higher universal—would be "made among these (ἐν τούτοις)" (cf. Hankinson (2011, 48)). For the items among which this stand is made are themselves universals (e.g. "such-and-such an animal" or "animal"), and it's natural to read "these" at 100b1–2 as referring back to the ἀδιάφορα which made the first stand. Bolton's alternative makes good sense, but the passage on which it rests speaks of moving from the universal to the particular, and this doesn't seem to sit well with the move from ἀδιάφορα to higher universals described here. (For more on this passage, see 4.6, below.)

stage we reach after we've already undergone a good portion of the cognitive development described in [22]. Indeed, given that one of the key stages in this development is described as that in which some *universal* has come to rest in the soul, there is good reason to identify the first stand with the grasp of a universal we develop *after* having progressed through the stages involving perception, memory, and experience. And of course Aristotle does describe these pre-universal states in some detail in other texts, so interpreting the ἀδιάφορα as I'm suggesting doesn't make his account incomplete.

So far, then, I've argued that each of the "stands" being described in [24] represents a separate use of induction, and that "induction" here is just the kind of process responsible for the first stand of a universal in our soul. I've further argued that this first stand represents our grasp of some *infima species*, and that it only occurs after we've progressed through three of the four cognitive states prior to νοῦς of first principles. I'm now going to consider what this first stand involves and what it has in common with subsequent stands in our soul, before trying to make sense of the claim that these should all count as *inductive* forms of cognitive progress.

3.4 The First Stand: Perception to Universal Knowledge

Aristotle thinks we perceive particular things in particular places at particular times. But there's nonetheless some sense in which perception relates us to the universals to which such particulars belong—as Aristotle notes in passage [24], in perceiving Callias we have a perception "of" *human being*, and presumably of some other universals Callias instantiates. I'll be considering these claims in greater detail in our next chapter. For now, it's important to keep in mind that perception is not meant to yield an *advanced* grasp of universals on its own—it's not merely by perceiving Callias that we're able to explain a range of zoological phenomena, or recognize what attributes must belong to any human, or suddenly know how to produce demonstrations involving human beings. Indeed, at the perceptual stage an inquiring subject may not even have the concepts necessary to articulate what it is she perceives, much less reason about it or its causes. What Aristotle is emphasizing here is only that a perceiving subject bears some relation to the universals instantiated by the things she perceives—and that this, together with the subject's other cognitive capacities, will allow her to develop a more advanced grasp of these universals.

Part of what makes this development possible is our capacity to achieve a form of *experience* on the basis of repeated perceptions of a certain type, retained as memories. Experience is a state Aristotle describes in some detail in *Met* A1, of which here is a key passage:[21]

> [25] To have a judgment (ὑπόληψις) that when Callias was ill of this disease this did him good, and similarly in the case of Socrates and in many particular cases, is a matter of experience; but [to have a judgment] that it has done good to all persons of a certain constitution, marked off in one class, when they were ill of this disease, e.g. to phlegmatic or bilious people when burning with fever, is a matter of craft. (*Met* A1 981a7–12)

Experience makes possible judgments of this sort, and, as Aristotle goes on to explain, thereby contributes to our practical success—an experienced doctor, on the basis of her past encounters with various particular patients and their various particular symptoms, will be skilled at determining the treatments that will cure patients she faces in the future (981a13ff, on which see further 5.2 and 5.3, below). But the diagnoses of such an experienced doctor are always rooted in and directed toward particulars. For instance, she doesn't pick a treatment by recognizing that Callias belongs to the type "phlegmatic human being," noting that he has a fever, and inferring that he must belong to the "malarial" type, and that "bloodletting with leeches" would therefore be a good treatment. Reasoning of this sort is only available to a physician capable of identifying the explanation for symptoms of some given type in some given type of patient, independently of any particular case presented to her—which, as Aristotle explains, is

---

[21] I follow Ross' translation, with a few minor modifications.

proper to the person who has universal, craft knowledge of medicine (981b6).[22]

So when Aristotle claims, in [22], that experience arises out of "repeated memories of the same thing" and that "many memories constitute a single experience," he is trying to explain how perceptual knowledge, whose objects are particular things in particular places and times, could ever provide a sufficient basis for the sort of reliable behavior displayed by those with experience. His explanation rests in part on the fact that perception is "of universals," even for perceivers who don't yet possess the concepts necessary to reason about the universals they perceive (on which point see 4.5, below). It also rests on the fact that animals endowed with memory can retain their perceptions, and that many memories of the same sort of thing might, in some of these animals, yield the kind of experience described above—as I will be explaining in greater detail in chapter 5. So, for instance, memories of a certain type of symptom and of some prescribed treatment's effects might constitute a "single experience" of some curing process, and an experienced doctor would presumably rely on a number of "experiences" of this sort.

Experience does require more than memory, since the experienced person has internalized some of the connections between her memories, and can associate new perceptions with her memories in a way that affords her a measure of practical success.[23] But it also remains a relatively basic state: the experienced person doesn't yet recognize the connections between her memories *as* connections between certain types which the remembered individuals instantiate. Though *we* might claim that an experienced doctor knows that all feverish phlegmatics

---

[22] More below on experience and its relation to such craft knowledge—on which see also Charles (2000, 151–56). There is some difficulty here in determining what role the constitutions Aristotle mentions are meant to play. As I understand his example, the patient's fever is the symptom, and fever in patients of some type (e.g. phlegmatics) is a sign of some disease (e.g. malaria). I thus take phlegmaticity, as it appears here, to be a disposition to exhibit certain symptoms when affected by certain diseases, rather than a disease itself. This seems in line with what Aristotle says at *EN* X.9 1181b5.

[23] For the sense in which such connections are "internalized" in an experienced subject, see Gregorić and Grgić (2006, 9–10).

should be leeched, the doctor herself (at least *qua* experienced) need not think of her patients or treatments in such terms.[24]

A physician possessing the craft of medicine differs from an experienced doctor in two significant ways: first, the physician can identify the *explanation* for some successful treatment, while the experienced doctor acts without explanatory knowledge, and second, the physician can recognize the effects of some *type* of disease in some *type* of patient, while the experienced doctor merely treats symptoms case by case. It may seem good to keep these points distinct, for one could presumably recognize patients as belonging to a certain type—as "phlegmatics," say—without yet knowing the explanation for the symptoms that phlegmatic people might display when affected by some disease. But here Aristotle assimilates the two: in the sense at play in this passage, universal knowledge allows us to think and draw inferences in general terms, and also makes clear explanatory relations between the universals in question.[25] So even if an ability to make judgments about types of individuals "marked off in one class" is a criterion for craft knowledge, as Aristotle suggests in [25], it's really our grasp of *explanations* which makes us wiser and allows us to "know

---

[24] On this point, see for instance Charles (2000, 152) and LaBarge (2006, 39), and see Hasper and Yurdin (2014) for a view on which the content of experience is dissociated from the particular discriminations it allows us to make. I disagree here with Johansen (2017, 109) and Schiefsky (2005, 351), who take experience to require some general *concept* because it involves many memories *of the same thing*. Again, it seems to me a mistake to think the experienced would recognize their memories of the same thing *as memories of the same thing*, even if they implicitly associate them with each other. Our describing their experience in general terms, from the outside, doesn't entail that the experienced themselves appreciate their generality.

[25] Compare for instance 981a5–7 and 981a16, where craft is associated with universals, with 981a24–28, where craft is associated with explanatory knowledge. See also 981b10–13, where knowledge of particulars is contrasted with explanatory knowledge (rather than *universal* knowledge). Bronstein has argued that Aristotle *does* distinguish these two forms of knowledge at 981a30–b6, when he separates the "manual worker" from the "master worker" (2012, 48–49). On his view the *master* worker has general explanatory knowledge, while the *manual* worker has general knowledge, but no grasp of explanations. This interpretation seems to me difficult to reconcile with the contrast drawn between particulars and universals in the rest of the chapter. For my purposes, however, all that matters is that a grasp of explanations be the real marker of rational progress; and Aristotle's dismissive description of manual workers acting as "lifeless things [τῶν ἀψύχων ἔνια], without knowing what they do" (981b2–3; cf. [52]) seems to me good indication that this is so even in the passage under consideration. On this point see also Moss (2012, 205–6).

in a stronger sense" (981a31) than someone with mere experience. The main mark of our cognitive progress beyond perception and experience is an *explanatory* form of understanding, manifested in an ability to give an account of what we are doing, and why.

Aristotle never explains the development of such understanding in much detail, but it doesn't seem too hard to fill out his account: an experienced doctor successful in her treatment of a range of particular patients might consider whether certain symptoms were common to certain types of patients, and whether some type of treatment was effective. If this kind of demarcation proves helpful, she might also be led to consider whether some type of disease (malaria, say) might account for the symptoms in question, and explain the treatment's effectiveness. And if she's successful in identifying the relevant disease, she'll have developed the kind of explanatory grasp proper to the craft of medicine. Her progress will consist in identifying some universal ("malarial") to which feverish phlegmatics, considered as a class, belong, and in seeing that their belonging to this universal explains their symptoms and the effectiveness of certain treatments. It's at this point, as I read Aristotle, that a universal will have "come to rest" in the physician's soul. For this is the first time our physician grasps universals *as universals*—the first time she is able to reason about what's "one and the same" in the many patients she encounters and prescribe a general type of treatment for some general type of symptom, recognizing both as such, that is, as "one apart from the many," as Aristotle puts it in [22].[26]

Now, a person in this state doesn't yet have νοῦς of medical principles. She doesn't yet know, for instance, whether the diseases she's identified are explanatorily basic or not. Nor could she situate any of her explanations in an axiomatic science of medicine.[27] At this

---

[26] Recall that Aristotle's concern here isn't to provide a method that would allow us to correctly identify explanatory universals. It's a difficult question what sort of method would lead to such discoveries, and indeed whether it's possible to identify any single method that would apply in all our inquiries. But Aristotle can describe the cognitive states involved in our learning without giving us a method to follow that would ensure their development, and even without committing himself to there being any such method.

[27] Here and below I will often characterize medicine as a science rather than a craft. In context, I don't take the distinction to be significant: Aristotle clearly indicates in

point she may not know if such a science is even to be found—it might not be possible to organize all medical explanations in the well-ordered fashion a demonstrative science requires. Still, she has made significant progress in this direction by reflecting on the experience she developed on the basis of a range of (remembered) perceptions. If my reading of II.19 is correct, the universal conclusions reached on this basis each represent a separate use of induction.

It's worth emphasizing that the resulting grasp of universals, as Aristotle describes it in *Met* A1, does not simply consist in an ability to form general judgments, or identify some group of individuals as members of a certain class. This is a necessary component of our advance from experience, but it isn't sufficient. Our progress beyond experience also consists in recognizing the *explanatory relations* between these universals—someone with the craft of medicine, for instance, won't just grasp that all feverish phlegmatics are cured by being leeched; she will understand that "feverish phlegmatics" belong to the class of "malarials," that their belonging to this class explains their fever, and the effectiveness of leeching as a cure. Someone with such craft knowledge could not yet be said to have νοῦς of the first principles of medicine, but she would at least have explanatory knowledge of some part of medicine—a step in the right direction.

So suppose, for now, that it's correct to call this kind of progress *inductive* (I'll be defending this claim in a bit). What does it have in common with the subsequent universal stands in our soul? Once

---

[22] that he takes his account of our epistemic ascent to hold for both theoretical and productive domains. I take it the explanatory structure of our knowledge would be similar in either case, with the difference being whether our understanding of this structure is theoretical or productive—that is, oriented toward our graping how things are, or rather our grasping what to do to fulfill some end. Thus the following demonstration might be a paradigmatic manifestation of medical science: "all feverish phlegmatics are malarials, all malarials are cured by leeching, so all feverish phlegmatics are cured by leeching" (assuming the premises here follow from definitions of diseases, symptoms, and their treatments). And something like the following reasoning would be a paradigmatic manifestation of medical craft: "all feverish phlegmatics are malarials, this patient is a feverish phlegmatic, so this patient is malarial—and malarials are cured by leeching, so this patient should be leeched," where the conclusion is known in a way that will issue in some action, and produce health in the patient. Though the aims of these arguments are different, they both invoke the universal *malarial* as an explanation—an explanation why something must be the case, and an explanation why something should be done, respectively. (I will have more to say about medicine as a craft on pp. 192–94.)

you've grasped certain portions of the science of medicine in the manner just described, how might you learn the basic principles of medicine, and recognize their explanatorily primitive role—and how does the progress from perception to medical craft knowledge compare with the progress from medical craft to νοῦς of medicine? I'll turn to these points in this next section.

3.5 Subsequent Stands: Universal Knowledge to νοῦς

Suppose you're an astronomer with a theoretically sensitive grasp of certain universals. You don't yet fully understand astronomical principles, and so you may not yet know how to produce proper demonstrations of all the astronomical events you've witnessed, but you can still explain some of them, and reason about them in universal terms. You might know, for instance, that shooting-stars are caused by a trail of vapor gleaming through the sky, that comets are caused by a fiery exhalation in the celestial sphere, and that the milky way is caused by a concentration of bright constellations outside the tropics.[28] In each case, you grasp an explanation for a range of perceived phenomena, and can reason about the explanation and the phenomena in general terms, without perceiving any one of their instances.

At this stage you only grasp distinct explanations for distinct types of astronomical phenomena. But you might seek some further explanation which would provide a more basic and unified account than the ones you currently have. For instance, you might come to see that the shooting-star's vapor and the comet's fiery exhalation are both instances of *condensation of the air*, and recognize that this condensation explains their behavior. And if you push the search further, you might come to see that the circular motion of the celestial sphere, together with some basic properties of air and fire, can explain

---

[28] These examples are from *Metr* I.4–8. See Lennox (1987) for a detailed treatment of Aristotle's search for explanations in *HA* and *PA*, and its relation to his methodological remarks in *APo*, and Lennox (2021) for a discussion of the relationship between these methodological points and Aristotle's claims about induction, with which I am in broad agreement.

this condensation as well as the presence of the Milky Way and a host of other astronomical phenomena. In doing so, you would come to recognize common explanations for a range of phenomena you were already able to explain in a piecemeal manner.

I claim that the cognitive development at play in this recognition is similar in structure to the one the experienced doctor undergoes when she learns the universal explanation underlying her treatment of a range of particular patients. Consider them side by side. The doctor's progress stems from the recognition that feverish phlegmatics are all malarial, and that this explains their symptoms and the effectiveness of having them leeched. Your progress as an astronomer stems from the recognition that vapor and fiery exhalation are both instances of a certain kind of condensation, and that this explains why they have the effects we observe them to have. In both examples, a universal is identified under which a range of cases are found to fall, and the fact that the cases instantiate the universal is supposed to explain their behavior. Why do vapor and fiery exhalation behave as they do? Because they're both instances of *condensation*. Why does leeching cure this feverish phlegmatic, and this other feverish phlegmatic, and so on? Because all these feverish phlegmatics are *malarial* (or, to put it more conspicuously, because they are all instances of malarial disease). If the medical example is a case of induction, there's good reason to think of your own astronomical progress as a case of induction, too.

Now, it's not yet clear how this kind of progress could yield νοῦς of first principles. What we have so far is a process which yields a grasp of certain universal explanations, and this alone won't tell us which universals *don't* admit of further explanation.[29] So one might think that even the robust sort of induction I've been describing would have to be supplemented to truly provide a grasp of principles as explanatory primitives.

---

[29] Nor has it yet been made clear how knowledge of an explanation, or even of a series of explanations, would translate into knowledge of a *demonstration* containing the relevant universal as its middle term. But finding demonstrations is easy once we grasp explanations: if we already know that feverish phlegmatics instantiate malarial disease and that this explains why they should be leeched, for instance, it's a small step to form a demonstration establishing as much (cf. n27).

But in fact this is unnecessary. To see why, it'll be important to consider a common Aristotelian assumption, namely that we can and should begin our inquiries by gathering all the scientific explananda relevant to some domain. Aristotle makes this point in a number of places, but here is a representative passage from *APr*:[30]

[26] The situation is the same in any other craft or science [as it is in astronomy]; once it has been grasped what belongs to each thing, at that point we will be prepared to make plain the demonstrations. For if nothing that truly belongs to the things has been left out in the collection of observations, we will be in a position to find the demonstration and demonstrate anything that admits of demonstration, and where there cannot be a demonstration, to make this evident. (*APr* I.30 46a17–27)

On Aristotle's view, then, our ability to find demonstrations and determine what cannot be demonstrated is dependent on an exhaustive survey of some domain of facts.[31] Once all the domain-specific facts have been gathered, we will have at our disposal all the terms necessary to describe the domain, and be ready to distinguish those attributes that belong to a subject's essence from those which are demonstrated on their basis.

The assumption that we have a comprehensive set of candidate explananda and explanantia at our disposal suggests a way induction could yield a grasp of principles as explanatorily basic. The idea is simply that repeated inductions would eventually reveal all the explanatory connections in the domain under consideration. And if induction repeatedly fails to produce a universal explanation for some fact (that the celestial sphere moves in a circular way, say), it will "make evident" (46a27) its explanatorily primitive status: since we've

[30] See also *APo* II.1 89b29–31, *HA* I.6 491a7–14, *PA* II.1 646a8–12, or *An* I.1 402b22–403a2. I follow Striker's translation here, with a few modifications.

[31] Aristotle does allow that we could provide provisional principles with an incomplete set of facts (*An* I.1 402b22–403a2). But ideally we would have all the facts at our disposal. Aristotle never explains how we would know we've amassed "all the facts" about some given domain, or how we would know which facts belong to which domain in the first place—a nontrivial point given that at this point in our inquiry we wouldn't have identified the principles definitive of any domain.

assumed that we have an exhaustive collection of facts at our disposal, no further observation could possibly serve to explain it. And insofar as induction makes this evident, it will yield an explanatorily sensitive grasp of the definitional principle expressing the fact in question. Though it won't *prove* its explanatorily basic status, there's a clear sense in which induction will reveal it.[32]

I've argued so far that there's good sense to be made of the claim that we come to know demonstrative first principles (and come to know them in a theoretically sensitive manner) by induction *if* induction is understood a certain way—roughly, if induction is understood as a form of cognitive progress from a range of particular truths to some universal explanation why all these truths hold. It's now time to defend the claim that this is in fact how Aristotle conceives of induction.

3.6 Induction and Universal Knowledge

In the *Topics*, Aristotle defines induction as "an advance (ἔφοδος) from particulars to a universal" (*Top* I.12 105a13–14). On its own, this doesn't tell us much. It's left open what the "advance" consists in, and just how it is we grasp the particulars from which it begins, and the universal in which it results.

Some commentators have suggested that the advance be understood as an inference beginning from particular premises to some general conclusion.[33] But this does not reflect Aristotle's typical and much broader usage of the term—the broader usage on which, for instance, all our learning can be said to come from perception,

---

[32] One might still want to know, of course, what allows us to establish explanatory priority *correctly* (e.g. to recognize that the presence of malarial disease in a subject explains the effectiveness of leeching, rather than the effectiveness of leeching explaining the presence of malarial disease). Aristotle is silent on this point, but he may simply think that there isn't much one could say about how to identify causes *in any science whatsoever*, because the methods and norms for establishing causal priority are often domain-specific (this is the suggestion advanced in Lennox (2011) and developed in Lennox (2021), cf. p. 42).

[33] Ross, for instance, singles this out as one of the key senses of the term ἐπαγωγή (1949, 481–87).

demonstration, or induction (cf. [18]).[34] For presumably Aristotle does not have in mind, in passages like these, that some specific sort of generalizing inference is responsible for all our nondemonstrative, nonperceptual learning.

Yet even if our inductive advance is not understood merely as a generalizing inference, one might worry that it must in some sense remain an advance from *particulars* to *universals*, and that this would already disqualify it from playing the role I suggested above. For example, when an astronomer induces that the shooting-star's vapor and the comet's fiery exhalation are both explained by their being instances of condensation, is she not advancing from *universals* ("vapor," "fiery exhalation") to some further *universal* ("condensation")? If so, it might be hard to see how this could count as a case of Aristotelian induction.

But such an objection rests on a mistaken interpretation of what Aristotle means by "particulars" and "universals" in this context. For Aristotle routinely invokes induction on *types*—indeed, right after defining induction he gives as an example that "if the skilled captain is the best, and [likewise] the skilled charioteer, then in general the skilled person is the best at her work" (*Top* I.12 105a15–16), and it's clear he's invoking captains and charioteers as types of skilled individuals here.[35] So the particulars from which induction begins and the universals to which it leads aren't meant to pick out specific logical categories—induction is not the move from knowledge of tokens to

---

[34] Aristotle does treat induction as a certain kind of syllogism at *APr* II.23, but he tells us at the outset that the inductive syllogism *arises* or *issues from* induction (it's a syllogism ἐξ ἐπαγωγῆς), and this leaves open a range of views concerning the relationship between inductive reasoning and the syllogism that arises out of it. In fact, the syllogism in question clearly *presupposes* some other form of inductive reasoning: the argument's *premises* (in his example, "longevity belongs to all Cs" and "bilelessness belongs to all and only Cs," for some animal genus C) are precisely the sorts of truths one would grasp inductively. See Caujolle-Zaslawsky (1987) and Engberg-Pedersen (1979) for further criticism of readings on which induction is a specific form of inference (and see Hintikka (1980) for a dissenting view). Commentators sympathetic to a broad reading of Aristotelian induction include Charles (2000, 270–72), Hamlyn (1976), McKirahan (1983), and Modrak (1981).

[35] See also *Rhet* II.20 1393b4–8, for an argument by example (which Aristotle says "has the nature of induction" at 1393a26) that operates on types and not tokens. Induction need not even yield a conclusion about types: in *APo* I.1 Aristotle describes someone inducing that some particular triangle *token* has angles equal to two right angles (71a21–24).

knowledge of types, or from a set of propositions about tokens to a general proposition about the type to which these tokens belong. The "particulars" and "universals" in question are better understood as descriptions of the *form* of our grasp before and after induction: we begin with some grasp of a range of facts which we understand *as particular cases*, that is, without recognizing any unifying feature they share, and we then induce such a unifying feature, which we grasp *as a universal* all the particular cases instantiate. And this sort of insight can be had regardless of the logical status of objects of our pre- and post-inductive knowledge—thus in Aristotle's example we recognize *skill* as the unifying type exhibited by various types of people we know excel in their field.[36]

Now, one might nonetheless object that grasping some conclusion *as a universal* does not mean grasping it *in its explanatory role*: we can have knowledge of some general conclusion without yet knowing anything about what this conclusion might explain. If induction served merely to secure the *truth* of general conclusions about a feature shared by some range of particular things, it wouldn't serve the purpose I've argued it must—though it might still be responsible for providing all the general *terms* featuring in the comprehensive survey of some domain (cf. p. 96), and thereby supply us with *candidate explananda*.[37]

But there are good reasons to think that induction does yield an explanatorily sensitive grasp of universals—or at least that it does so

---

[36] A consequence of this reading is that "particular" and "universal," in this context, are not absolutes: our knowledge can be more or less universal, and universal relative to some knowledge yet particular relative to some other knowledge. For instance, before the inductive advance Aristotle gives as an example was even possible, we must have known that skilled captains are best—a conclusion reached, presumably, from our knowledge of various individual captains. That initial knowledge was more particular (less universal) than the knowledge that "the skilled captain is the best," which itself is more particular (less universal) than the knowledge that "the skilled person is best." And after recognizing that skill makes people best at their work, we might induce some further, more universal explanation that would account for skill and a range of other cognitive features—perhaps some psychological explanation emphasizing certain features of our rational soul. This is compatible of course with some knowledge not being universal at all: knowledge that is not grasped as an explanation for anything else. For more on Aristotle's conception of particular and universal states, see 4.4.

[37] This line of thought is an important motivation for deflationary readings of *APo* II.19 (see Bronstein (2012, 46–47) for an explicit endorsement of such an interpretation). Thanks to Gisela Striker for pressing me on this point.

in the context of *A Po*. For when Aristotle speaks of grasping *universals* in *A Po* the grasp in question typically involves a grasp of *explanations*: someone grasping something καθόλου doesn't merely grasp some general proposition or term, but grasps a universal explanation for a range of particular facts. Consider for instance Aristotle's explanation of perception's contribution to scientific knowledge, at *APo* I.31. After having explained why perception doesn't (by itself) yield the kind of knowledge of universals required by scientific understanding, Aristotle describes how perception does contribute to our grasp of universals:[38]

> [27] Some features [of problems] are such that if we perceived them, we would not seek; not because we know by seeing, but because we grasp the universal from seeing. For instance, if we saw the glass having been pierced and the light going through it, it'd be plain why it does, too, even if we see separately in each particular [case] but think at a single time that it's such in every case. (*APo* I.31 88a12–17)

The case presented here is an example of our grasping some universal based on what we see: we see a pierced piece of glass, and understand why light goes through glass. How exactly this is supposed to work is not something I wish to address here (I'll say a bit more below, p. 119). I only want to draw attention to the fact that our perceiving light going through the glass is supposed to make clear *why* it does, and that this is meant to exemplify our grasping something universal from what we see—when we judge "that it's such in every case" we also learn *why* light refracted as it did in each of the particular cases we observed. A similar remark is made later on in *APo* II.2, when Aristotle notes that our witnessing a lunar eclipse from the moon would help make plain both the fact that and the reason why the eclipse is occurring, because (γάρ) "we'd come to know the universal from perceiving" (90a28–29).[39]

---

[38] The text for this passage is problematic, but not in any way that would affect the use I am making of it here. I follow Barnes' reading of the manuscripts.

[39] Aristotle never explicitly labels these cases as instances of induction, but in context it's clear that they should be taken this way—as Engberg-Pedersen (1979, 309) and Ross

In cases like these, grasping the universal does not just mean grasping general facts. It means grasping the universal *in its explanatory role*. In this sense, someone could have *general* knowledge about triangles (say) without yet having *universal* knowledge about them, as Aristotle illustrates at *APo* I.5:[40]

[28] Even if you prove of every triangle, either by one demonstration or by different demonstrations, that each has two right angles— separately of the equilateral and the scalene and the isosceles—you do not yet know of triangles that they have two right angles, except in the sophistical way; nor do you know it of triangles universally, not even if there are no triangles aside from these. For you do not know it of triangles as triangles, nor even of every triangle, except in number: [you do not know it] of every triangle according to the form ["triangle"], even if there is no triangle of which you do not know it. (*APo* I.5 74a25–32)

Thus even if we can prove of each and every species of triangle that it has two right angles, we won't thereby know that triangles have two right angles *universally*. What's missing is the realization that these species of triangles are *exhaustive* of their genus, and that it's *because* they belong to the genus triangle (or "according to the form" triangles share) that they have the angular sum they do. As above, the proper, non-sophistical grasp of the universal is an explanatorily sensitive one—not merely one that is general enough to cover all triangles.[41]

The grasp of a universal resulting from our inductive advance should (I suggest) be understood along similar lines—as the grasp of some universal *as an explanation* for a range of particular cases. So, in

---

(1949, 599) both note. In *APo* Aristotle almost never mention induction by name. On the lunar eclipse passage, see also Robin (1942, 477).

[40] I follow Barnes' reading of the manuscripts and slightly adapt his translation. See also Hasper and Yurdin (2014, 131–32) for a reading of this passage along similar lines.

[41] See further, in a similar vein, *APo* I.4 73b33ff and I.24 85b23–27. This association between καθόλου knowledge and explanatory knowledge is not restricted to *APo*. Recall (p. 91) that Aristotle contrasts craft knowledge and ἐμπειρία by noting that the latter has particular objects, while the former requires an understanding of *explanations* which is assimilated to our grasp of certain universals (*Met* A1 981b10–13; see also *Met* A2 982a24–25 and *Phys* I.5 189a5–8).

Aristotle's example, induction won't merely tell us that skillful people are good at their work. It will also tell us that it's because of their skill that skillful people are good at their work. Note that induction need not *always* be taken yield such explanatory knowledge; my claim is only that it's natural to read it this way in the context of *APo*, where universal knowledge is often identified with a knowledge of universal explanations.[42]

One last objection.[43] The kind of induction described in II.19 seems to involve a rise from the less to the more *general*—recall the progression from "such-and-such an animal," to "animal," to "something partless and universal" (100b1–3). Even granting that induction leads to a grasp of these more general universals in some explanatory role, one might worry that this will leave out key cases of explanatory priority. For instance, suppose triangles are essentially three-sided rectilinear figures—so that "triangles are three-sided rectilinear figures" is an explanatorily primitive geometrical principle. One of the properties we would want to explain about triangles is their angular sum, and it's a key part of Aristotle's view that their angular sum be *explained* by their three-sidedness, rather than the other way around. But in this case all *and only* three-sided rectilinear figures have angles equal to two right angles. If induction requires a progression through more *general* universals, it isn't clear how it would allow us to see the three-sidedness of triangles as explanatorily prior to their angular sum.

I think the best reply here is to deny that the increasing generality of the universals described in II.19 is an important part of Aristotle's account. I've already argued (p. 85) that the structure of Aristotle's argument in this passage doesn't depend on the increasing generality of the universals Aristotle describes. And note that Aristotle tells us

---

[42] I concede that there are exceptions: at *APo* I.13, induction is said to establish that "what doesn't twinkle is near" (*APo* I.13 78a34–35), in an example specifically meant to illustrate the premise of a *non-explanatory* demonstration. And at *APo* II.7 92a37 induction seems to result only in knowledge *that* something general is the case. But typically something καθόλου, in *APo*, is something explanatory, and knowing something καθόλου is knowing it an explanatorily sensitive way. If induction yields such knowledge it's natural to think of it in the more robust way I've been defending here. For a similar line of thought, see Hamelin (1900, 43–45).

[43] Thanks to Ben Morison for bringing this issue to my attention.

at *APo* II.13 97b28–29 that the particular is *easier* to define than the universal, and that this is why we should move from the former to the latter—which suggests that moving toward "higher" universals could simply be a matter of expediency. But there's also some philosophical motivation to think generality unimportant. The motivation is simply that it should be possible for an *infima species* to be a first principle: the definition "human beings are rational animals" is presumably a biological or zoological first principle, even though it appears at the lowest rung of the universals mentioned by Aristotle. What counts as a scientific first principle is determined by some given set of explananda, and we would expect the definitions of various kinds of animals to be explanatorily basic relative to some set of zoological phenomena. If this is correct, the progression through higher genera in II.19 may simply reflect a decision to illustrate our inductive progress for an especially broad set of explananda—perhaps the broadest possible set of explananda, if we understand the "partless and universal" things as basic categories of being.[44]

To sum up, then, I think there's good reason to think of induction in the context of *APo* as the process by which we move from a grasp of a set of particular facts to a unified explanation thereof. The facts in question need not be expressed in propositions with a specific logical form, and the universals involved in their explanation need not apply more generally, to facts distinct from those whose explanation we sought. But induction in this sense does yield a grasp of something universal in precisely the sense in which the term is typically used in *APo*, that is, a grasp of some universal which is sensitive to its explanatory role.

If this is right there's no reason to scoff at Aristotle's claim that induction would lead us from perception to νοῦς. And so there's no reason to think he must have invoked some brute intuitive insight to sanction our principles, or that he must have implicitly circumscribed the ambitions of his inductive account. Even taking into consideration the very demanding constraints placed on our knowledge of scientific first principles, the claim that we would learn them by induction is a sensible and informative response to the challenge Aristotle sets

---

[44] As Bronstein (2012, 59) and Ross (1949, 678) suggest.

himself. None of this is to deny that certain methods are a good way for us to discover explanations and establish definitions—Aristotle may well think that collection and division, say, are good ways to come to know definitions noetically.[45] But as I see it, this would mean they are good ways to bring about our *inductive* advance, in the same way a geometry lesson with Socrates is a good way for Meno's slave to (begin to) recollect.

At this point, of course, I've presented inductive learning in a rather schematic way: moving from a range of particular facts to some universal, unified explanation of these facts. Aristotle indicates that our initial knowledge of particulars would be supplied by perception. But that leaves it open what other cognitive capacities would be required to move forward from this initial perceptual knowledge. Clearly, coming to grasp universal explanations is something that involves our intellect in some way—as Aristotle tells us, it takes a quick *intelligence* (ἀγχίνοια, *APo* I.34 89b10) to hit upon explanatory middle terms. So induction requires more than our perceptual and mnemonic capacities, even broadly construed. In our next two chapters I'll be examining just how far these perceptual capacities get us, and how we should understand the role they and our intellect respectively play in our learning.

---

[45] For different accounts of the ways these tools might be put to use, see Bronstein (2016a, 108–30), Charles (2000, 234–39), Ferejohn (1991, 23ff), Modrak (2001, 93–94), or Rodriguez (2020), and see Lennox (2021) for a detailed account of the general methods found in *APo* and some of the more specific ones found in Aristotle's scientific works.

4

Perception and Perceptual Contents

I've argued so far that perception, for Aristotle, serves as a starting point for our learning—not only because it's a *sine qua non* for the development of more advanced cognitive states, but also because it provides the knowledge on which the rest of our learning must be based. I've further argued that this learning results from the sort of inductive development Aristotle outlines in *APo* II.19: induction supplies us with an understanding of definitional principles on the basis of the knowledge perception affords us. It's now time to consider more closely the role perception is meant to play in this inductive account—what it is Aristotle thinks we can learn from perception itself, and how our perceptual knowledge relates to the more advanced states we develop on its basis.

It should be noted at the outset that these are points Aristotle does not address directly. It's clear enough that our perceptual beginnings play a central role in his epistemology. But it's far less clear what exactly Aristotle thinks we can experience perceptually, and what kind of knowledge perceptual experience is meant to afford us. Of course we do find in *De Anima* an account of perception on which a restricted set of sensible qualities play a privileged role: qualities like color, hardness, or motion, which Aristotle calls perceptible *per se* (καθ᾽ αὑτά).[1] But then Aristotle also speaks of perception in far more expansive ways. In *De Anima* already he allows for *accidental* (κατὰ συμβεβηκός) perceptibles, which would merely coincide with things perceptible *per se*—his main examples are "the son of Cleon" or "the son of Diares" coinciding with some pale surface.[2] And elsewhere Aristotle freely

---

[1] Where *per se* perceptibles include both *special* perceptibles (objects perceived by a unique sense modality—colors, sounds, and so on) and *common* perceptibles (objects perceived by more than one sense modality—motion, shape, and so on).

[2] Perceptibles that are not perceptible *per se* are perceptible accidentally. At any rate this is how things are categorized in *An* II.6: Aristotle also calls accidental (at *An* III.1

Aristotle's Empiricism. Marc Gasser-Wingate,
Oxford University Press (2021). © Oxford University Press.
DOI: 10.1093/oso/9780197567487.003.0004

speaks of our perceiving eclipses, refracting light, planets, triangles, oxen, and hares, and of our perceiving that we are perceiving, or that something is pleasant, or nearby, or twinkling, or that it's a loaf of bread, and whether or not the loaf is baked.[3] The relationship between *per se* perceptibles and these richer perceptual contents is never fully articulated: Aristotle doesn't spell out how we would get from the sort of bare sensation central to his psychology to perceiving the son of Cleon or a loaf of bread, or perceiving that the son of Cleon is here, or that some loaf is baked. This makes it hard to see exactly what Aristotle took to be available to perception. And this in turn makes it hard to assess his claim that perceptual knowledge serves as a foundation for the rest of our learning: it's hard to determine what knowledge perception could afford us without a clear account of what we might experience perceptually.

Now, one might think that he at least makes it clear that we must perceive particulars rather than universals—setting aside exactly which particulars we perceive, and what we perceive about them. But there are difficulties even at this more abstract level of description. For recall that Aristotle also tells us that "although we perceive particulars, perception is of universals; for instance of human being, not of Callias-the-human-being," and that this is one of the reasons he takes perception to provide an adequate basis for our inductive learning (*APo* II.19 100a16–b1; cf. [24]). In another passage, Aristotle tells us that we must perceive particulars and *not* universals (*APo* I.31 87b29–30), which suggests that the universals our perceptions are "of" must not be the objects we perceive. But then it's not obvious how we are to make sense of the thought that perception is "of" something other than its objects. Even supposing we somehow grasp universals when we perceive some particular, we'd like to know what relation we bear

425a20ff) the perception by some sense of some quality that naturally affects a sense different from it (e.g. seeing something sweet). But this won't affect what I have to say here.

   [3] Examples abound—for these see *APo* I.13 78a33–35, I.31 88a1, I.31 88a15, *EN* III.3 1113a1, III.10 1118a17ff, VI.8 1142a28–29, VII.6 1149a35, *An* III.2 425b12–25, III.7 431a8ff. Of course Aristotle also uses "perceive" to mean "be aware of," in a very general sense that would not pick out some specific mode of apprehension. But in the cases listed above he intends to oppose perception to various other cognitive powers, and so presumably does not have the generic sense in mind.

to these universals when we do so—and whether this relation is borne to just any universal, or only to some. In the case at hand, for instance, we'd like to know what exactly we're meant to learn about the universal *human being* when we perceive the particular Callias and thereby have a perception "of" this universal, and whether we perceive just this universal or also perceive the many other universals he instantiates.

The difficulty here reflects a broader tension in Aristotle's views on perception's epistemic role. As we saw, the general strategy behind Aristotle's rejection of innatism depends on perception's being a *basic* cognitive capacity—a capacity we share with lower animals, and which yields a form of knowledge that doesn't depend on the use of our rational capacities. If perception were not basic in this way, Aristotle's critique of innatist accounts of our learning would lose its force: part of the point was that we would avoid positing (absurdly, Aristotle thinks) the innate existence of advanced forms of knowledge. And yet, as I'll be arguing in more detail below, Aristotle's own account of our learning depends on our ability to discriminate things perceptually, and develop a relatively robust form of practical experience on this basis—achievements that may seem to require far more than perception itself. So on the one hand, perception alone must not supply us with overly sophisticated forms of knowledge. On the other, it must do enough to serve as a plausible foundation for the more complex forms of knowledge we're meant to develop on its basis.

I'll be trying to resolve this tension over the next two chapters. First, by arguing that Aristotle had a rich conception of perceptual contents, extending far beyond the basic sensible qualities identified in his psychological works, and moreover that he thought perception could be trained in ways that would transform what's conveyed to us by what we perceive. Then, by arguing that his claims about the particular and universal aspects of perception can be reconciled in a way that helps explain perception's contribution to the development of practical experience—and that this can be done without making perception too sophisticated a state to ascribe to nonrational animals. And finally (in our next chapter) by considering in more detail the zoological and physiological views that motivate his account of our perceptual responsiveness to universals—in particular the ways in

which perception, *phantasia*, and desire contribute to purposive locomotion, and how these capacities manifest themselves in the behavior
of rational and nonrational animals alike. Taken together, these points
will yield an account of perception and perceptual knowledge that
is expansive but nonetheless compatible with Aristotle's anti-innatist
commitments.

4.1 Perceptual Objects and Contents: A Broad View

I noted above that Aristotle is not always clear about what he takes to
be perceptually available to us: he seems to speak of perception in both
very narrow and very broad ways. But it might seem that Aristotle has
more to say on this matter than I've been letting on. For we do find
in *De Anima* II.5–12 an account of perception on which perception
involves an assimilation of our senses to the sensible qualities of
physical objects (those of their qualities perceptible *per se*). Now,
there are contentious interpretive debates about whether perception
just *is* this kind of assimilation, or rather something *realized* by
assimilation—and a range of further issues concerning the nature of
the assimilation in question. But however exactly these matters are
settled, it might seem clear enough what the *objects* of perception are
meant to be: we perceive whatever is the proper object of some sense,
or whatever object multiple senses have in common. Oxen and baked
loaves of bread are not the proper object of any sense, and so these, it
may seem, must be "perceived" only in some looser, derivative sense—
likewise for the son of Cleon and anything else Aristotle marks out
as an "accidental" perceptible, and *a fortiori* whatever it is we might
perceive about such accidentals. Strictly speaking, perception is just
the sensation of colors, sounds, and so on.

The difficulty here is not (or not merely) a matter of terminological
precision. It's true of course that Aristotle sometimes characterizes
some object as an αἰσθητόν when he really has in mind some
sensible quality of that object—just as we might sometimes speak of
smelling baked bread in contexts where we really mean smelling the

smell of baked bread.[4] But even setting this aside, there remains a question concerning the sorts of things Aristotle thinks our perceptual experience presents us with—whether in perception we are presented solely with an array of sensible qualities (red, sweet, etc.), or rather with an array of sensible qualities structured in some way, for instance by being experienced as a complex unity (red and sweet, as a cluster), or as qualities *of some object* (red and sweet as qualities something instantiates). On the former view, we would perceive only sensible qualities, which we might then combine or associate by other means. On the latter we would also perceive, at a minimum, something about the arrangement of these qualities, and perhaps also perceive the object whose qualities they are, and perceive this object's qualities as being instantiated by that object. Our perceptual experience itself would have predicative structure—so that we might experience *that some beet is red and sweet*, say, or at least that something is exhibiting the qualities red and sweet.[5]

I think there are good reasons to favor these latter, more expansive readings of the contents of perceptual experience. To begin with, note that Aristotle thinks perception is the capacity responsible for animal survival (see for instance *Sens* 436b18–437a3 and *An* III.12 434a30ff). So even for the most basic animals, it must convey enough to perceivers for them to pursue prey and flee predators. And surely this already requires more than the mere unstructured perception of sensible qualities. The lion must perceive the ox is near when it hears its lowing, the dog where the hare is when it detects its scent (*EN* III.10 1118a18–21). It wouldn't be sufficient to simply hear some sound or

---

[4] I take it that typically we speak of smelling bread, not smelling smells of bread—my point here is only that we could use the former locution even if, after some theoretical reflection, we came to believe only smells are truly smelled. See *An* II.6 418a25 or *An* II.12 424a29 for some examples where Aristotle's perceptible objects are clearly the perceptible qualities of certain objects. And see also Hicks (1907, 360–61), Kahn (1992, 368), or Shields (2016, xxxiv) on these terminological issues.

[5] Maybe there are ways of spelling out the perception of clusters of properties without saying that perception has predicative structure. I do think the sort of combination Aristotle considers necessary for almost all perception can plausibly be taken as a sort of predication, as I'll be explaining below (though not a form of predication that requires any conceptual grasp of its terms—cf. Tuozzo (1994, 527)). But I won't be defending this in full detail, since my primary aim here is to move us away from thinking of perception (or perception proper) as the bare sensation of *per se* perceptible qualities.

smell some scent—to hunt the animal must minimally recognize the sensible quality as belonging to some prey, and perhaps also recognize the prey as a source of pleasure.[6] So if perception is going to serve the role Aristotle describes in these passages, it must at least convey to us that some object exhibits a range of sensible qualities, and so do more than Aristotle's account of *per se* perception would allow.

Now, one might reply that this sort of animal perception must involve more than mere perception. On a common interpretive line, hunting animals need *phantasia*, and when characterizing them as perceivers Aristotle is implicitly relying on certain other capacities that would enrich what we perceive: perception delivers the sensible qualities, and other faculties operate on this input to yield something more. But while it's true that *phantasia* plays a key role in explaining animal behavior, and also true that it can assist perception in various ways, it seems to me mistaken to think it is required for anything beyond the mere sensation of qualities perceptible *per se*. For note that even when he describes the most rudimentary forms of perception in *De Anima*, Aristotle freely moves from the perception of some *x* ($\alpha\check{\iota}\sigma\theta\eta\sigma\iota\varsigma$ *x*) to the perception *that* something or other about *x* is the case ($\alpha\check{\iota}\sigma\theta\eta\sigma\iota\varsigma$ $\acute{o}\tau\iota$ *p*, where *p* is something that can be true or false). For instance, he tells us that when seeing a color or hearing a sound we (infallibly) perceive that whatever we see is a color, and whatever we hear a sound ($\acute{o}\tau\iota$ $\chi\rho\hat{\omega}\mu\alpha$... $\acute{o}\tau\iota$ $\psi\acute{o}\phi o\varsigma$, *An* II.6 418a15), and that we also (fallibly) perceive what it is that has color or emits sound, and where that thing is (418a16).[7] Later on,

---

[6] Where such recognition need not be understood as a *conceptual* exercise: a lion can be taken to recognize an ox *as a source of pleasure* merely in virtue of being disposed to respond to the ox's behavior in various ways—ways I will be specifying in more detail in our next chapter. See on this point *Sens* 443b20–26, where certain odors are said to be pleasant (or unpleasant) *accidentally*, yet where the pleasantness of the odor is nonetheless critical to the pursuit of food.

[7] See further *An* III.6 430b29–30, on seeing that the white thing is (or is not) human, and *An* II.3 414a29–b16, where Aristotle tells us that even the most basic animals must perceive pleasure and pain, and also pleasurable and painful *things*—and, further, perceive *food* when they perceive *per se* perceptible qualities through touch (more on such perception in our next chapter). Recall also (from [25], [34]) the association between the particular-directed, broadly perceptual state of experience and judgments "that when Callias was ill of this disease this did him good." On the propositional structure of perception in these cases, see Moss (2012, 87–88), Sorabji (1996, 315–16), and Tuozzo (1994, 528–32).

at *An* III.3 428b21ff, he distinguishes between the perception of *per se* perceptibles (e.g. perceiving white), the perception of something's being an attribute of something else (e.g. perceiving that *this* or *that* is the white thing), and finally the perception of further perceptible attributes of such perceptible things (e.g. perceiving that *this (white) thing* is *moving*).[8] And since one of Aristotle's ambitions in *An* III.3 is to distinguish *phantasia* from various other cognitive capacities, and in particular from perception, which is closely associated with it, we should take him at his word when he says we perceive these things (i.e. perceive them in a manner that would not require the assistance of *phantasia*).[9] So it seems Aristotle is happy to speak of our perceiving not only sensible qualities, but also the objects that instantiate them, and of our perceiving *that* (our having αἴσθησις ὅτι) these objects are what they are, and where they are—and that he speaks this way even when we would expect him to be careful about his labels, and even when he is describing perception in its most basic form.

Why resist this conclusion? Two related reasons are usually adduced. The first is simply that Aristotle does draw a distinction between things perceptible *per se* and things perceptible accidentally, and that there must therefore be some sense in which the former are basic. A natural thought is that they are basic because our perception of anything more complex would have to be derived or inferred on the basis of *per se* perceptible qualities: we only *really* perceive what's perceptible *per se*, though we might of course interpret these perceptual data by other, non-perceptual means, and come to form judgments that something or other is the case on their basis—perhaps in a very immediate way that would coincide with our perceptual activity. The second reason is that Aristotle's examples of accidental perception seem geared to emphasize their nonperceptual features.

---

[8] Each level introducing further opportunities for error. He also tells us at *Met* M10 1087a19–20 that sight sees the universal *color* accidentally, just because whatever sight sees is some particular color. It's not always easy to see the common thread in all these cases, but I take it to be clear that they all involve our perceiving objects, and our thereby perceiving that they are something or another (or some way or another).

[9] In fact he tells us right after describing these three levels of perception that *phantasia* is "a motion brought about by active perception" (429a1–2), whose truth or falsity will be partly determined by the sort of perception that brought it about (428b24–30). So the initial perception must be possible without the assistance of *phantasia*.

For we do not see that someone is *Cleon's son*, for instance, by closely attending to certain features of our perceptual experience. We must have learned on non-perceptual grounds that this person was Cleon's son (e.g. from Cleon's telling us: here's my son).[10] So the paradigmatic cases of accidental perception may seem to depend on something more than what perception itself can deliver.[11]

On its own, the first of these points seems to me to have little force. For Aristotle doesn't generally think that an accidental *x* is not an *x* at all, or not *really* an *x*. Accidental causes, for instance, are still *causes*: it's true to say that Polyclitus, or some human being, or a living creature is the cause of a statue, even if the *per se* cause of the statue is *the sculptor* (*Phys* II.3 195a28ff). Likewise, accidental predicates are still *predicates*: it's true to say that "log" is a predicate in the statement "the white thing is a log," even if, on Aristotle's view, it isn't a predicate *per se*

---

[10] Now of course we must *hear* what Cleon is telling us in this scenario, and so some form of perception is involved in our learning from him who his son is. But the words we hear aren't responsible for our learning here—what's responsible for our learning is what's expressed by these words. Aristotle makes this point most clearly at *Sens* 437a11–15, where he tells us that hearing indirectly contributes more to the development of our intelligence than our other senses, because it allows us to hear what others are saying, and thereby allows for the communication of some vocalized λόγος. But as he emphasizes, it's this λόγος that is the cause of our learning, not the words used to convey it. A similar point is raised by Plato at *Theaetetus* 163b1–c3, where it's agreed that hearing a foreign language or seeing letters of an unknown script should be distinguished from our learning what the spoken or written words express—something we do not achieve by perception alone. (Note that Aristotle does think nonrational animals can *signal* things: one can convey meaningful sounds without conveying a λόγος. But even in these cases, the sounds animals emit and hear are not on their own responsible for their communication—in Aristotle's terminology, animals can produce sounds (ψόφοι) without having voice (φωνή), and they can have voice without having language (διάλεκτός). Insects emit sounds, animals with lungs and windpipes communicate by voice, and only humans use language—on which points see *An* II.8 420b5ff, *HA* IV.9 535a29ff, or *Pol* I.2 1253a7ff.)

[11] For views in this direction, see for instance Block, who claims of accidental perception that it "is not really perception at all but an association of ideas connected with direct [i.e. *per se*] perception" (1960, 94), Hicks, who claims that "we really perceive whiteness, [while] we think and say we perceive Cleon" (1907, 361), or Ross, who tells us that "the 'perception' of Cleon's son [...] is not really the perception of Cleon's son, but the perception of a white object which happens to be Cleon's son" (1961, 271). (How exactly we are meant to perceive a white *object* rather than just perceiving white Ross does not make clear.) For the view that nonperceptual capacities must be involved in accidental perception, see Kahn (1992, 367–68), Scheiter (2012, 261–64), and Taylor (1990, 127–28). Different interpretations on which we do perceive accidentals can be found in Cashdollar (1973), Everson (1997, 227), Modrak (1987, 69–71), Moss (2012, 39–40), Reeve (2012, 28–40), Shields (2016, 227), or Sorabji (1992, 196).

(*APo* I.22 83a1ff; see also *APr* I.27 43a33).[12] In both cases, we can still say that there is some sense in which the accidental case is derivative. On Aristotle's view some human produced a statue only because the sculptor produced the statue, and the white thing is a log only because the log is white. Still, the human is a cause and "log" is a predicate, even if presenting them as such might obscure some causal or predicative order we might, in certain contexts, hope to preserve.

A similar thought seems to be at play in Aristotle's characterization of accidental perceptibles. Consider for instance the following passages:[13]

[29] Something is said to be an accidental perceptible if, for example, the white thing should be the son of Diares. You perceive him accidentally, because he coincides with the white thing, of which there is perception. Thus you are not affected by an object of perception insofar as it is such a thing [i.e. such a thing as the son of Diares]. (*An* II.6 418a20–24)

[30] We perceive the son of Cleon not because he is the son of Cleon, but because he is white, and his being the son of Cleon coincides with this white. (*An* III.1 425a25–27)

In both cases we are indeed said to *perceive* accidental perceptibles (the son of Diares, the son of Cleon). It's true that we perceive them because

---

[12] "Log" is not a *per se* predicate in this statement because the statement doesn't mirror the natural metaphysical order, according to which "white" is predicated of "log," and not the other way around (*APo* I.22 83a1–17). Aristotle does say that "if we must legislate, let speaking this way [i.e. as when we say "the log is white"] be predicating, and speaking in this other way [i.e. as when we say "the white thing is a log"] not be predicating at all, or not predicating *simpliciter*, but rather accidentally" (83a14–17). However it's clear from the prior discussion that there *is* a sense in which accidental predication is predication: we can speak *truly* (if somewhat circuitously) when we say "the large [or white] thing is a log" (83a1–4). So the fact that this predication doesn't mirror the metaphysical order does not disqualify it as a predication—even if, in some contexts, it might be useful to speak as though it did ("if we *must* legislate. . .").

[13] The translation here is adapted from Shields (2016). His rendering of κατὰ συμβεβηκός as "co-incidental" seems to me right in this context—and brings out nicely the connection with the συμβέβηκεν at 425a26. I've stuck with "accidental" only to be consistent with Aristotle's broader usage, which includes a range of cases where that translation wouldn't straightforwardly fit.

of the sensible qualities with which they coincide—they affect us *qua* white, not *qua* sons. So saying that we perceive a white humanoid surface might make more perspicuous the causal underpinnings of these perceptual episodes, by revealing what makes these perceptibles perceptible. But it remains true that we really perceive the son of Cleon or Diares, just as a human really does sculpt a statue though they do not sculpt it *qua* human.[14] So Aristotle's distinction between accidental and *per se* perceptibles doesn't in itself suggest that we don't perceive accidentals, or that these accidentals are things we should somehow derive or interpret from what we actually, strictly speaking, perceive.

One might still wonder, however, what entitles Aristotle to think such entities perceptible—especially since the fact that some person was Cleon's son is something we plainly must have learned from someone else. Even a less elaborate case, like seeing that some humanoid thing is *human* (*An* III.6 430b29–31), might seem to require more than what perception can supply. At any rate, this isn't something revealed to us merely by concerted reflection on what perception presents as a humanoid thing.[15] Thus to some it will seem that our rational capacities must somehow be involved in such cases: without them it isn't clear how we could be said to perceive that someone is Cleon's son, or even just a human being.

Here, however, it will be helpful to distinguish perception from perceptual recognition.[16] In English as in Greek, it might be true to

[14] See Everson (1997, 188), Johansen (2012, 180–85), and Modrak (1987, 69) for an account of accidental perception as a case of accidental causation, and see Cashdollar (1973) for an account of accidental perception as a reflection of the accidental predicative order in our perceptual contents. I am sympathetic to the former view, but I won't defend it here. For my purposes any account on which accidental perceptibles are full-blooded perceptibles will do.

[15] That is, concerted reflection won't reveal whether we are really being presented with a human rather than, say, a non-human entity of humanoid appearance. Nor, when we perceive Cleon's son, will concerted reflection on our experience reveal that we are indeed being presented with Cleon's son.

[16] A distinction Everson (1997, 187–93) is right to press against more demanding interpretations of accidental perception, *contra* Cashdollar (1973, 160), Modrak (1987, 70), and Tuozzo (1994, 529), among others. I follow his extensional reading of accidental perception here. Recall that we raised similar considerations when presenting Aristotle's notion of experience: we can characterize an experienced doctor as knowing that all malarials should be bled without implying that she could recognize them as such or reason about the causes and effects of malarial disease (3.4 n24).

say that someone perceives an *x* though she does not recognize that *x* as such. For instance, you might rightly be said to see an *elm tree* despite not recognizing it as such, or knowing what makes it an elm, or even what distinguishes it from other trees. Likewise, to claim that you perceive the son of Cleon is not yet to claim that in doing so you recognize that he is the son of Cleon. What Aristotle says is only that we perceive the son of Cleon because he coincides with a white thing that's perceptible *per se*—and that leaves it open that we haven't yet learned anything about the person whose qualities are acting on our senses. To classify the son of Cleon as an accidental perceptible is thus not to say that we recognize him, just on the basis of our perceiving him, as the accidental perceptible he is.[17]

There is, admittedly, some difficulty in capturing the thought that we might also perceive *that* the son of Cleon is approaching (for instance) without knowing who the son of Cleon is.[18] For to perceive *that* something is the case is usually taken to entail our recognizing what is the case as such.[19] So one might go along with the thought that we can perceive the son of Cleon without knowing who he is, but deny that we can perceive *that* the son of Cleon is approaching without knowing who he is. But whether or not this point is true in English, it can't be true in Aristotle's Greek. For recall that Aristotle thinks we perceive *that* something is a color (ὅτι χρῶμα, *An* II.6 418a15) when we sense some particular color—where the sort of perception at play is presumably not meant to require an ability to recognize what we perceive as a color.[20] So we need not think that perceiving that the son of Cleon is approaching would require the prior knowledge necessary

---

[17] A good example of this usage can be found at *An*.3 414b6–10, where Aristotle claims that "touch is perception of food: all living things are nourished by dry and wet and hot and cold things, and touch is perception of these." Whether or not we take animals to be capable of recognizing food as such, Aristotle's explanation for their ability to perceive food is extensional: they perceive food simply because they perceive the proper sensibles that coincide with their food.

[18] One of the forms of perception Aristotle describes at *An* III.3 428b22–23.

[19] For what it's worth, I don't share this intuition: it seems to me right to say that I saw that the elm in my yard was shedding its leaves even if I never recognized that it was an elm. But I'm told this is not how "perceiving that" talk is usually heard. I'm happy to concede the point, as long as αἴσθησις ὅτι *p* (however rendered in English) not be taken to require that the perceiver recognize as such the terms featuring in *p*.

[20] Presumably not because this is meant to describe one of the most basic forms of perception, available to all animals alike (or at least, in this case, all animals with vision),

to identify Cleon's son—at least if "perception that" is simply meant to reflect Aristotle's use of αἴσθησις ὅτι in *De Anima*.

Now, no doubt someone's being the son of Cleon *is* just the sort of thing you might learn about them. And, once learned, it's the sort of thing you would recognize perceptually: once you know who he is, you see the son of Cleon as the son of Cleon, and not just as another Athenian, or just some other person. But in choosing this example Aristotle need not be read as emphasizing that we *must* recognize accidental perceptibles perceptually, or that the objects of accidental perception must always be transparently conveyed to the perceiving subject. His point might in fact be precisely the opposite, namely, that we can be said to perceive things even if perception itself doesn't allow us to recognize them as the things they are. A descriptor like "the son of Cleon" would be an especially good illustration of this point, since patrilineage (or patronymics) is obviously not accessible to us by perception alone.[21]

As I read Aristotle, then, accidental perceptibles are perceptible merely in virtue of their coinciding with certain sensible qualities— whether or not we have the cognitive resource to recognize them for what they are. It's sometimes objected that extensional readings of this

---

and I take it that basic nonrational animals do not recognize, when they perceive some color, *that it is a color*.

[21] It might be objected here that Aristotle suggests that accidental perception is prone to error in a way that our perception of *per se* perceptibles is not, and that this must mean some sort of recognition is required on the part of the subject—for, as he puts it, "[the perception] that there is white cannot be false, while [the perception] that this or that other thing is what is white can be" (*An* III.3 428b21–22, see also *An* II.6 418a11–16, *Sens* 442b4–9, or *Met* Γ5 1010b2ff). But in fact it's far from clear that *being accidental* is what makes our perceptions prone to error in these cases. Aristotle's point could simply be that we are more often mistaken about accidentals because our perceptions of accidentals are frequently informed by our background knowledge or beliefs about them. So you might believe Socrates is at the market, and so think you see him there when in fact you see Callias. The mistake here doesn't stem from Callias' or Socrates' being an accidental perceptible. It stems from the fact that your beliefs about Socrates' whereabouts (erroneously, it turns out) what your perception conveyed to you when you saw Callias. Since we have more beliefs about accidentals like Socrates and Callias than we do about *per se* perceptibles, accidental perception is more prone to errors of this sort (but not *because* it's accidental). As Aristotle says at *Insomn* 458b31–33, misperceiving occurs when someone perceives something that is real but not what they suppose it to be (οὐ [...] τοῦτο ὃ οἴεται). I take it we suppose things about accidentals more than we do about sensible qualities. If that's so it's no surprise the sort of mismatch alluded to here would be more common in the accidental case.

sort make perception overly broad: all sorts of things coincide with sensible qualities, and counting them all as perceptibles might seem to make perception little more than a generic form of cognition.[22] But this is a mistake. For on Aristotle's view *essences* do not coincide with any particular set of sensible qualities, and so on this account they would not count as accidentally perceptible, or indeed as perceptible in any way (as we learn at *An* III.4 429b12–18, on which more below— but see also *Met* Z10 1035b32ff). Thus we might perceive some human accidentally, and in doing so perceive the son of Cleon and the grandson of Cleanetus (and an Athenian, and so on) if these are things this human happens to be. But *what it is to be human* does not coincide with this human or any other human we perceive—and so will not be perceptible by that token. So identifying accidental perceptibles as whatever coincides with *per se* perceptibles does not entail that we can perceive anything whatsoever—even if we do not insist that the perceiver recognize accidentals as such. There will always remain a critical kind of entity Aristotle takes to be accessible only by rational means.[23]

If this is right, accidental perception need not be taken to depend implicitly on other, more advanced capacities—and our perceiving its many objects should therefore not be supposed to require something beyond perception itself. This is not to say, of course, that our perceptions *cannot* be affected by such capacities. Whether or not you recognize the son of Cleon when perceiving him will indeed depend on your prior knowledge about him—knowledge you did not acquire by purely perceptual means. Whether or not you recognize an elm tree when you see one will likewise depend on your prior knowledge of elms, or at least on your having some conceptual resources you might bring to bear on your experience. What perception *conveys* to a perceiver, for Aristotle, often depends on that perceiver's prior knowledge: I might see a bird and recognize it as a bird, while an ornithologist would see the same bird and recognize it as a kestrel, and

---

[22] This sort of worry is voiced for instance by Cashdollar (1973, 158); cf. Everson (1997, 189–90).

[23] This holds whether or not we think essences are somehow dependent on their perceptible instances: whatever their ontological status, we do not *learn* about essences by perception alone.

her cat recognize it as lunch. In all these cases perception presents us with the same bird, but our existing cognitive resources (conceptual, theoretical, or broadly mnemonic) affect what is conveyed to us when we perceive this bird.

For some perceptual content to be "conveyed" to a perceiver, as I understand it, is for the content to be available to this perceiver in a way they could use to form beliefs or guide their actions.[24] There's a nice example at *An* III.7 431b5–6, where someone seeing a moving fire is said to thereby recognize it as an enemy beacon. To perceptually recognize the beacon, in this case, is for the content of the perceiver's experience to be conveyed to them in a way they can use to, say, determine where to move troops, or form beliefs about the enemy's location, or else simply flee. In the former cases what's conveyed is affected by some existing knowledge of signals and warfare, while in the latter case it might simply depend on past memories of beacons and subsequent enemy attacks, and of the pain these attacks brought about, which the perceiver now associates with the sight of beacons, and which prompts them to flee (more on such associative responses below—and more on their psychological underpinnings in our next chapter).

Now, it's natural to wonder at this point just how we should understand the interaction between our perceptions and the background knowledge at play here. For if what perception conveys to us is affected by our background knowledge, then it may seem we could never truly be said to learn by perception alone: our past memories or existing knowledge or conceptual resources would always influence what we recognize perceptually, and thus always influence what we learn when we perceive something. And this might appear to threaten Aristotle's broader account of our learning, which, as I understand it, relies centrally on the idea that we share with other animals perceptual powers whose operation does *not* depend on any form of advanced knowledge or thought. But this appearance is misleading. For Aristotle does not take perception to *necessarily* depend on our rational powers, even

---

[24] In using this terminology I am following Siegel (2010, 51). I am using "belief" here in a generic sense, which may not correspond to any single state Aristotle describes in his psychological works—though on this point see Moss and Schwab (2019).

if he does think our background rational knowledge can sometimes influence what perception conveys to us. He can therefore allow for a form of perceptual learning that does not depend on any rational knowledge or thought. And indeed Aristotle takes such perceptual learning to be widespread even in subjects endowed with rational capacities, and to constitute an indispensable part of our cognitive development. Or so I will be arguing in what follows.

4.2   Perception and Rationality: A Nontransformative View

Many of Aristotle's remarks about perception suggest that he thought perception could be influenced by a wide range of cognitive states—or, as the point is sometimes put nowadays, that perception would admit of "cognitive penetration" from a number of different sources. We already encountered an example of this phenomenon in passage [27], where Aristotle suggested that seeing light going through some piece of glass would make clear *why* the light behaves as it does. Of course he doesn't mean that we learn such an explanation from perception alone: he is explicit that we do *not* know the explanation merely by seeing the light's behavior (*APo* I.31 88a13). What he has in mind is that some observation might lead us to an understanding of some explanation *given our existing background knowledge of the properties of glass and light*, which makes what we see relevant in a way it would not be to someone without this background knowledge.

In a similar vein Aristotle tells us that if we were witnessing an eclipse from the moon "we would seek [to determine] neither whether it is coming about nor why: these would be clear at the same time. For from perceiving we would come to know the universal as well" (*APo* II.2 90a26–29). Of course he doesn't mean that we learn the universal explanation for lunar eclipses *just* from some singular observation. What he must intend here is that witnessing the shadow cast by the earth would quickly allow us to recognize the earth's screening as the reason why eclipses occur *given our prior understanding of astronomy*. Someone without any background in astronomy would probably just be confused by what they see—all the more so because witnessing an eclipse from the moon would be quite different from witnessing it from earth.[25] But someone with some prior knowledge of planetary motion and the casting of penumbral shadows would quickly appreciate its significance.

In both of these cases, the significance of what we perceive is informed by some existing theoretical knowledge. But a similar phenomenon occurs in practical contexts as well. For instance, Aristotle tells us that only humans can perceive things as good or bad, or as just or unjust, rather than merely perceiving them as pleasant or painful, and that they can do this because they are capable of a sort of speech (λόγος) unavailable to nonrational animals (*Pol* I.2 1253a7–18). Again, I take it perception would not *itself* allow us to recognize anything as just or unjust. But our capacity to speak and appreciate the speech of others enables us to learn (from parents, fellow citizens, or laws, say) what is just or unjust. And this sort of learning expands the range of qualities we can subsequently recognize perceptually—and thereby allows for the prompting of rational desires that are directed toward the good rather than the merely pleasant.

These cases are sometimes taken to show that perception is not only potentially informed by rational forms of knowledge and thought, but that our soul's rational capacities necessarily transform our perceptual ones. If this is right human perception would always be an inherently rational exercise: merely by being human we would perceive differently from nonrational animals. Thus Joachim tells us that rational thought "permeates all [our] being and doing" (1951, 2), and Kahn holds that any form of perception beyond bare sensation is in fact a "conjoined action of sense and intellect" (1992, 368).[26] And if our

---

[25] From the moon, an observer sees a solar eclipse. So they would have to be able to imagine how this solar eclipse would appear from earth to appreciate the universal explanation Aristotle has in mind—which is not at all an obvious thing to do, and indeed seems to depend on our already having some understanding of solar eclipses. In *APo* I.34, Aristotle describes the talent one might have at working out such explanations: *quickness* (ἀγχίνοια) is the skill someone displays when, for instance, "upon seeing that the moon always has its bright side toward the sun, they quickly see why this is so: because it gets its light from the sun" (*APo* I.34 89b11–13). Again, I take it this sort of insight is only possible for someone whose perception is informed by some understanding of astronomy.

[26] In a similar vein, Whiting holds that our practical intellect might not only inform what we perceive, but that it "belongs to [the] perceptive or locomotive soul" (2002,

rationality does indeed transform the perceptual part of the soul in this way, it's not clear there is any form of perceptual knowledge we would share with other animals. Indeed it's not clear there is any form of knowledge that would count as *perceptual* in the first place, if this is meant to contrast with knowledge that would depend on more advanced cognitive powers. For the sort knowledge perception affords us would always—except perhaps for cases of bare sensation—depend on the rational transformation of our perceptual soul.

I think such transformative views are a mistake. There are some direct interpretive reasons for resisting them: in many of his arguments Aristotle invokes a distinction between broadly perceptual modes of cognition and their rational counterparts. For instance, he begins *Insomn* by asking whether dreams are presented to the perceptual part of the soul or to the part of the soul responsible for thought. This is plainly meant to be a disjunction: if the thinking soul isn't responsible for dreams, then the perceptual soul must be (*Insomn* 458a33–459a10). Likewise, in the opening lines of *Mem* Aristotle asks to which part of the soul memory and recollecting belong (*Mem* 449b4–8), and again the two options he considers in the ensuing argument are the thinking and perceptual parts of the soul—recollection belonging to the former and memory to the latter. It's not clear what sense there is to be made of arguments of this sort if it turns out that perception, in humans, must always involve the joint operation of our rational capacities. For that would undermine the very distinction Aristotle invokes when classifying our cognitive powers.[27]

There are also broader reasons for doubt. For Aristotle plainly thinks perception plays a key role in the survival of animals of every sort—by allowing them among other things to pursue what's good for

198). See also Keil and Kreft (2019, 8–16) and Rabbås (2015, 100). We find views along similar lines in the commentary tradition as well, in the context of debates concerning the unity of the soul and its parts. Here for instance is Aquinas: "just as an animal, as such, is neither rational nor nonrational—a human is rational and a brute nonrational—so too is the perceptual soul, as such, neither rational nor nonrational: it's rational in a human but nonrational in a brute" (*Quaestiones Disputatae de Anima* 11, ad 19). For a recent development of this view, see Boyle (2012, 409–16) and Boyle (2016).

[27] See Lorenz (2006, 152n7), where these same points are pressed against views that would assimilate the thinking and perceptual parts of the soul.

them and avoid what's bad for them. Nowhere does he suggest that humans would perceive any of this in a distinctively human sort of way. Of course, only we humans can appreciate reasons *why* something is good or bad, and recognize what's good and bad as such, as noted above. But on Aristotle's view we often respond to the situations we face in nonrational ways, without relying on any form of deliberation that would require our intellect. That we are capable of doing so is shown, for instance, by the fact that we display complex modes of behavior even when our rational modes of cognition are temporarily inhibited or obstructed, as Aristotle tells us at *An* III.3 429a4–8 and in *EN* VII.3—and by the familiar cases in which we find ourselves desiring things and effectively pursuing them without ever thinking them good, and even while thinking them bad.[28] We should therefore allow that nonrational perception is available to humans, and is often used in a way that does not involve any of our rational powers. Reading Aristotle this way will also allow for the kind of continuity between human and animal cognition he emphasizes in his zoological works (e.g. at *HA* VIII.1 588a18ff, and in the passages in our next chapter) and at various points in his description of our learning (e.g. at *Met* A1 980a28–b28 and in passage [21]).

This is of course not to say that our rational and perceptual capacities would operate alongside each other in some wholly self-contained, independent manner. Plainly this is not Aristotle's view. To my mind the examples above already show it is not—but one could also point to the general remarks Aristotle makes at *An* II.3 414b19–33 about the relationship between our nutritive, perceptual, and thinking capacities, where each lower capacity is said to be potentially in the higher, for the sake of which it exists.[29] Presumably this is the sort

[28] On which see further *EN* VI.5 1140b11–21, and also Cooper (1999), Lorenz (2006, 196–99), and our next chapter.

[29] Aristotle compares the parts of our soul here to the way triangles are potentially in quadrilaterals, quadrilaterals in pentagons, and so on. Part of his thought, I take it, is that more complex figures can be built up from more basic ones, on which they depend for their existence, and yet still count as figures of their own, rather than, say, a mereological sum of triangles. Likewise our capacity for rational thought would depend on our capacity to perceive for its existence, but our soul would be a functionally unified whole, rather than a mereological sum of soul parts. What provides for this unity is a teleological ordering between these parts—the nutritive soul exists for the sake of the perceptual, and the perceptual for the sake of the rational. For readings along these lines,

of teleological subordination that manifests itself in the fact that humans can perceive things as grounds for the development of more advanced forms of knowledge, rather than just perceiving them with an eye toward survival and reproduction—and in the related fact that humans can experience the pleasures of learning for its own sake, which other animals cannot.[30] Thus, for instance, the role perception plays as a source of *conviction* in our inquiries (as described on pp. 36–37) would plausibly be a role it only plays in human perceivers: only humans can take some observation to be convincing, or take it to serve as evidence for or against some broader scientific theory (cf. *An* III.3 428a19–24).

So the use we humans make of what we perceive can indeed be affected by our rational nature. And human perception is subject to cognitive penetration by rational forms of knowledge in a way that is not possible for nonrational animals. What I think we should resist is the thought that human perception is an inherently rational exercise, which *must* operate in a way that reflects our rational nature, or *must* be informed by rational forms of knowledge or thought. As I see it, our rationality merely expands the range of states that can inform what we perceive, and the uses to which perception can be put. Nonrational animals use perception to survive, and perceive in ways that are informed by mnemonic association. Humans use perception to survive and also to contemplate, and perceive in ways that are informed by mnemonic association and also higher forms of rational understanding. What our rationality does not do is transform perception in a way that would make it necessarily rational: humans can perceive rationally, but they can also perceive in ways that are not at all influenced by their rational natures, or informed by rational forms of knowledge or thought. Indeed, Aristotle thinks our learning

see Corcilius (2015, 42–44), Hicks (1907, 357), or Johnson (2008, 9), and see Leunissen (2010, 59ff) for a dissenting view, on which our lower capacities are not for the sake of our higher (but note also *MM* II.10 1208a13–21). The key point here is that this teleological ordering does not entail that the rational part of the soul must always affect the operation of our perceptual powers.

[30] On which point see *Met* A1 980a20–27 and [37], which I will discuss below. See also Whiting (2002, 188), who points out that perception can be altered and informed in the ways I suggest here, but who, I think, is more easily read as adopting a transformative view of the sort I reject.

begins in just this way—on the basis of knowledge we develop by nonrational means, through the use of our perceptual and mnemonic powers only.

In our next chapter I'll be considering more closely what such nonrational perceptual cognition might involve, how it might be informed by our mnemonic powers, and what sorts of knowledge we might plausibly take it to supply. For now, I hope to have defended a broad reading of perceptual contents, on which we perceive not only certain sensible qualities, but also the objects of accidental perception, which will include anything that coincides with these sensible qualities—and that in perceiving such accidentals we also perceive *that* they exhibit certain qualities. To say that we perceive such accidentals is not to say that we recognize them as such, or that the contents of some perceptual experience are always transparently conveyed to the perceiver. And so it's no objection to this view that identifying the son of Cleon as the son of Cleon is something we cannot learn by strictly perceptual means. Nor is it making perception an intellectualized faculty to allow that we might perceive kestrels, eclipses, and refracting light. What our perceptual experiences convey to us can be affected by our prior knowledge, but need not be, and perceptual activity need not therefore rest on any prior or occurrent intervention of the intellect. Nor, finally, is calling perception of this sort "perception" an empty point, or something that makes perception so broad it could not be distinguished from generic cognition. For the contents of our perceptions will still pertain only to things that coincide with sensible qualities, and Aristotle thinks there's a critical difference between entities of this sort (which he takes to be particular material entities external to us) and the sorts of entities that are distinctive objects of thought.

One final note. The picture I've presented so far does not seek to explain how perceiving sensible qualities would allow us to learn about accidental perceptibles. To some this will no doubt be a disappointment: commentators often expect from Aristotle an account detailing the derivation of any sort of knowledge from our most basic

apprehension of *per se* perceptible qualities.[31] But these expectations
are misplaced. For Aristotle, *per se* perceptibles are fundamental in
a psychological sense: they serve to define the few sensory capacities
whose operation underlies all perceptual activity. It does not follow
from this that they are fundamental in an epistemological sense, too—
that our *knowledge* of *per se* perceptibles should be taken to serve as an
exclusive basis for all our learning, or as the sole "given" from which
we must infer other forms of knowledge.

Aristotle's descriptions of our cognitive development make it clear
this is not the role he assigns them. Recall that in [24] he describes
our epistemic ascent as something that begins with our perception
of *Callias*, and not a pale humanoid surface, or whatever his *per
se* perceptible qualities might be.[32] Likewise at *Phys* I.1 184b12–
14, he tells us that "young children first call all men father, and all
women mother, and only later distinguish each of them." Setting
aside for now what this learning involves, it's plain that young
children, as described here, would perceive *persons* even before they
can adequately recognize which persons are their parents (on this
example see pp. 148–49, below). Nowhere, then, is it suggested that
our learning would have to begin from raw sensory data—and in the
few places Aristotle describes the early stages of our learning he seems
to think of *accidental* perception as our starting point. So whatever
one might want to say about the sense in which *per se* perceptibles

---

[31] The absence of any such derivation is a key source of concern for Anagnostopoulos
(2009, 106n5), Barnes (1993, 266), Goldin (2013, 203), Stein (2009, 32), Taylor (1990,
128; 137–42), and Wedin (1988, 156–57). And the implausibility of such a derivation is
one of the considerations motivating the thought (most explicit in Kahn (1992, 367ff))
that our noetic capacities must be involved even at the earliest stages of our cognitive
development. On these points see also Biondi (2004, 212–13).

[32] I am thus unconvinced by the suggestion in Scheiter (2012, 263) that accidental
perception requires experience, and that the cognitive development described in *APo*
II.19 must have begun from mere sensation. Plainly Aristotle thinks our cognitive
development begins with Callias, not his sensible qualities. In fact this is something his
description of experience seems to require, rather than explain—witness his description
of an experienced doctor as forming a range of judgments of the form "when Callias
was ill of this disease this cured him" (*Met* A1 981a7–8). For similar reasons I am
unconvinced by the suggestion in Nussbaum (1978, 259) that *phantasia* is needed to
"actively focus on something in our environment, separating it out from its context," or
the suggestion in Caston (1996, 42) and many others that *phantasia* is needed for the
perception of accidentals.

are fundamental and accidental perceptibles derivative, we should not expect from Aristotle an explanation how knowledge of the former would lead to knowledge of the latter. That would reflect a sort of fundamentality he never intended. (To his credit, I would add: why ascribe him such an insane *tabula rasa* view if we could avoid it?)

So we shouldn't assume, as commentators often do, that Aristotle takes what's psychologically basic to be epistemically basic as well. One might of course still worry about the psychological framework on its own terms—Aristotle doesn't say much about how the perception of objects (or the perception that something is the case, where some predicative combination is involved) would emerge from the operation of our sensory apparatus. And so one might worry that Aristotle may not have the psychological resources to account for his expansive view of perceptual contents. But I won't consider these difficulties in any detail here.[33] What I hope to have shown is that the sort of perception Aristotle considers epistemically basic involves far more than the bare sensation of qualities—and that he nonetheless (and nontrivially) takes it to be a form of perception, rather than something that would implicitly require the use of more advanced modes of cognition, even if these more advanced modes of cognition can, once developed, inform our perceptions and affect what's conveyed to us by what we perceive.

4.3 Perceptual Experience and Conceptual Resources

As I argued above, Aristotle doesn't seek to explain our learning starting from some initial encounter with colors and shapes. He thinks we perceive Callias and other human beings (and in doing so perceive that they exhibit certain perceptible features), and seeks to explain our cognitive development from there. But even once we agree to this, it's

---

[33] See Johansen (2012) and Marmodoro (2014) for recent attempts to address them, which depend on different views of the nature and role of Aristotle's common sense. I agree with these commentators that Aristotle's common sense is meant to account for our perceiving accidentals and their various qualities, and our perceiving their combination. But it would take us too far afield to consider the merits of various accounts of this common sense here, given that my focus is on Aristotle's account of our learning, and this account, as we've seen, takes it for granted that we perceive objects like Callias.

not entirely clear how we should conceive of perception's contribution to the sort of inductive learning described in our previous chapter. On the reading defended above, perceiving Callias (or whatever else we perceive) doesn't itself entail the *recognition* of Callias as such—that is, a recognition of Callias that would inform our interactions with him, and perhaps serve as a basis for the beliefs we form about him. How then do we come to recognize what it is we're perceiving? And how do we move from there to knowing what would explain what we perceive, or to an understanding of essences we do not perceive?

Aristotle doesn't say much on these points, and what little he does say is telegraphic and confusing. He tells us, for instance, that perception leads to universal knowledge because perception itself is "of universals" despite the fact that we perceive particulars—so that when we perceive Callias our perception is "of human being" (*APo* II.19 100b1; cf. [24]). But this claim is problematic for at least two reasons. First, it seems to flatly contradict what Aristotle says everywhere else, which is that we perceive particulars and do not perceive universals. Second, it seems to undermine his critique of innatism. For this critique requires that perception be a *basic* capacity—a capacity we share with lower animals, and which yields only an unsophisticated form of knowledge. And it's natural to think that one of the things that makes perception so basic is the particular character of its objects.[34] But then it's hard to see how this could be consistent with our having any perceptual grasp of universals: perception is supposed to be basic because we perceive particulars *and particulars only*, and this should rule out any perception of universals from the start.

Now, it has been suggested (e.g. by Scott (1995, 153–55)) that we should pay close attention to the phrasing of Aristotle's remark: he tells us we *perceive* particulars and that *perception* is "of universals," not

[34] It's natural to think this because Aristotle thinks it's our grasp of universals that sets us apart from other, nonrational animals, and serves as the key mark of epistemic progress. Perception, though a helpful way to know that fire is hot or that Socrates looks pale, say, would never yield the sort of wisdom ascribed to those who grasp universal causes (*Met* A1 981b10–13; cf. p. 91). See also *Met* A2 982a11–12 on perception's basic character, and *EN* VII.3 1147b3–5 for Aristotle's argument that lower animals cannot be akratic because they lack universal knowledge.

that we perceive particulars and universals, or that our perception is of both (αἰσθάνεται μὲν τὸ καθ'ἕκαστον, ἡ δ'αἴσθησις τοῦ καθόλου, APo II.19 100a17). What this phrasing tells us, the suggestion goes, is that any particular perceptual act has a particular object, but the capacity to perceive is nonetheless defined in general terms.[35] But I don't think this can be right. First off, note that Aristotle says not only that we do not perceive universals, but also that *perception* is not of universals (APo I.31 88a2, cf. McKirahan (1992, 253)), and not only that we perceive particulars, but also that *perception* is of particulars (APo I.18 81b6). So we shouldn't read too much into the phrasing of his remark. More importantly, while it is of course true that there is a distinction between perceiving and the capacity to perceive, and that the objects of the latter can be described in general terms, this doesn't in itself explain anything about why perception's universality would contribute to our learning. A Platonic opponent could very well agree that the objects of perception can be described in general terms ("what participates in the Forms," say, or maybe "what participates in the Forms and isn't a Form"), without for all that considering perception an adequate starting point for our learning—except in the trivial causal sense.

Another common approach rests on a distinction between the objects perception relates us to and the contents of our perceptual experiences.[36] For restricting perception to particular objects, like Callias or some particular figure, does not preclude universals from featuring in a full expression of the contents of our experience when perceiving these particulars—the sorts of contents we might express

[35] This is meant to explain our learning, Scott tells us, because Aristotle thinks universals are *in* perceptible forms—so that he would be reminding us here that in perceiving particulars we nonetheless perceive particular "such-and-suches" (1995, 155). But I don't see how this helps: whether universals are in perceptible forms or not, we would still like to know how our perceiving particular "such-and-suches" would help us recognize "such-and-suches" for what they are. A Platonist might well agree that we perceive particular such-and-suches, but deny that this is any help: we perceive things as hot and cold, as long and short, as equal and not. What exactly we learn from this is far from clear.

[36] See Barnes (1993, 266), Bronstein (2016a, 245), Caston (2015, 46–47), Ferejohn (1988, 105), McKirahan (1992, 249), Modrak (1987, 168), and Moss (2012, 153–54) for recent examples, and see also Sorabji (2010, 3–26) for some precursors in the commentary tradition. I think versions of this reading can be found in Eustratius (*In APo* 266.14–29), Philoponus(?) (*In APo II* 437.15–438.2), and Themistius (*In APo* 64.2–9).

in propositions like "Callias is a human being," or "this figure is a triangle."[37] So one might interpret Aristotle's remark along the following lines: perception relates us to particular objects, but these objects must instantiate certain universals, and so perception will be "of universals" at least insofar as universals are always encoded in the contents of our perceptual experiences. For instance, when you stare at the sunset you perceive a particular: *the sun*. But a universal nonetheless features in the content of your perception: you perceive that the sun is *red*. Perception would thus, on this reading, be "of" the universal red, even though in perception you are related to some particular thing—the sun.

The challenge is then to explain what it would mean for certain universal types to "feature" or "be encoded" in the propositional content of some perceptual experience. The claim could be understood in (at least) two different ways. On one reading, Aristotle would be telling us that

(PCS) Perception is a conceptual state. To have a perception "of human being" is to recognize a human being as such, and this requires (at a minimum) the ability to *think* of human beings as entities of some kind and draw certain *inferences* about them.[38]

Interpretations along these lines have been defended, but they seem to me inadequate for two reasons.[39] First, we saw above that Aristotle's rejection of innatism relies on the thought that perception

---

[37] In what follows I will sometimes refer to these perceptual contents as *propositional*, but this shouldn't be taken to imply that we always perceive something that can be assessed for truth just as a proposition would. It seems, for instance, that our perception of *per se* perceptibles is true in a different sense, which does not require subject-predicate combination (*An* III.3 428b18–22, cf. *An* III.6 430b27–29, *Met* Θ10 1051b17ff). As in our previous section, I mean the "contents" of our perceptions to simply pick out *p* when we have αἴσθησις ὅτι *p*, keeping in mind that for Aristotle we can perceive ὅτι λευκόν without recognizing that something is white, or that *this* or *that* is white (*An* III.3 428b21).

[38] What exactly is required will depend on one's views concerning concept possession. We might take as a plausible minimal requirement for conceptual thought the generality constraint presented in Evans (1982, 100–5).

[39] Defenders of some form of (PCS) include Goldin (2013, 203), Kahn (1992, 368), and Taylor (1990, 127–28). Unsurprisingly, this kind of view is often endorsed by interpreters who think of perception (or at least perception that is not mere sensation) as a capacity transformed by and inherently dependent on our rational powers—cf. p. 120.

is a relatively basic capacity, which *all* animals possess (as Aristotle emphasizes at *APo* II.19 99b32–35). But animals cannot think or draw inferences. So (PCS) seems unlikely in this context. Even if Aristotle's account were restricted to humans only, part of the point of *APo* II.19 is to describe how we could ever come to develop the concepts at play in scientific demonstrations—assuming that they are already available to us in perception would simply be circular.[40]

The second reason is that Aristotle explicitly says at *Met* A1 981a7–12 (=[25]) that thinking and drawing inferences (e.g. about diseases) in general terms is something distinctive of craft knowledge—a state we reach *after* perception, memory, and experience on our path toward scientific understanding. This strongly suggests that even states more advanced than perception would not require the ability to engage in conceptual thought of the sort (PCS) demands—and therefore *a fortiori* that perception itself would not require such an ability. If this is right we have good grounds for resisting interpretations that would make perception a conceptually demanding cognitive achievement.

It seems plausible, then, that perception in this context is meant to be a non-conceptual state: even perceivers without the concepts needed to articulate what they perceive might have perceptions "of" universals. So we might think that Aristotle is telling us instead that universals feature in the contents of our perceptions in the following sense:

> (PCC) Perception has conceptual content. To have a perception "of human being" is to be related to some proposition containing "human being" as one of its terms—e.g. the proposition *that Callias is a human being*. We can be so related even if we cannot articulate or understand the proposition or its terms: it's sufficient that the propositional content *could* be understood (by someone with the appropriate conceptual resources) using the universal concept "human being."

On this interpretation, Aristotle would be telling us something about the content of our perceptions—in particular, that this content will

---

[40] As Goldin fully recognizes (2013, 202–3).

contain universal types, even for a perceiving subject who cannot recognize them as such. Thus on (PCC) an infant might see an otter at the zoo, and have a perception "of otter" even though she hasn't yet developed the concepts relevant to her observation. Once she develops her conceptual repertoire she might return to the zoo and perceive the otter *as such*—that is, she might perceive the otter in a way that allows her to *articulate* and *think* (and perhaps draw inferences and form beliefs) about what it is she perceives. But on this reading her perception was "of otter" even before this: the universal "otter" was encoded in the content of her perception before she acquired the concepts that would allow for this content to be conveyed to her, and enable her to articulate and think about what she perceived.[41]

Now, I think the idea that perception has conceptual, universalizable content captures an important part of Aristotle's treatment of perception. As I argued above, the contents of Aristotelian perceptions are quite rich—we perceive Callias and loaves of bread, and perceive that Callias is human and that the loaves are baked. Surely a full expression of these contents will require type-level terms. Once we separate perception from perceptual recognition, as is implicit in (PCC), and as I argued we should, I see no reason to deny that Aristotle means what he says when he tells us we perceive that Callias is human, that a loaf is baked, and so on. Quite apart from Aristotle's usage, it seems odd to think he would deny this.[42] For that would imply that our perceptual experiences are not only particular, but moreover such that they simply could not be expressed—even from the outside, as it were—in universal, type-level terms. Some contemporary philosophers do think that perceptual contents resist conceptual description, but it's hard to see what alternative view Aristotle could have been arguing against here. I therefore think we should endorse the view that perception has universal content in the

---

[41] On this way of speaking about content, her learning changes the relation she bears to the content of her perception, but not the content itself: she perceived *that there is an otter* both before and after she developed the conceptual tools necessary to articulate what she perceived. What her conceptual development changes is what is conveyed to her from having an experience with this content. See Bronstein (2016a, 245), Modrak (1987, 168), or Moss (2012, 154) for views in this direction.

[42] As Irwin is right to point out (1988, 320–21).

sense articulated by (PCC), that is, content that *could* be expressed in general terms.

It's a further claim, however, that this is what Aristotle means when he tells us that perception is "of universals." I think there are good textual grounds to resist this further claim, which I will discuss below. But note, as a preliminary reason for doubt, that (PCS) and (PCC) tell us very little about how a subject would be perceptually related to universals. On (PCS), a perceiving subject would already have to have certain conceptual resources to perceive universals at all—so our perception's being "of universals" doesn't itself explain how we might come to grasp universals. On (PCC), the content of our perceptions would be something we *might* understand in universal terms—but that explains little about the *actual* relation a perceiving subject would bear to the universals her perceptions are of.

Neither view, moreover, accounts for the fact that we perceive universal causes, specifically—that the universals our perceptions are of are not just any type whatsoever, but rather the very ones we might go on to understand scientifically. Recall that Aristotle's claim occurs as part of his description of our epistemic ascent, which involves a series of universals making consecutive "stands" in our souls, where, as I argued in our last chapter, each stand marks a grasp of the relevant universal in its explanatory role (cf. [24]). Perception is said to be an adequate starting point for the development of such explanatory knowledge *because* (γάρ) it relates us, in some way, to universals like "human being." But neither (PCS) nor (PCC) explains why these explanatory universals, rather than any general type, would be the ones our perceptions are of.[43]

The explanatory role played by universals is in fact a point of emphasis in Aristotle's discussion of particular and universal states in *APo* I.31, to which I now turn.

---

[43] Note that this concern arises even if I haven't convinced you that the universal "stands" in Aristotle's account reflect an explanatorily sensitive grasp of explanatory universals. For even if our perception of universals is invoked to explain something less sophisticated, one would like to know why the universals our perceptions are of are, specifically, the ones we might eventually understand scientifically, as explanations for some range of phenomena (e.g. some range of human features or behaviors).

4.4 Particularity and Universality: *APo* I.31

Both (PCS) and (PCC) share a common assumption. The common assumption is that Aristotle's remark about our perceiving particulars (and our perceptions being of universals) concerns the *logical status* of certain perceptible entities. Specifically, Aristotle would be telling us that we necessarily perceive, of some token *x*, *that x is F*, for some type *F*. The two interpretations differ on what it takes to perceive this. But they agree on this: to say we perceive particulars is to say we perceive *tokens* (things that are *not* "predicated of many things") and to say our perceptions are of universals is to say they are perceptions of *types* (things that *are* "predicated of many things," *Int* 17a38–40).[44]

But this assumption does not sit well with Aristotle's discussion in *APo* I.31—the only other text in the corpus that explicitly mentions perception's particular and universal aspects. Consider how perception is distinguished from scientific understanding:

[31] You can't understand anything through perception. For even if perception is of what is such-and-such and not of what is this so-and-so, you must still perceive a this so-and-so at a place and at a time. It's impossible to perceive what's universal and in every case, for that's not a this at a certain time ([if it were] it wouldn't be a *universal*, since we call universal what's always and everywhere). Thus since demonstrations are universal and universals impossible to perceive, it's clear it isn't possible to understand anything through perception. (*APo* I.31 87b28–35)

Aristotle begins his argument in this passage by echoing the thought voiced in passage [24], namely that perception is "of what is such-and-such," but that we nonetheless perceive "this so-and-sos" at some definite time and place.[45]

---

[44] See also Wedin (1988, 157) on this point.

[45] I'm assuming here that Aristotle is using "what is such-and-such" (τὸ τοιόνδε) to denote universals and "this so-and-so" (τόδε τι) to denote particulars. This isn't always the case, but in this context it's clearly what Aristotle has in mind: in this passage already he freely moves from "what is such-and-such" to *universal*, and later in *APo* I.31 he names *particulars* (καθ᾽ ἕκαστον) as objects of perception (87b38, see also 88a4).

So the fact that we always perceive "a this so-and-so" (i.e. that we perceive particulars) is supposed to disqualify the things we perceive from being universals, since, as Aristotle puts it, universals exist "always and everywhere." Now Aristotle cannot mean by this that universals exist independently of their perishable instances, or that universals are somehow always instantiated. After all, think of the universal "eclipse," which Aristotle treats as a paradigmatic object of scientific understanding. We can understand eclipses even if they don't in fact occur always and everywhere.[46] Thus his point here is not that universals are literally "always and everywhere," but rather that we can only understand phenomena that are *eternally recurring*, and that scientific demonstrations primarily explain general, unchanging facts about these eternally recurring phenomena. This is a point familiar from *APo* I.8, where Aristotle argues that we cannot demonstrate facts about perishable entities, because "nothing holds of them universally, but only at some time and in some way" (75b24–26).

Thus it's not because we only perceive tokens that it's impossible to perceive universals. The reason we can't perceive universals is that our perception is always tied to a specific time and place, and that it therefore can't tell us about universals *universally*, that is, *as* the sorts of entities that might explain a range of eternally recurring phenomena. In other words, Aristotle's argument in [31] isn't based on the logical status of the sorts of things we perceive or understand, but rather on the *manner* perception and understanding put us in touch with their objects: perception only tells us about things *as they are here and now*, understanding about things *as they are always and everywhere*.[47]

This point is vividly brought out by the subsequent discussion of perception's limitations:

[32] Rather, it's plain that even if it *were* possible to perceive that triangles have angles equal to two right angles, we'd seek a

---

[46] Note also that Aristotle thinks some *token* entities are eternal and unchanging, like the sun—in fact οὐρανός is even characterized as a token entity that's eternal and unchanging and *everywhere* (*Cael* I.9 278b3–7). So not all scientifically relevant types are "always and everywhere," and some things that *are* "always and everywhere" are not types. (See also *Met* Λ3 1073b5–6.)

[47] On this point note also *Top* V.3 131b21–30.

demonstration, and not, as some say, already understand it. For we must perceive particulars, but understanding is by knowing the universal. (*APo* I.31 87b35–39)

In this passage, Aristotle is asking us to suppose that we could perceive that triangles have angles equal to two right angles (henceforth: "2R"), and noting that even this wouldn't yield the kind of knowledge we have when we grasp a demonstration—and again, the reason invoked is that perception has particular objects, while understanding is reached by knowing universals.[48]

It's clear that in this counterfactual we're meant to be perceiving a general fact about all triangles, and not a fact that concerns only some given triangle token. So passage [32] is good evidence that Aristotle can't just be saying that our perception of triangles is particular because it only tells us about tokens and doesn't tell us about all triangles, or because it doesn't really relate us to the type *triangle*. For his thought here is that *even if* we perceived a general fact about all triangles, our perception would still be the perception of particulars, and therefore wouldn't yield understanding on its own.

In this case too, Aristotle is best understood as making a point about the *manner* in which perception puts us in touch with its objects. The point is that merely perceiving that all triangles have 2R wouldn't tell us what the connection is between being a triangle and having 2R, and that understanding the universal triangle *as a universal* requires some grasp of this connection. This is consistent with his earlier remarks about universal knowledge, which we discussed above (p. 97ff). For recall that Aristotle tells us ([28]) that we might fail to know that triangles have 2R universally even if we have a series of proofs showing, for each species of triangle (equilateral, isosceles, etc.), that triangles of that species have 2R: we would still need to recognize that being *triangles* is what makes it the case that all these species of triangles have 2R. Separate proofs might establish this for all

---

[48] The point of the counterfactual here is not that it's impossible to perceive triangles, and thus, *a fortiori*, impossible to perceive that triangles have 2R. For the assumption isn't just that we can perceive triangles, but that we can perceive of triangles *that they have 2R*. And the thought is that even if we somehow perceived this, we still wouldn't understand it. For we would still be perceiving particulars.

instances of triangles, but not for all triangles *qua triangle*, and so, as Aristotle puts it, not for the universal triangle (καθ' ὅλου τριγώνου, *APo* I.5 74a29).

In the counterfactual scenario we're being asked to consider in [32], then, perception (rather than a series of proofs) tells us that each and every triangle has 2R. But it doesn't tell us that these are all the triangles, and that it's precisely because they are triangles that they have 2R. And it therefore fails to yield knowledge of the universal *triangle*: it only tells us of the triangles we're currently perceiving that they have 2R, and it just happens to be the case that these are all the triangles there are. Thus perception fails to yield universal knowledge because perception is a capacity whose exercise depends on the presence of its objects—or, as Aristotle puts it in this context, because "we must perceive particulars."

APo I.31 is the only place outside *APo* II.19 where Aristotle explicitly discusses perception's particular and universal aspects. So it's especially significant that in this chapter perception's particularity is tied to the manner in which it relates us to its objects, rather than the logical status of these perceived objects. When Aristotle argues that we never perceive universals, he doesn't simply point out that we don't perceive general facts, or that we perceive tokens and not types—recall that on Aristotle's usage here we would be perceiving particulars *even if* we could perceive a general fact about triangles. Nor, when discussing our scientific understanding of universals, does he tell us that we only understand general, type-involving facts. Here too, his emphasis is on our grasping universals *universally*, in a manner sensitive to their explanatory role.

I think there are two related conclusions to draw from this evidence. The first is that the claim that we perceive particulars is not just the claim that we perceive tokens. It is, rather, a broader claim about the limitations of perception as a mode of apprehension, whatever its objects may be. Because its exercise is tied to present circumstances, perception cannot yield an understanding of the universal causal connections governing eternally recurring phenomena—this is what makes it a particular capacity, and an appropriately basic starting point for our cognitive development.[49]

This shouldn't really be a surprising result. It's clear from Aristotle's psychological theory that perception is supposed to be a capacity whose exercise is realized in a material process, when some perceptible object impinges on our sense-organs—this, as I argued above, is what makes perceptibles *perceptible*. Thus Aristotle often identifies perceptible objects as those that occupy space and subsist in matter, and infers from this that we perceive particulars (see for instance *Cael* I.7 275b5–11 and I.9 278a10–11, or *An* III.4 429b10ff). He tells us at *An* III.3 427b22–24 that we perceive particulars, and that this explains why perception is triggered by external objects, and thus why it isn't up to us to perceive whenever we wish, and he tells us at *Met* Z11 1036a2–7 that perception wouldn't tell us whether circles exist when we are not actively perceiving them.[50] So it's natural to read the claim that we perceive particulars as closely connected to the process by which we perceive things: we perceive through a *material* process, which is necessarily always tied to some specific time and place, and therefore only perceive particulars, that is, only perceive things as they appear to us at some time and place.

The second conclusion is that the sort of universality attributed to cognitive states like understanding is tied to the role universals play as explanations for a range of eternally recurring phenomena. On the way of speaking Aristotle adopts in passages like [31] and [32], perception cannot yield a grasp of universals because it cannot yield a grasp of universals *in their explanatory role*. This lends further support to the point defended above (p. 97ff) about induction: the cognitive state resulting from our move from particulars to universals should be understood as a form of *explanatory* knowledge. It also serves as evidence for the preliminary critique of (PCS) and (PCC) voiced

[49] On some conceptions of the token/type distinction, it might *follow* from this that perceptual objects must be tokens. My claim is only that this is not what Aristotle intends in *APo* I.31. For more on Aristotle's conception of particulars, see Harte (2010).

[50] In that passage Aristotle draws the same conclusion about our *thinking* particular circles, in abstraction from their sensible manifestations. Even such abstract circles, he tells us, have intelligible matter, and so are only known when we actively think them. It's only by some universal account that can we state and know how circles *always* are (1036a7–8). See further *Met* Z11 1036b33ff and Λ3 1070a9ff.

above. For the fact that types feature in perceptual contents, though correct as far as it goes, fails to capture the relevant aspect of Aristotle's conception of universality, at least as it plays out in these texts, which is that universals explain, and particulars do not.

In what follows I'll develop an interpretation of our perception of universals that does justice to these considerations. For now I hope to have established that Aristotle's treatment of particular and universal states tells against the shared assumption motivating (PCS) and (PCC). Aristotle's focus when discussing perception's universality is not on the logical status of whatever terms feature in perceptual contents. His focus is, rather, on the manner perception presents its objects to us: we perceive things as they are at some time and place, not as they are always and everywhere, and this is what distinguishes perception from universal states, which would enable us to explain why things are what they are, and appear as they appear to us to be.

4.5 The Perception of Universals

Aristotle makes it clear that perception alone won't provide any theoretical understanding of universals—perception doesn't yield any knowledge of the causal or explanatory relations between universals, or any grasp of universals as they are "always and everywhere." As he puts it elsewhere, we don't learn these things by just observing something and pointing our finger at it (*APo* II.7 92b2–3). In what sense, then, could perception be "of" such universals nonetheless? Aristotle never directly answers this question, but I think we can reconstruct a plausible view by considering his other descriptions of the relationship between universal and particular cognitive states.

Consider, for instance, how he distinguishes perception from thought in this passage in *An* III.4:

[33] We discriminate flesh and what it is to be flesh by different means. [...] It's by means of our perceptual capacity [τῷ αἰσθητικῷ] that we discriminate hot and cold, and those things of which flesh is the account [λόγος]. But it's by means of something

else [i.e. by means of our capacity for rational thought] that we discriminate what it is to be flesh. (*An* III.4 429b12–18)

Aristotle tells us here that we perceive hot and cold, and the qualities of which flesh is the "account," but that this account itself—what it is to be flesh—must be grasped by some other, rational means. We are, in other words, perceptually responsive to the sensible qualities *caused* by certain formal features of flesh—we sense hot and cold the way we do because flesh is what it is. Psychological theorists might seek an account of what flesh is, and investigate its sensible effects. But even for those of us innocent of psychological theory, our perceptions of hot and cold, on any particular occasion, are what they are because flesh is structured the way it is (and our perceptual organs structured the way they are). This, on the view I will be spelling out below, is just what it is for our particular perceptions to be "of" the universal flesh: we do not perceive the universal itself, and need not understand it independently, but are nonetheless perceptually responsive to its effects—that is, to perceptible features explained by what flesh essentially is.[51]

Now, Aristotle's discussion of flesh doesn't explicitly mention particulars or universals.[52] But his treatment of experience and craft in *Met* A1 rests on a similar distinction between theoretical, thought-involving cognitive states and their non-theoretical counterparts—and there the states are picked out as having universal and particular objects, respectively. Recall (from [25], repeated here) his characterization of experience as judgments on associated particular cases:

---

[51] A related case: Aristotle tells us even the most basic animals have the perception "of" nourishment (τῆς τροφῆς αἴσθησιν ἔχουσιν), because "all living things are nourished by dry and wet and hot and cold things," which are the proper objects of touch (*An* II.3 414b4–9). To say that our perception is "of nourishment" is thus to say that certain things appear dry or wet (or hot or cold) *because* they are nourishing—and that we are responsive, through touch, to the perceptible features distinctive of such nourishing things, where this does not imply any handle on the notion of nourishment itself.

[52] He does say flesh is "not without matter" and "a this in a this" in the elided portion of [33]. What he means is that flesh, though we can study it theoretically, is nonetheless material—and so should not be treated as an entity separate from its material manifestations. This is in line with his early programmatic remarks in *An* I.1 403a3–b19. But I won't attempt to fully explain the hylomorphism at play here.

[34] To have a judgment (ὑπόληψις) that when Callias was ill of this disease this did him good, and similarly in the case of Socrates and in many particular cases, is a matter of experience; but [to have a judgment] that it has done good to all persons of a certain constitution, marked off in one class, when they were ill of this disease, e.g. to phlegmatic or bilious people when burning with fever, is a matter of craft. (*Met* A1 981a7–12)

And consider the contrast he draws between such experience and craft knowledge:[53]

[35] We think that knowledge and expertise belong to craft rather than experience, and we take those with craft knowledge to be wiser than the experienced [...] because the former know the [universal] cause, but the latter do not. For the experienced know the [particular] "that" but don't know why, while the others know the "why" and the [universal] cause. (*Met* A1 981a24–30)

So an experienced doctor would (*qua* experienced) recognize patients and their symptoms at some determinate time and place, and know what to do to cure them. Experience is thus a *particular* state, in the sense articulated above: the doctor is responsive to things as they are here and now, on the basis of her remembering how they were then and there. Her capacity to remember that leeching cured Callias, leeching cured Socrates, and so on, enables her to respond appropriately to patients in need of leeching (981a14). Someone with craft knowledge of medicine, by contrast, reasons (i.e. engages in λόγος-involving thought) about types of patients and treatments without reference to any particular case. She understands certain diseases and their effects, and so understands *why* certain kinds of patients should be treated some way, rather than merely recognizing *that* some treatment is called for in this or that case. She thus knows universals universally.

---

[53] See 981b10–13 for the association of the "that" with particulars (and the association of the "why" with universals) that I am supplying here.

As we saw in our discussion of inductive learning, Aristotle thinks craft knowledge of medicine emerges from medical experience: we begin with a practical, particular grasp of medicine, and eventually come to understand the universal causes underlying our practice— for instance, by recognizing that the patients we cured by leeching were *malarial*, and that this is what explains the effectiveness of treating them with leeches. So there's a close connection between the universal objects of craft knowledge and the particular practice of those with experience: a craft treats theoretically and in explicit terms the explanatory structure that underpins the reliably successful practice of those with experience—just as, in Aristotle's example later in the chapter, a master worker in some craft knows "the causes of things done" by manual workers, who simply act as they do out of habit (981a30–b6).[54]

The contrast between practical experience and craft is nicely articulated in the opening lines of the *Rhetoric*:

[36] To some extent, everyone tries to examine arguments, to formulate them, to defend some positions and criticize others. Some people do these things at random, others from a disposition acquired by habit. Since both are possible, it's clear these matters can also be treated systematically.[55] For it's possible to study the causes accounting for the success of those who succeed—whether they do

[54] Craft knowledge is not a purely theoretical exercise, of course, since unlike scientific understanding it is oriented toward production (thus one might distinguish, as in 3.4 n27, above, between medical science and medical craft). But craft knowledge nonetheless requires our understanding some λόγος—our being able to explain or account for what we do—in a way experience does not. So while craft and science both require explanatory knowledge, the import of this knowledge, in the case of craft, is understood relative to the product one seeks to bring about. For instance, the doctor understands she should avoid circular surgical cuts because circular wounds are slower to heal (and her aim is to produce health). But she doesn't necessarily have the further geometrical understanding of circles that would explain why this would be true (*APo* I.13 79a10–15). Nor does she necessarily have any philosophical understanding of the nature of health (*Sens* 436a17–b1). So she does understand some theory, but her aims are not theoretical: the scope and extent of her understanding is dictated by her overarching aim, which is to promote the health of her patients—as are the modes of reasoning she employs in her craft, which will typically not be demonstrative in the strict sense laid out in [7] (cf. *EE* I.5 1216b16–25). For more on this point see Annas (2011, 108–12) and Johansen (2017, 121–28).

[55] Reading ὁδῷ ποιεῖν here, with Ross and Kassel.

so through habit or spontaneously. And everyone would already agree this is the function of craft. (*Rhet* I.1 1354a4–11)

Aristotle argues here that rhetoric admits of systematic treatment.[56] His evidence is that people obviously practice rhetoric (we all formulate arguments, seek to defend them, and so on), and that some are better than others at doing so, either because they've honed their skills through practice or just because they're naturals.[57] Aristotle thinks that something must ground this practical success: if people are indeed skilled at arguing there must be some explanation *why* they are skilled. And this shows that rhetoric can indeed be treated as a craft—we can give a systematic account of the reasons why certain argumentative practices reliably succeed.

I think the contrast between practical experience and craft knowledge suggested by these passages provides a helpful model on which to think of our perception of universals. Recall that experience, for Aristotle, is a state that emerges from the operation of our perceptive and mnemonic capacities—he tells us that experience arises out of "repeated memories of the same thing," and, even more strongly, that "many memories constitute a single experience" (*Met* A1 980b28–a1; *APo* II.19 100a4–6). So for instance many memories of some range of symptoms and corresponding treatments would constitute a single experience of some disease—and an experienced doctor would presumably rely on many such experiences, formed through her ability to associate various memories. The experienced doctor is thus meant to be *perceptually* responsive to her patients, *seeing* them each as feverish, and such that they should be leeched. And in doing so she is perceptually responsive to features these patients have *in virtue* of being malarial—though she doesn't know this, it's *because* they have malaria that Socrates and Callias are feverish and cured by

---

[56] The opposing view was plainly in the air—it's advanced in the *Gorgias*, for instance.
[57] Though he doesn't label it as such, it seems to me plausible to think of such skill as a kind of argumentative *experience*. As noted above, succeeding through habit is said to be characteristic of workers who have experience but no craft knowledge (*Met* A1 981b5). The case of spontaneous success is a bit harder to understand—but setting it aside won't affect the present argument. (For a related discussion of luck in practical matters, and its relationship with craft, see *EE* VIII.2 1247a3ff and also Gasser-Wingate (2020).)

leeching. In general, someone with experience in some domain will be perceptually responsive to the features certain things have *because* they instantiate some universal—which is just to say (on the reading I'm suggesting here) that their experience results from their repeated perceptions "of" the universal in question.

In the case under consideration, some sort of medical training is presumably necessary to form the relevant experience. We don't just intuit out of nowhere that leeching would be a good cure for some patient. The doctor's seeing that Callias should be leeched is thus an instance *trained* perception—perception informed by her other cognitive resources (of which we saw other examples above, p. 119). But this doesn't threaten the main contrast Aristotle seeks to draw between particular and universal states. For the required training is presumably meant to be non-intellectual—at least in the sense that it does not require any understanding of universal causes, or any account articulating what malaria is. We can, after all, be trained to leech malarial patients without understanding *why* leeching is the right remedy, and without understanding that it's the right remedy because they're malarial. The training might come from someone with craft knowledge, who could point us in the right direction as we hone our skills at handling malarials (still without identifying them as such). But it might also be largely self-directed, based on our own successes and failures, or on the successes of others who do not yet appreciate why they succeed.[58] It's therefore a kind of perceptual responsiveness we could plausibly ascribe to less sophisticated animals, as Aristotle himself suggests: a lion perceiving a buffalo might perceive it as something to be hunted, to be avoided when in groups, and so on. As with our experienced doctor, it would perceive the buffalo this way *because* the buffalo is a certain kind of animal, though of course a lion couldn't recognize that this is the case. And by interacting with buffalo, retaining what occurred, and associating its past memories, a lion could plausibly be taken to form a kind of practical experience structurally similar to the one possessed by a human doctor.

---

[58] It's good to keep in mind that not all our successful practices are fully articulated—and that diagnostic practices, for instance, are typically developed before we understand what accounts for their success.

Now, Aristotle does not think nonrational animals form experience in just the same way humans do: he tells us that they have only "a small part of experience" (980b26–27). This is perhaps because they retain less than humans, or because some of their senses are less developed than ours, or generally oriented toward survival behavior rather than the development of knowledge (980a20–27; see also *An* II.9 421a7ff). It is not, however, because the development of experience requires the use of our rational powers. In our next chapter I'll be considering in more detail what's required for this development—and why Aristotle took it to be a broadly perceptual exercise. For now, what's significant is that Aristotle draws the line between human and nonhuman animal cognition somewhere else: our ability to grasp universal causes and account for what we perceive depends on our rational powers, our ability to develop a reliably successful a form of practical experience does not.[59] So human experience might be more complex and wide-ranging than the sort of experience developed by other animals, who might generally be too busy surviving and reproducing. But the development of experience remains a psychological possibility for them, even without the capacity to engage in reasoning about universal causes.

An experienced subject, then—human or otherwise—perceives some particular *x* (something as it appears to them *here and now*), but there is some universal Y such that their behavior is responsive to features *x* has in virtue of being a Y. This, I suggest, is just what it means for the subject's perception to be *of* the universal in question. So to say that a lion has a perception *of* the universal "buffalo," on this reading, is just to say that the lion's behavior is responsive to a range of features the buffalo displays *qua* buffalo. To say that an experienced doctor has a perception *of* the universal "malarial" is just to say that the doctor's behavior is responsive to a range of features her malarial

---

[59] As I will explain in more detail below, this conception of our rational powers aligns with Aristotle's claim that perception and *phantasia* share the same objects (*An* III.3 428b10ff), and that the φανταστικόν and αἰσθητικόν parts of our soul are the same, and to be distinguished from parts of our soul responsible for intellectual thought (*Insomn* 458a33–b2 and 459a8ff). (For a similar point about the distinction between rational and nonrational as it plays out in Aristotle's ethical works, see Cooper (1999, 244–49) or Moss (2011).)

patients display *qua* malarial. Our perceptions are of universals when we are perceptually responsive to the features or phenomena these universals explain.[60]

This kind of responsiveness is something Aristotle often emphasizes when discussing perception's role in animal behavior. Here is a representative passage:[61]

> [37] The non-contact senses—i.e. smelling and hearing and seeing—belong to all self-moving animals. In all these animals they are present for the sake of their preservation: based on past perceptions they pursue their food and shun things that are bad or destructive. But in animals who also have intelligence (φρόνησις) they are present for the sake of their good: they report many distinctive qualities of things, from which both theoretical and practical wisdom is generated in the soul. (*Sens* 436b18–437a3)

Perception is a means of preservation, then, because it tells us what's to be pursued or avoided. In animals equipped with more advanced cognitive capacities it's also the basis for more advanced forms of knowledge: we humans perceive not just for the sake of our survival, but in a way that allows us to develop practical and theoretical knowledge. Perception provides this basis (I suggest) not by delivering a theoretical or conceptual grasp of universals from the start, but rather by conveying the many "distinctive qualities" things around us have *in virtue* of instantiating various universals—and doing so in a way that solicits a certain set of behaviors on our part, and thus allows us to develop *experience* about them, and eventually come to understand the relevant universals *as causes*.

---

[60] It's worth remembering that dogs can be trained to detect cancer and malaria—so there is no restriction, in principle, on the sorts of universals to which the perceptions of nonrational animals might be responsive. When sniffing out cancerous patients, dogs are responding to scents caused by cancer, and so have perceptions "of" the universal *cancerous*—all this of course without grasping an account of what cancer is, and indeed without the concept *cancer*. A similar case might be made for astronomical universals: animals are responsive to seasons, tides, and various other meteorological phenomena with astronomical causes, as Aristotle knew full well (cf. for instance *GA* IV.10 777b24–778a2).

[61] The translation here is partly based on Beare's.

How exactly these distinctive qualities are perceived and which action they solicit will plainly depend on a range of factors. For instance, a lion might appear to a hunter as something *to be hunted* and to a buffalo as something *to be avoided*—both because of features it has in virtue of being a lion. So facts about the perceiver's nature and general situation will affect how the perceived qualities are experienced.[62] And of course the *background knowledge* of the perceiver will matter, too—as noted above, a patient won't appear as something *to be leeched* to someone without any medical training.[63] In both cases, however, we remain perceptually responsive to features these patients or lions have in virtue of being malarial or some kind of big cat—and in both cases our behavior is so responsive without requiring an *intellectual* grasp of the universals in question, that would be sensitive to their explanatory role and depend on some account of what it is to be malarial (or a big cat).

Our perception is "of universals," then, because we are naturally constituted so as to be perceptually responsive to the effects of certain universal forms—in ways that allow for the development of the sort of experience described above. The fact that our perception is of universals explains how we can develop any such experience on the basis of our perceptions: if there were no universal causes in virtue of which things reliably appeared to us the way we perceive them to, we would never form the coherent sort of practice typified by the experienced doctor described in *Met* A1. The first steps of our epistemic development would therefore not be possible were it not for our perception of universals—and so neither would the universal "stand," as Aristotle indicates in [24].

So when perceiving Callias, to return to our main example, we might perceive Callias as someone to have a conversation with, to

---

[62] On which point see Freeland (1994, 48).

[63] Not *everything* depends on background knowledge acquired by training or habituation: elephants start breastfeeding the moment they're born (*HA* VI.27 578a22–24), some newborn vipers eat their way out of their eggs (*HA* V.34 558a30), and a range of animal reactions to predator and prey are presumably innate. (Allowing for this kind of innate responsiveness does not threaten Aristotle's critique of innatist views—recall that what Aristotle finds objectionable in [19] is the existence of innate *advanced* knowledge. It's quite open to him to allow for innate knowledge of a primitive sort, *contra* Fine (2010, 153).)

be treated as a living being capable of a range of virtuous activities, and so on.[64] If Callias appears to us this way *because* he is human, our perception will be a perception of the universal human being. And it will be a perception of the universal human being even though its object is Callias as he appears to us here and now—that is, even though what we perceive is the *particular* Callias. By perceiving Callias and other human beings we might develop *experience* of the universal "human being," that is, develop a grasp of human behavior that informs how we deal with the various humans we encounter, but doesn't require us to reason about them as human beings, or even to think of humans apart from the ones we face at some particular time and place. It follows from this reading that the universals our perceptions are "of" are precisely the ones we could understand in a scientific context, when they come to a "stand" in our soul—the ones that play some role as universal *causes*, that is, rather than any generic type.[65]

If this is right, Aristotle's remark extends a familiar point about perception's teleological role. It's widely acknowledged (and made explicit in [37] and at *An* III.13 435b19–24) that perception serves the good or well-being of the creature in which it is present. This must mean, at a minimum, that perception tells us what to pursue and avoid for the sake of our survival. But in human creatures the point goes further: perception tells us about the world in a way that would allow us to *understand* it, by developing a perceptually

---

[64] Aristotle never makes it clear exactly what our knowledge of the universal "human being" would serve to explain—but presumably the explananda would include some set of distinctively human behaviors and pursuits.

[65] Objection: does it not follow that explanatory universals are part of the content of perception after all—allowing, as on (PCC), that the perceiver need not be able to articulate or understand the universals in question? And if so does this not conflict with the claim (cf. pp. 45 and 117) that perception does not supply us with any explanatory sort of knowledge, or any knowledge of explanatorily basic essences? Reply: Yes and no. Explanatory universals are indeed part of our perceptual contents: we perceive that Callias is human, and are responsive to his humanity. But it does not follow that perception yields any explanatory knowledge or any knowledge of essences. For recall (from p. 17) that explanatory knowledge, as Aristotle understands it, requires an understanding of explanations as explanations—and an understanding of essences as explanatorily basic. And though we might be perceptually responsive to Callias' humanity, we do not, as I have argued here, perceptually recognize what it is we are responding to, or what his humanity might serve to explain. That requires induction, and the use of our intellect.

based form of practical experience from which a theoretical grasp of universal causes—our highest end as rational creatures—might emerge. It does so by enabling us to respond to the features caused by these universals in a manner that coherently solicits some behavior on our part. Perception can do this without engaging in any λόγος-involving thought, and despite always depending for its exercise on the presence of its objects. It thus remains an appropriately basic starting point for our epistemic development, as Aristotle's rejection of innatism requires.

4.6 Discrimination, Recognition, and Compound Universals

We might of course still raise some further questions about this account. For suppose we interact with Callias in the ways I suggested above—that is, by being perceptually responsive to features he has in virtue of being a human. We might still wonder how the recognition of Callias *as Callias* would come about from such behavior, or even how we would learn to identify Callias by name, rather than just responding to him as we would any other human. And that might seem to be a very first step if indeed we are to move from our experience with various particular humans (Callias, Cleon, and others, say) to an understanding of the universal "human" that would explain their shared features. It may seem, in other words, that Aristotle has not yet said enough about the sort of knowledge of *particulars* perception would provide—even if we allow for the sort of perceptual relation to universals outlined above.

In fact Aristotle is sensitive to this concern. Early in the *Physics*, he explains that[66]

> [38] The things which are first clear and plain to us are those which are compounded (τὰ συγκεχυμένα). It is only later, by taking these apart, that we know elements and principles. That is why we must proceed from the universal to the particular. For the whole

[66] The translation here is partly based on Charlton's.

is what's better known by perception, and the universal is a sort of whole: it embraces many things as parts. Words stand in a somewhat similar relationship to accounts. A word like "circle" indicates a whole indiscriminately, whereas the definition of circle divides it into particulars. And young children first call all men father, and all women mother, and only later distinguish each of them. (*Phys* I.1 184a21–b14)

Now, this passage has often troubled commentators, since it associates universals with what's better known to us and closer to perception, and particulars with what we discover later on. Elsewhere, as we've seen (e.g. in [9]), Aristotle treats what's particular as what's better known to us (but less well known by nature) and closer to perception, and what's universal as what's less well known to us (but better known by nature) and farthest from what we perceive. But I think there's good sense to be made of this passage in terms of our broader perceptual response to universals, as I've presented it above. For the thought here is not that we somehow directly perceive universals like human, and then go on to perceive particulars like Callias—recall that Aristotle is unambiguous that the objects of perception are particulars and particulars only. His thought must be, rather, that we begin by responding perceptually to undifferentiated "wholes," and only later learn to separate out the parts that make them up.

Thus in Aristotle's example, young children might begin with an undifferentiated whole ("men") from which they would later distinguish the parental and nonparental parts ("fathers," "other men").[67] That they call all men father is evidence that these children begin by being responsive to the broader category despite not yet being able to differentiate its parts: they are tracking *something* when they call all men father, even if they use the wrong word for it. Likewise, the

---

[67] I disagree with Scott's interpretation of this example, on which the initial whole would be "a mixture of the forms man and father" (1995, 122). It seems to me hard to imagine what it would be to grasp such a mixture. And it's hard to see how we would then understand the analogy Aristotle draws with our defining a circle—for the definition would presumably involve separating out genus and differentia as component parts of some existing thing, rather than sorting out some mixture that does not reflect any part of the structure of reality. (I am otherwise sympathetic with Scott's reading of this passage.)

term "circle" might be used pretheoretically to pick out some broader category—any roughly circular or elliptical figure, say.[68] We might then go on to make our talk more precise, and separate this category into circles and other elliptical figures. By articulating the definition of a circle ("figure extending equidistantly from some center," say, or something approximating this account) we would differentiate the undifferentiated whole (whatever we labeled "circle" pretheoretically) into separate parts ("circles," "other elliptical figures"). We might then recognize that circles are in fact a special subset of the things we used to label "circle," just as a child will come to recognize fathers as a special subset of the things they used to label "father."[69] In each case, our progress is progress *toward* universals, in the sense that it involves articulating *accounts* of certain things—accounts that would spell out their permanent features, and, in the ideal case, their essential ones. But it's also progress toward a more precisely delineated understanding of the universals to which we are perceptually responsive—and so a move toward the particular, as Aristotle uses the term here.[70]

---

[68] It's worth remembering that κύκλος can be used in all sorts of everyday contexts, where the shapes are not strictly circles, and are in fact sometimes just semicircles or vaguely elliptical arrangements (people standing around, amphitheaters, shields, eyes, city walls, and so on). And of course we ourselves commonly call such things circular, or round, without expecting geometrical precision. I take it there is some pretheoretical category these locutions pick out—even if the category would need a good deal of refinement to be of any mathematical use.

[69] A child might of course do this with far less than full understanding of some essence-giving definition of fatherhood: any nominal definition would do (cf. *APo* II.10 93b30–31), as would any preliminary account of the sort discussed in Bronstein (2016a, 159–62) and Charles (2000, 35ff). And of course a child's learning to discriminate their parents from other humans should not be taken to depend on their ability to *articulate* any such an account—the discrimination would presumably occur well before they develop the relevant linguistic resources.

[70] To say that "we must proceed from the *universal* to the *particular*" is perhaps not the best way to capture Aristotle's meaning here, as I understand it—though I've stuck with this translation for consistency. What he has in mind here is moving from some universal we grasp only in some indiscriminate way toward a more precisely differentiated understanding of this universal. This move does in fact depend on our initially perceiving various *particulars* that instantiate the universal in question—the starting point of the sort of inductive development I described in our previous chapter. The resulting grasp of differentiated parts of the universal (our understanding of *fathers* and *circles*, say, where these are distinguished from other men and round shapes) might then be the basis for further inductive progress, which might eventually lead to a complete understanding of the universal to which we were initially responsive (a full understanding of the universals *man* or *woman*, in Aristotle's example).

It's quite natural to think that we respond to universals in this way—
that we begin with relatively indiscriminate responses which we later
develop and refine through experience, teaching, or theory. And if we
think of the universals in question not as objects of perception but
rather as those universals perception is "of," there is no conflict in
describing our progress as something that would begin with universals, as Aristotle does here. We perceive various particular men and
women, but in so doing we respond to features they possess *qua* men
and *qua* women, and so have perceptions "of" some ("compounded")
universal we will gradually differentiate into various categories, each
signified with some label, and each corresponding to some account
we might go on to articulate (accounts of "father," "mother," and so
on). For perception reports many distinctive qualities, as Aristotle
frequently reminds us (e.g. at *Met* A1 980a27 and in [37]), even if it
is often quite hard to articulate what exactly these distinctive qualities
are, and what they are distinctive of. "Just as the eyes of bats are to the
blaze of day, so is the reason in our soul to the things which are by
nature most evident of all," as he puts it in a rare moment of eloquence
(*Met* α1 993b9–11).

For our purposes, what's significant is that Aristotle suggests we
operate with pretheoretical and prelinguistic forms of knowledge from
the earliest age—well before we manage to articulate anything in
an account. For even though their response to them is unrefined
and indiscriminate, and whatever exactly they call them, Aristotle
plainly thinks young children can differentiate and identify men and
women.[71] I submit that our perceptual encounters with Callias and
other humans at the start of our cognitive development should be
understood in similar terms, so that we might well identify Callias
and differentiate him from others without any deep understanding of
Callias' features, or of who Callias really is—and even, one might allow,

---

[71] I agree with Bronstein (2016a, 17n26), *contra* Fine (2010, 150), that there is no
reason to think the young children in Aristotle's example have any false *opinions* or *beliefs*
(δόξαι). The children here are not confused about who their parents are (or who is a
man or woman). They just do not yet know the right terms to pick them out. Indeed,
depending on their age it's not clear to me they would count as having opinions at all—
for opinions, on Aristotle's view, must be responsive to rational persuasion (*An* III.3
428a19–24). But whether or not infants opine at all, they should not be taken to opine
falsely in Aristotle's example.

without knowing Callias by name. In other words, the knowledge required to perceive Callias, Cleon, and others at the start of our cognitive development need not be taken to be the sort of knowledge that would allow us to *fully* differentiate them from any other person, or give a complete *account* of each of them, whatever exactly such an account may be.[72] It's sufficient that we perceive them as distinct from each other in some way or another, and as nonetheless sharing certain features we might eventually recognize as consequences of their humanity—just as a young child distinguishes various individual women but appreciates some of their shared features, which they might later recognize as consequences of (what Aristotle would take to be) their womanhood.

To fully work out what is distinctive about some individual, then, would indeed require more than perception can supply. But it's not required for the sort of learning stemming from our initial responsiveness to universals. What's required for such learning is just the basic ability to identify Callias and distinguish him from others. And this is something that's available to all sorts of animals, including very basic ones: Aristotle tells us that birds imitate their parents' song, that newborn pipefish cluster around their mother, and (somewhat more dubiously) that scorpions kill their parents the moment they can swarm them (HA IV.9 536b14–17, VI.17 571a4–6, V.26 555a23–26). So very basic animals can recognize their parents, even without the resources necessary to pick them out in language, or understand much of anything about them—and thus too the young children in Aristotle's example in [38]. They do so in virtue of their capacity to retain perceptual impressions of their parents, in a way that allows them to associate what they retain with what they initially perceived:

[72] Callias, as a perishable, contingent being, would presumably be an object of practical understanding rather than the sort of theoretical understanding that has been our focus (cf. EN VI.1 1139a6–8)—though we might allow that we could understand the universals he instantiates scientifically, and thereby understand *him* in an accidental way (as APo I.8 75b24–26 seems to suggest). To fully understand Callias in the practical way, I take it, would be to understand him in a manner that informs the deliberations that concern him—to recognize the features of his salient to our deciding how to act or interact with him in various settings, and appreciate what about him we should take as a given in the deliberative context. Of course there is a good deal of room between this sort of understanding and the minimal knowledge required to distinguish Callias from Cleon and others, and recognize each of them on various occasions.

memory, as Aristotle conceives of it, is a capacity to retain what we perceive *as a likeness of something else*, and so a capacity that would allow us to recognize what we currently perceive as something we've perceived in the past (*Mem* 449b22–23, 451a14–16). This does involve more than *mere* perception, which, as we noted above, is always of the present.[73] But knowing who your parents are (or who Callias is) in this way is something that Aristotle still takes to be the province of the perceptive, nonrational part of our soul, as his account of our learning requires, and as he emphasizes at *Mem* 449b24–30, 450a14, and 451a16–17, and in further passages I will be discussing in our next chapter.[74]

So here's what I've argued so far. Aristotle's psychological theory posits as basic the perception of certain sensible qualities (qualities perceptible *per se*). But he also allows for the perception of accidentals that would coincide with these sensible qualities—and for the perception *that* these accidentals are some way or another. So we see red and taste sweetness, but also perceive the son of Cleon, and perceive that the son of Cleon is approaching, and that he is human. These perceptual contents are indeed *perceptual*, and shouldn't be taken to rely on some implicit use of the intellect, or even the assistance of some less sophisticated capacity like *phantasia*. For to say we perceive the son of Cleon is not yet to say we *recognize* the son of Cleon as such, or recognize that he is approaching, or human: what features in the content of some perceptual experience might not be transparently conveyed to the perceiver. Indeed, Aristotle frequently suggests that our background knowledge (rational or not) would inform our response to what we perceive—spotting a rare bird might be of theoretical interest for an ornithologist, of predatory interest for her cat, and probably wouldn't even register for me. In each case, we do perceive the same bird: what changes, and what depends on our

---

[73] Thus Aristotle tells us memory is not available to animals who cannot perceive time (*Mem* 450a16–19). But presumably these are quite few—perhaps Aristotle has in mind here the sorts of grubs that do not even have *phantasia* (cf. *An* III.3 428a10–11), and of whom it's not implausible to think that they would not recognize their parents. More on these animals below.

[74] For more on memory and the association of likenesses, see Everson (1997, 193–210) and Modrak (1987, 103–7), and also Alexander's commentary on *Met* A1.

respective background knowledge, is what's conveyed to us when we do so.

Allowing for such expansive perceptual contents doesn't yet explain what we learn from perception: we'd still need to know how we come to recognize the things we perceive for what they are. But it does allow us to distinguish the sorts of things perception might teach us about from entities accessible only to rational modes of thought. For perceptibles must coincide with sensible qualities, and *essences* do not coincide with anything we can sense—individual humans are perceptible, what it is to be human is not. Because perception is realized through material processes, whatever we perceive must remain *particular*, in the sense that we perceive it as it appears to us at some time and place. Scientific understanding, by contrast, concerns *universal* features— and reflects a knowledge of these features as they are (in Aristotle's terminology) "always and everywhere."

How then does perceiving particulars contribute to our learning? Part of Aristotle's view is that in perceiving particulars we are also responsive to the features they possess in virtue of instantiating certain universals—the universals our perceptions are "of," and which induction, as I argued in our previous chapter, might lead us to understand in their causal role. So even though we perceive things as they are at some time and place, certain universals will determine some of the features to which we're perceptually responsive at that time and place—and at other times and places. Perception allows us to discriminate these features, and respond to the many different ways things appear to us in different situations. In animals who can remember things, repeated perceptions of some type can develop into a certain kind of productive or practical skill—for instance, in the human case, the skill someone with medical experience has to leech people, or, in the animal case, the skill a lion has to hunt isolated buffalo, avoid them when in herds, and so on. Perception's being "of universals" explains this part of our cognitive development by explaining how perception can yield such experience: some things regularly appear to us some way *because* they belong to some universal, and this (together with our mnemonic and associative capacities, as I will spell out in what follows) explains how it might be possible for us to become reliably responsive to perceptions of some given type.

As Aristotle emphasizes, this perceptual response to universals is still, in an important sense, *indiscriminate*. We respond to humans in reliable ways, but perception itself does not tell us what humans are, or why we respond to them as we do, or even what features we are using to determine our responses to them in various cases. Articulating any of this is a difficult, intellectually demanding task. But it's something that depends on our being able to form reliable (if indiscriminate) response to universals in the first place—and to do so on broadly perceptual grounds, without positing innate knowledge of the universals in question. Thus Callias, Cleon and others are entities we can perceive, but they are also entities we can come to recognize, on broadly perceptual grounds, as humans—in a way that allows us to respond to them as humans even without having any deep understanding of who they are as individuals, or of what their shared humanity consists in.

This, at any rate, is what Aristotle needs to show if he is to have a plausible response to Platonic innatism. That is, Aristotle needs to make the case that nonrational modes of cognition can give rise to sophisticated practices and behaviors—that we can indeed become *experienced* without relying on our rational powers, and without grasping universals as such, or being able to articulate what these universals are. In fact Aristotle has good zoological and psychological grounds to believe just this: his ambitious take on nonrational learning is motivated by his broader conception of the role perception and *phantasia* play in directing purposive animal behavior. Or so I'll be arguing in our next chapter.

But first, a brief look back on Aristotle's rejection of Platonic innatism, now that we have the structure of his account of our learning in better focus. Recall that one of the key ideas motivating Aristotle's rejection of innatism is the thought that perception is an epistemically valuable state, rather than a fetter on our learning. Yet it may seem that his account of our learning, as I've been presenting it here, is not after all so different from the Platonic one he seeks to reject.[75] After all, Aristotle does think perception is deficient insofar as it does not supply us with any explanatory knowledge, or any understanding of universals as universals. And he does think our intellect must step in to help us achieve any such explanatory knowledge, which perception alone cannot provide.

Now, I think we should agree that Aristotle shares with innatists the thought that perceptual knowledge is deficient relative to the sort of explanatory understanding that constitutes our epistemic ideal. And I think we should further agree that our intellect, for Aristotle as for an innatist, plays an ineliminable role in moving us toward this epistemic ideal. Still, I think the views differ in two significant ways. First, recall that on the Platonic view perception presents things to us in ways that are outright *incoherent*, or at least ways that can be shown to be incoherent once we reflect a bit on what we perceive—and that perception's contribution to our learning stems precisely from its incoherence (cf. point (b), p. 62). Aristotle, by contrast, plainly thinks that perceptual knowledge is highly coherent, and that perception is a reliable guide to the truth even without the assistance of the intellect—and that this plays a key role in its ability to contribute to our learning. The second point is a consequence of the first: Aristotle thinks that perceptual forms of knowledge serve as a *foundation* for more advanced explanatory understanding, rather than something to turn away from in our learning, once our intellect has been summoned (cf. point (a), p. 62). Thus, to put the point somewhat metaphorically, Aristotle's view is that we build upon and try to understand what we learn perceptually, while on the Platonic view our learning consists in recognizing what makes our perceptions deficient, and then dismissing whatever we learn perceptually to engage in the sort of pure intellectual work that would contribute to recollection.

So as I understand him, Aristotle is not giving up on every aspect of Platonic innatism—but he is, importantly, seeking to reject a view on

---

[75] Where, again, I do not insist that this is Plato's considered view, or the only view of our learning we find in his dialogues. In fact I think we find different accounts of our learning across Plato's works, some of which are in many ways much closer to the sort of view we find Aristotle defending. There are many ways of being a Platonist—Aristotle may well endorse some and reject others.

which perception is not only a relatively basic mode of apprehension, but an inherently deficient one as well, and conducive to our learning only because it is so deficient. His doing so is what allows him to dispense with the claim that we are born with innate advanced knowledge—a claim he finds absurd—and with the associated view that perception is useful only as a precursor to the intellectual work that makes this latent knowledge manifest.

5

Perception, Experience, and Locomotion: Aristotle on Nonrational Learning

In our last chapter, I considered one of the reasons Aristotle explicitly invokes for thinking perception a sufficient basis for the rest of our learning: the fact that our perceptions are "of" universals despite having particular objects. I argued that we should understand this as a claim about our perceptual responsiveness to certain universal causes—Aristotle's point being that certain things regularly appear to us some way because they belong to some universal, and that this helps explain how it might be possible for us to become reliably responsive to their perceptible features, without yet being able to articulate what these features are, or why they appear to us as they do.

I take it these views are motivated by some of Aristotle's broader metaphysical and teleological commitments—views about the explanatory structure of reality, and the corresponding cognitive structure with which various animals find themselves equipped. But the motivation does not issue from teleology alone. The thought that perception could ground the development of experience is also based on Aristotle's psychological and zoological views, and in particular on his views concerning the cognitive and affective underpinnings of animal locomotion.[1] As I argued above, Aristotle has an expansive conception of perceptual contents, and takes our background knowledge to inform what's conveyed to us by what we perceive. The background knowledge in question could well

---

[1] Some of these views, as we will see, are themselves teleologically inflected. My claim here is just that Aristotle's conception of our learning doesn't issue *merely* from some large-scale teleological assumptions about our cognitive architecture and its correspondence with the structure of reality.

Aristotle's Empiricism. Marc Gasser-Wingate,
Oxford University Press (2021). © Oxford University Press.
DOI: 10.1093/oso/9780197567487.003.0005

be theoretical in nature—as when an astronomer's knowledge of planetary motion and the casting of shadows informs her observation of an eclipse. But it's critical for Aristotle that it could be nontheoretical as well—that we and other animals might develop a sophisticated kind of responsiveness to the world (the sort of responsiveness distinctive of those with experience) on broadly perceptual grounds, without yet being able to understand our practices or account for their underlying causes.

In this chapter my aim is to consider more closely how Aristotle sought to account for nonrational learning of this sort—and to vindicate the suggestion, implicit in much of the preceding, that this learning be considered broadly perceptual in nature. Again, this is not something Aristotle spells out in any single place. But I think a plausible view can be reconstructed from what he does say about perception, *phantasia*, and animal locomotion in *MA* and various parts of *An* III. As I see it, the view is guided by two main ideas. The first is a conception of perception as a capacity that not only presents certain things as being the case, but is also, thanks to its affective characteristics, capable of soliciting some behavior from the perceiving subject—so that a lion wouldn't just perceive that a buffalo is brown and scruffy, say, but also perceive that it's something *to be hunted when hungry, to be avoided when in herds*, and so on. The second is the auxiliary use of *phantasia* as a means of storing and associating nonoccurrent perceptions, in a manner that would allow the retention of past perceptions as memories, and the projection of future scenarios on the basis of these past memories. I'll argue here that, taken together, the ability to associate perceptions and appreciate perceptual solicitations provides a basis for the sort of coherent, purposive forms of animal behavior Aristotle takes to reflect our nonrational responsiveness to universals—a basis that is, in an important sense, perceptual in nature.

5.1 Discrimination, Pleasure, and Desire

Here is Aristotle on the origins of animal movement:[2]

> [39] The affections suitably prepare the organic parts, desire suitably prepares the affections, and *phantasia* the desire. And *phantasia* comes about either through thought or through perception. (*MA* 8 702a17–19)

In this passage Aristotle identifies a series of causes (a "chain of movers," as it's often called) leading to the sort of preparation of an animal's "organic parts" (bones and sinews) that would produce a certain sort of movement on their part: affections, desire, and *phantasia* that issues from either perception or thought.

Now, the exact contribution of each of these movers is something Aristotle does not make entirely clear. For one thing, he doesn't seem to think *phantasia* strictly necessary for desire. Indeed, he tells us elsewhere that some animals do not have *phantasia*, but that all animals must at least have the basic desires necessary for their survival—for instance, desires for the pleasant, which directly follow from their capacity to perceive (cf. *An* II.3 414b1–6, III.3 428a8–11, on which more below, and recall also [21]). Animals can thus desire things without the "preparation" *phantasia* is meant to supply. Nor is desire necessary for bringing about affections of just any sort. For perception and *phantasia* already have an affective component on their own, independent of the further movements they might produce when coupled with some desire (cf. *An* II.5 416b33–34, *MA* 7 701b16, *Mem* 449b5ff, *Insomn* 459b1ff).[3] So the movers on Aristotle's list should not be taken as necessary conditions for each other *in*

---

[2] Translations from *MA* are adapted from Nussbaum (1978) unless otherwise noted.

[3] Presumably it's only in the presence of some desire that our perceptions or thoughts produce *chills* and *dread*, and the further movement of limbs involved in *flight* or *pursuit* (*MA* 7 701b16ff). Still, perception and thought produce heating and cooling around the heart on their own (*An* III.9 432a29–433a1; *MA* 7 701b28–32), and so move us "up to a point" without relying on desire (*An* III.12 434b30). For different accounts of the connection between thought and the movement of animal limbs, see Charles (2015), Cooper (2020), Corcilius (2008b, 326–46), Fernandez (2014), and Moss (2012, 23ff). I'll be considering perception's affective profile and motivational role in more detail below.

general. Nor should they be taken as necessary conditions for animal movement of just any sort. They should be thought of, rather, as jointly characterizing the etiology of a specific kind of *purposive* animal movement—to "suitably prepare" one of the movers is to provide it what it needs to help bring about animal movement which is directed toward something that isn't immediately available, and which might thus be conceived of as fulfilling or realizing some end.[4]

The movers in [39], then, are jointly responsible for purposive animal movement, but not necessary conditions for one another in general, or for animal movement in general. Their contributions, Aristotle explains in the following, fall into two broad categories:[5]

[40] We see that the movers of animals are thought, perception, *phantasia*, decision, wish, spirit, and appetite. And all of these can be reduced to thought and desire. For *phantasia* and perception hold the same place as thought. For they are all discriminative [capacities], though they differ in the ways discussed elsewhere. (*MA* 6 700b17–22)

On this simplified view, then, there are two components to locomotion: discrimination and desire. Each of these components can take a rational or nonrational form. Thought is a form of rational discrimination, while perception and *phantasia* serve as its nonrational counterparts (they "hold the same place" as thought in the production

---

[4] Conceived of by us, that is: the animals themselves need not be taken to conceive of their movement as directed toward some end. I'll be calling goal-directed movement of this sort "locomotion" (cf. *MA* 4 700a8, *MA* 5 700a26, *An* III.9 432a17, 432b8, III.10 433a13), though sometimes I will follow Aristotle and just use "motion." Locomotion should be distinguished from movements like reflexes or other forms of uncontrolled bodily change (*MA* 11 703b8ff). Animals engaged in locomotion aim toward spatially distant ends, and so move their limbs—though presumably in lower animals the movements are quite rudimentary, as they are for the imperfect animals mentioned at *An* III.11 433b31–434a5. And of course Aristotle was aware that some animals are sessile (*An* I.5 410b18–20, III.10 432b19–26): this account does not apply to them.

[5] I agree with the reading of the manuscripts defended in Lorenz (2006, 130n19). But for my purposes not too much hangs on this—what matters is that *phantasia*, perception, and thought supply the sort of discrimination necessary for locomotion, on which point there is no controversy.

of purposive movement). Wish is a form of rational desire, while spirit and appetite serve as its nonrational counterparts.[6]

At times, Aristotle presents the desire component of this simplified picture as what's *primarily* responsible for initiating locomotion. At any rate this seems to be the upshot of his discussion in *An* III.9–10, where he denies, in turn, that our capacity for nutrition (III.9 432b7–19), perception (III.9 432b19–25), and thought (III.9 432b25–433a6) would suffice to initiate motion, and concludes that our capacity for desire must do so instead (III.10 433a31–b1). Indeed he often speaks as though desire had the power to move our limbs directly, regardless of the conclusions we reach by reasoning or through other forms of discrimination (see e.g. *EN* VII.3 1147a34–35; III.12 1119b8–10). But this shouldn't be taken to imply that the discriminative component of his account is somehow dispensable or secondary. After all, to desire something is to take it to be desirable in some way—the *objects* of desire are things that appear pleasant to us, or which we think good (cf. *An* III.10 433a28–29, 433b8–10, and [42]–[45] below). So desire is dependent on some sort of discernment of the object one desires—we must recognize something as pleasant or good in order to desire it. In fact this is precisely what Aristotle goes on to emphasize, telling us that the *object* of desire is what "initiates motion without being moved, by being grasped by thought or *phantasia*," while our capacity to desire both moves us and is itself being moved by our grasping its object (433b11–12, 433b13–18). All of this corroborates his characterization, at *MA* 10 703a4–5, of desire as an "intermediate" in the production of locomotion, causing us to move our limbs while itself being prompted by something prior—and ultimately by our apprehending something desirable, since "the first mover is the object of desire and the object of [practical] thought" (*MA* 6 700b23–25). The sort of primacy Aristotle ascribes to desire should therefore not

---

[6] Decision (προαίρεσις) depends on wish and practical thought, and so falls on the rational side of things as well. Aristotle offers no nonrational analogue of decision here—but the sort of perceptual association enabled by *phantasia* might play a similar role, as I will argue below. In this chapter I will use "thought" for νοῦς and διάνοια as they appear in *MA* and *An* III.9–12. These should be understood quite broadly, as including any form of cognition available to rational creatures (so not just reasoning about explanations, or understanding definitional principles in a theoretically sensitive manner).

be taken to imply that desire might in some cases produce locomotion without some prior discrimination, or indeed without the rest of the movers mentioned in [39].

In what sense *is* desire the "primary" cause of locomotion, if our movement doesn't in fact originate from it? Aristotle's point might be that a desire (once active) initiates a physiological process that results in locomotion and can only be derailed by physiological processes of the same type—that is, processes prompted by other, conflicting desires.[7] For the dictates of the discriminative component of locomotion can be undermined not only by further discrimination, but also by the effects of some disruptive desire. This is most clear in the case of thought: we might think that something should be done and work out how to do it, and yet not act in accordance with these thoughts, as occurs in common cases of akrasia (*An* III.9 433a1–3).[8] And one of the key causes of akrasia is precisely the disruption caused by nonrational desires, as Aristotle explains for instance at *EN* VII.6 1149a24–b2. Now, there is considerable dispute concerning the nature of the disruption at play here, and whether it's compatible with the rest of Aristotle's treatment of akrasia in *EN* VII. But however the details are worked out, I take it the possibility of akrasia prompted by appetitive desire is sufficient to show that our practical thoughts can be disrupted by something other than further thoughts—while there is some evidence our desires will lead to bodily movement unless impeded by some desire pulling us some other direction.[9] If this is right, the sense in which desires are primary

---

[7] See Cooper (1999, 239) for a similar suggestion, *contra* Labarrière (2004). I set aside here external disruptions: a bear might of course grab your legs before you can run.

[8] This is unproblematic when it comes to purely theoretical modes of thought, which do not produce locomotion at all (cf. *MA* 7 701a10–13; *An* III.9 432b26–433a1). It's plain enough that *theorizing* about virtue doesn't alone yield virtuous action—the vicious can be, and have been, great ethical theorists. The more significant point is that even the dictates of practical modes of thought, which do generally determine how we act, might sometimes fail to do so. (Though Aristotle does not tell it, we can imagine a similar story in the nonrational case: typically perceiving something as an object of pursuit leads to its pursuit, but in some cases an animal might be distracted by some active desire for something else—e.g. a desire to avoid a predator even while hungry and spotting some prey.)

[9] One might object here that thought can override desires as well, as Aristotle tells us right after mentioning akrasia ("nor is desire in control of motion, since the self-controlled (οἱ ἐγκρατεῖς), though they desire things and have appetites, do not act as

is a limited one: their primacy reflects the superior force of their physiological manifestation, and in particular their ability to distract us (temporarily, at least) from what we think we ought to do, or what we perceive as an object of pursuit.

What it does not reflect—and what I think we shouldn't take it to reflect—is the provision of a certain sort of motivational force wholly independent of our discriminations.[10] Admittedly, some of Aristotle's characterizations of animal locomotion might seem to suggest such a division of labor. For instance, he offers the following syllogism to describe an animal being moved to drink:

[41] "I should drink," says the appetite. "This is something to drink," says perception or *phantasia* or thought. Immediately it drinks. (*MA* 7 701a32–33)

This sort of description might seem to indicate that perception (or *phantasia* or thought) makes an instrumental and purely cognitive contribution to locomotion: desire presents us with something to be done ("drink!"), and we then discriminate something that would help us do it ("this is something to drink"). On this sort of picture our appetitive desire to drink would be something like a pro-attitude: it would provide a nonrational analogue of Aristotle's "premise of the good," setting the end we seek to realize, while our discerning some drink would supply the "premise of the possible," serving only to determine a way to realize that end (cf. *MA* 7 701a23–25). The drinking itself would then result from (or, on some views, be constituted by) the putting together of some desire to drink with an

desire would have them, but are guided by their thoughts instead," *An* III.9 433a6–8). But Aristotle doesn't say here that thought *alone* would be "in control of" the actions of the self-controlled. His view might simply be that the self-controlled have rational desires (i.e. wishes) that conform with their thoughts, and outweigh their nonrational desires—they act as they think they should, but not just by thinking they should. Though our text is somewhat corrupt, this seems consistent with the description of akrasia at *An* III.11 434a12–14.

[10] For a convincing argument against this view see also Moss (2012, 11–19). Though I agree with Moss on the central role evaluative perception plays for Aristotle, I am not convinced by the further claim that nonrational animals perceptually recognize certain things *as good*, rather than just recognizing them as pleasant—as will become clear below.

awareness of some specific drink ready-at-hand—the former serving a purely conative role and the latter a purely cognitive one.[11]

One should keep in mind, however, that for Aristotle even basic appetites of the sort portrayed in [41] are directed toward things we perceive as pleasant. He tells us, for instance, that while different animals perceive food by different means they all "have the appetitive desire for food because they have perception of the pleasure that comes from food—for the object of appetitive desire is pleasure" (*PA* II.17 661a6–8). In a similar vein, he explains that[12]

[42] all animals have at least one sort of perception, [i.e. perception by] touch. And that which has perception also has pleasure and pain, and both the pleasant and the painful. And where there are these, there is also appetite. For appetite is a desire for what is pleasant. (*An* II.3 414b3–6)

Aristotle is telling us here that creatures with the capacity to perceive also "have" pleasures and pains, as well as "both the pleasant and the painful." What I take him to mean is that perceptual creatures (i.e. animals) can *experience* feelings of pleasure and pain, and that in perceiving things they experience such feelings—and thus experience what they perceive *as* pleasant or painful, in a sense I will further specify below. The fact that they can perceive things this way explains the existence of appetitive desire in these animals, which is a state directed toward things perceived as pleasant—e.g. toward food, if an animal is hungry.[13] As he puts the point elsewhere,

[43] wherever there is perception, there is also both pain and pleasure; and wherever there are these, there is necessarily appetite as well. (*An* II.2 413b23–24)

---

[11] See Labarrière (2004) or Nussbaum (1978, 261–65) for a reading along these lines.
[12] See further *Top* VI.8 146b9–12.
[13] There is no doubt some teleology implicit in the sort of explanation we find here and in [43]. But I won't attempt to fully work out these condensed arguments, since we find a more elaborate (if more difficult) discussion of the connection between pleasant perception and desire in [45].

166 ARISTOTLE'S EMPIRICISM

Thus appetitive desires, on Aristotle's view, are just desires for what is pleasant. These desires are present in all animals, and their presence is explained by the fact that animals are perceivers, and that perceivers experience pleasures and pains. Below I will consider in more detail the relationship between our perceptions and pleasure and pain, and how we should conceive of the role certain perceptions play in generating appetitive desires and prompting locomotion. For now my point is simply that we should not conceive of our appetites as brute pro-attitudes or dispositions to (e.g.) satisfy our hunger and quench our thirst, and our perceptions of food and drink as yielding only an awareness of food and drink. For Aristotle makes it clear in [42] and [43] (and in [44] and [45], below) that our perceptions do not merely make us aware of some object, but also present that object in a pleasant and painful manner, and that this fact plays a central role in generating our appetitive desire for that object.[14] So either pleasant and painful perceptions bring some desire into existence, or else they serve to activate some standing desire (to drink when thirsty, say, or more broadly to pursue what's pleasant) by assigning it a determinate object, which they present as a desirable thing—that is, as something *to be pursued*.[15] In either case they do more than simply make us aware that something is food, or that something is drink.

---

[14] To represent our desires and discriminations as Aristotle does in [41] does, I think, obfuscate this. But it's important that in [41] Aristotle is not attempting to provide a complete account of the factors that would move us to drink. His aim is only to explain how in some cases we do not need to pause and think about how to realize certain ends, but rather do them "quickly and without calculation" (701a28–29). So it's no surprise he would not fully spell out the perceptual underpinnings of our desires: his point is only that when we already have a desire for drink, and see some drink, we do not pause and take the time to calculate just how pleasant it would be to do so (we just drink). Nonetheless, as I will argue below, the perceived pleasures of quenching our thirst are responsible for our desiring to drink, and so for the assertion that "I should drink" we find attributed to the appetite in [41].

[15] On the former view we would retain a sharper separation between perception and desire, while on the latter the content of our desires would be fully determined by our perceptions of pleasant and painful things. For a defense of this latter view, see Charles (2006) and Whiting (2002, 173ff). I agree with Moss (2012, 19), however, that our evidence leaves it unclear which of these options Aristotle endorses: he plainly wants to separate desire and discrimination in passages like [39] and [40], and yet what he says in [45] suggests they might in some cases not be so different after all.

Two key passages make this latter point in more detail. The first follows Aristotle's description of the physiological effects leading from affections in our sense organs to the movement of limbs:

[44] So the object of pursuit or avoidance in the sphere of action is a principle of motion, as we have said. But the thought and *phantasia* of these are necessarily accompanied by heating and chilling. For the painful is to be avoided and the pleasant to be pursued, and [the thought and *phantasia* of] the painful and the pleasant are almost always accompanied by chilling and heating. (*MA* 8 701b33–702a1)

Thus heating and chilling occur (around the heart—cf. *MA* 7 701b28–32) when we discern certain objects, through thought or *phantasia*, as objects of pursuit or avoidance. Before this passage Aristotle indicates that these are just the physiological effects that eventually lead to full-blown animal locomotion ("a small change at the beginning makes several big differences farther along" 701b24–6). He adds here an explanation (γάρ, 701b36) why our perception of objects of pursuit and avoidance would have such effects: our discernment of the pleasant and the painful (through thought or *phantasia*) is almost always accompanied by heating and chilling, and since the pleasant is to be pursued and the painful to be avoided, our discernment of objects of pursuit and avoidance will do the same.[16] This already suggests that our perception of pleasant and painful things is intimately connected (perhaps even identical) with our recognition of certain objects as things to be pursued or to be avoided—that is, as objects of desire—and that such perception serves, through its physiological manifestation as chilling and heating, as a basic initiator of locomotion.

Aristotle elaborates on the relationship between pleasure, perception, and desire in the following passage:

---

[16] Almost always, I take it, because on Aristotle's view humans can experience pleasures unconnected with locomotion—e.g. aesthetic pleasures, when smelling flowers (*Sens* 443b27ff), or intellectual pleasures, when learning for purely theoretical ends (*Met* A1 980a22–27). Such pleasures might have physiological effects of their own, but I take it they would not yield the sort of heating and chilling that occurs in cases where perception leads to locomotion.

[45] Perceiving, then, [45a] is similar to simply stating or thinking. [45b] But whenever it [=the perceived object] is pleasant or painful, [the soul], as if it were affirming or denying, pursues or avoids [that object]. [45c] And to be pleased or pained is to be active with the perceptual mean in relation to what is good or bad insofar as they are such. [45d] And actual avoidance and pursuit (ὄρεξις) are the same as this [activity with the perceptual mean]; and the capacity for pursuit and the capacity for avoidance do not differ either from one another or from the capacity to perceive, though they do differ in being. (*An* III.7 431a8–14)

So Aristotle is telling us here that perceiving is like "simply stating or thinking," but that perceiving something pleasant or painful leads to the soul's pursuing or avoiding that thing, and that in doing so the soul is acting "as if it were affirming or denying." He then adds that our feeling pleased or pained amounts to our being "active with the perceptual mean in relation to what is good or bad insofar as they are such," and that actual avoidance and pursuit are the same as this activity, and that our capacity for avoidance is the same (though different "in being") as the capacity for pursuit, and as the capacity to perceive. Aristotle's train of thought is far from clear, and his phrasing is somewhat obscure and compounded by some textual difficulties.[17] But here is how I understand him.

The first part of the passage contains a contrast between ([45a]) "simply stating or thinking" and ([45b]) "affirming or denying," the former being assimilated to perceiving and the latter to pursuing or avoiding. Now, what we state or think, in this analogy, is a singular term—some object or quality—while what we affirm or deny is a combination of such terms into a complex propositional whole (*Int* 17a16–26). So part of Aristotle's point here is that some combination must occur before any pursuit or avoidance can take place: just as

---

[17] I follow the manuscripts with τοῦτο at 431a12, indicating that avoidance and pursuit are the same as the sort of perceptual activity Aristotle mentions in the preceding lines. An equally well-attested alternative is to read ταὐτό, which would indicate that avoidance and pursuit are in some sense the same as each other—on which see Corcilius (2011, 132–38). One could arguably read the passage as I do even with ταὐτό; cf. Charles (2006, 20n3).

affirmation and denial require a combination of terms into something we can affirm or deny, pursuit and avoidance require some sort of combination—a combination that enables us to actually pursue or avoid something.

It's not immediately clear what the simples being combined here are meant to be, nor what the combination would amount to. On a widespread view, the combination amounts to a recognition (in the positive case) that the perceived object is *good*, with the simples being the perceived object and its goodness, respectively, and the pleasure in [45c] the form this recognition takes in nonrational animals.[18] This last point is significant: since [45] is concerned with nonrational pleasures and desires, we should not take the combination to reflect any sort of discernment that would depend on our rational powers.[19] Thus our pursuing or being pleased by something should not be taken to depend on our *judging* or *understanding* anything about it, e.g. our judging that it is good, where this would require our having some handle on the concept "good." Nonetheless, proponents of this interpretation hold that animals recognize the good *as good* when they are pleased by what they perceive. To be "active with the perceptual mean in relation to what is good or bad insofar as they are such," they argue, is to perceive the good or the bad as such, and not just to perceive (and be pleased) by things that are in fact good or bad for us. Even if such perception does not amount to a judgment, it does require that the perceiver subjectively find something good—which is why Aristotle specifies that we are active in relation to the good or bad "insofar as they are such."

I am unconvinced. Note, first, that Aristotle's "insofar as they are such" clause in [45c] need not be understood as a marker of intensionality. As Corcilius has argued, Aristotle might mean that animals are pleased when they perceive what is good or bad for them

---

[18] For recent expressions of this view, see for instance Achtenberg (2002, 161–63), Moss (2012, 31ff), Richardson (1992, 395), or Tuozzo (1994, 535–36). A similar view is defended on different grounds in Broadie (1991, 329–30).

[19] On the restriction of [45] to nonrational pleasures and desires, see Corcilius (2011, 127) and Lorenz (2006, 140n7).

insofar as it is good for them in their current condition.[20] Thus a thirsty lion is pleased when it perceives water because it perceives something good (water) insofar as it is good (insofar as the water will quench its present thirst). This would reflect a relational fact about the lion, its thirsty condition, and the properties of the water it perceives, but would not require that the lion recognize the goodness of the water, or perceive the water *as* something good. There is, in addition, some direct evidence against the view that nonrational animals could perceive goods in this way: Aristotle tells us at *Pol* I.2 1253a10–18 that nonrational animals perceive pleasure and pain, but that only humans perceive the good and the bad.[21] Since [45] can be read in a way that is compatible with this passage, I think that's the way we should read it.

There are also broader reasons for resisting the sort of interpretation sketched above. For it isn't clear what perceiving the good as such (or "finding something good") would amount to for nonrational animals, if indeed this perception merely amounts to their being *pleased*. As I see it, to perceive the good "as such" is to perceive something good and recognize the good in doing so—in a way that makes the goodness of what one perceives subjectively available to the perceiver. One way for it to be available is for it to serve as a basis for some judgment or belief (the belief *that this water is good*, say). But this would of course not apply to nonrational animals, who do not recognize anything as grounds for some belief. Another way for it to be available is for it to guide our actions—for our behavior to be responsive to our awareness of the goodness of what we perceive. But on the interpretation above, animals are guided by the pleasures and pains that accompany (or partially constitute) their perceptions, not by an awareness that what they perceive is good. Indeed it's precisely because their awareness of the good *takes the form of pleasure* that the perceptions of nonrational

---

[20] Nonrational pleasures are directed toward objects that are only qualifiedly good for an animal (i.e. good for an animal only under certain circumstances). So to say that an animal is pleased by some perceived good would be imprecise: one has to specify that the animal is pleased by some perceived good insofar as it is, given its present circumstances, a good for it. For a defense of this reading, see Corcilius (2011, 124–32).

[21] I assume that the claims in this passage must be read intensionally. It would be insane to claim that only humans perceive things that are in fact good for them: the claim must be that only humans can perceive good things and in doing so recognize them for what they are.

animals are motivating.[22] If this is right, however, I do not see what is gained by adding that these pleasurable perceptions are also perceptions of the good as such, rather than simply being perceptions of the *pleasant* as such, and motivational just in virtue of the pleasures that attend them (where of course it would be true that, as a general rule, an animal is pleased when it perceives what is in fact good for it in some way, and so normally perceives as pleasant what is good).[23]

This is in fact how I think we should make sense of the combination at play in [45]: as a combination between some perceived object and the feeling of pleasure or pain that attends our perception of this object. Thus a thirsty lion will perceive some water (which is like "simply saying," on the analogy introduced in [45a]), and in doing so experience pleasure. The combination necessary for pursuit or avoidance is just the combination of this experience of pleasure with the perception of water—the lion's pursuit of water ([45b]) results from its perceiving water and feeling pleased at what it perceives, just as affirmation results from our saying or thinking something and then asserting something about the thing said or thought. It's natural to think this is the sort of combination Aristotle would have in mind. For on his view pleasure, while not strictly a form of perception, is something so closely connected to our perceptions that it is tempting to assimilate the two:[24]

[22] Thus Tuozzo tells us that "[t]he unconceptualized mental experience of the good is the experience of being pleased" (1994, 536), and Moss that "perceiving something as good [...] *is* the state of feeling pleasure," and that the nonrational part of the soul "cognizes the good only through pleasure," so that for nonrational animals "perceiving something pleasurably amounts to perceiving it as good" (2012, 35; 109). Likewise, for Achtenberg, "pleasure is perception of something good as good (not as white, or a triangle, or large, etc.)" (2002, 161). For all these authors this fact plays a central role in explaining the motivational powers of nonrational perception.

[23] For this view, see also Charles (2006, 27), Vasiliou (2014, 353–67), and Whiting (2014, 38–39). Of course animals are also sometimes pleased by things that are bad for them—on which more below.

[24] See further *EN* X.4 1174b14ff. Aristotle also tells us at *Phys* VII.3 247a16–17 that pleasures and pains are alterations of the perceptual part of the soul. At *PA* III.4 666a11–13 he adds that the physiological manifestation of pleasure and pain, just like the physiological manifestation of our perceptions, takes place in the heart. So pleasures and pains belong to the same part of the soul and affect the same organ as our perceptions. I do not think we should take it to follow from this that pleasures *are* perceptions, however, as is suggested for instance in Achtenberg (2002, 161). Admittedly [45c] might be taken to suggest this—but I do not think Aristotle is trying to give anything like general definition of pleasure in that passage. In any case, for the purposes of my

[46] The pleasures involved in activities are [...] so inseparable from them that it's disputable whether the activity is not the same as the pleasure. Still, pleasure does not seem to be thought or perception. That would be absurd. But because they are not found apart they appear to some to be the same. (*EN* X.5 1175b30–35)

Aristotle already told us in [42] and [43] that even the most basic animals will have feelings of pleasure and pain, merely in virtue of their having the capacity to perceive. What we learn here is that pleasures or pains *accompany* perceptual activity, and are so intimately connected with this activity that they might appear identical with it. But Aristotle emphasizes that there is in fact a combination of two factors when a pleasurable perception occurs: the cognitive apprehension of some object, and the feeling of pleasure that attends it. It's when this combination occurs, as I understand [45b], that the perceived object becomes an object of *pursuit* for the perceiver: to perceive some water *as pleasant* (i.e. to perceive some water and experience pleasure in doing so) just is to perceive the water as something desirable, or to be pursued.

What then of the claim, in [45c], that to be pleased is to be "active with the perceptual mean" in relation to what is good "insofar as it is such"? To say that we are "active with the perceptual mean" in to relation to what is good is just to say that we perceive what is good.[25] To add that we perceive what is good "insofar as it is such," on the reading I favor, is just to specify that we perceive that aspect of something good that is in fact good for us in our present condition (e.g. the thirst-quenching aspect of water if we are thirsty). I think all of this should be understood extensionally: we are pleased, in the context relevant to animal locomotion, when we perceive what's good for us in some respect, but in doing so need not be taken to recognize that what we perceive is good for us in that respect (or in any other respect). Now, on the way I've been speaking of perceptual contents this does

argument a more modest point will suffice: the sort of perceptual discrimination critical to animal locomotion is necessarily attended by feelings of pleasure and pain.

[25] For this technical formulation see *An* II.11 424a2–10 and II.12 424a28–b3. And see Charles (2006, 23–26) and Corcilius (2011, 128) on the possible significance of Aristotle's use of this formulation in [45].

mean that things good for us feature in the contents of our perceptions (cf. pp. 114–15). But it does not follow from this that their being good is something conveyed to us as perceivers, or subjectively available to us in a way we could use to form beliefs or guide our actions.

What perception *does* allow us to do is recognize certain things as pleasant or painful, and thus as things to be pursued or avoided. This is possible because perception is itself an affectively loaded form of cognition—an awareness of something combined with attending feelings of pleasure or pain. What Aristotle is telling us in [45c] is that these feelings track what is good or bad in some way for the perceiver. Thus the sight of meat is pleasing to a hungry lion, but isn't pleasing (and might be displeasing) to a lion who has just fed—and is presumably neither pleasing nor displeasing to buffalo, giraffes, and other herbivores, for whom the meat is neither good nor bad.[26] This is a sensible thing for him to say at this point: he has just claimed that what we perceive can serve as an object of pursuit or avoidance because of the pleasures and pains that attend our perceptions. He is now specifying the sorts of things which, when perceived, lead to these pleasures and pains—good and bad things respectively (in that

---

[26] For the impact of our degree of hunger on our perception of food, see *Sens* 443b20–26. Our broader affective state also bears on the pleasures and pains attending some perception—in ways that might result in a coward running from anything that resembles an enemy, say, or a lover running toward anything that resembles his love (*Insomn* 460b3–8). There will therefore be a number of cases where pleasures and pains lead us to act in ways that are not conducive to our own overall good. Does this contradict the claim that we are pleased by what is in fact good for us in some way? It does not. For what is good for an animal *in some way* need not be what's good for it *overall* or *unqualifiedly*. Consider for instance a rat eating some sugar-coated poisonous bait, which is pleasant but bad for the rat (for this example, and a broader treatment of the issue of misrepresentation faced by extensional readings of [45], see Corcilius (2011, 138–43)). What the rat is being pleased by in this case is not the poison, but the sweetness: it perceives and consumes the bait *qua* sweet thing. And sweet things are, normally, good things for rats to consume (sweet things usually have sugar, and sugar is a source of energy). So it would be correct to say in this case that the rat is being pleased by something that is good for it in some way, even if that thing is unqualifiedly bad for it. Aristotle can even allow for cases in which something is perceived as pleasant that is bad for an animal in *every* way, so long as that is not the norm. Thus a rat eating sweet poisonous bait where the sweetness is artificial, and therefore not a source of energy, is pleased by something that is not good for it in any respect. But such cases are presumably abnormal, and would require some manipulation of the rat's natural environment (if they were the norm, rats would not survive for long). For a similar treatment of these difficulties, see also Freeland (1994, 56–59).

respect in which they are indeed good or bad for the perceiver). Thus nonrational perceivers are normally pleased or pained by what's good or bad for them in some way, as the sorts of creatures they are and in the specific situations and conditions they find themselves in, and this feature of their perceptions allows them to behave in ways that are conducive to their own flourishing—a familiar teleological point.[27]

Aristotle adds, in [45d], that actual pursuit and avoidance are in fact the same as these perceptions, and that the capacity for pursuit and avoidance are the same, and furthermore identical to the capacity for perception. This suggests that our desires just are pleasurable perceptions—to perceive something and feel pleasure in doing so is to perceive that thing as something *to be pursued*, which is just to desire what we perceive. Now, we saw that in passages like [39] and [40] (and [41], [42], and [43]) Aristotle wants to keep separate the contributions perception and desire make to locomotion—which is in tension with what he is telling us here. I will not try to settle this difficulty.[28] What matters for my purposes is the intimate relationship between our desires and pleasurable and painful perceptions. What this relationship shows is that our perceptions—or at least, the ones relevant to animal locomotion—are more than purely cognitive acts: perception tells us what is the case, but also, thanks to its affective characteristics, solicits some behavior from us. It follows that perception does not merely reveal to us, say, that the nearby spring water is *something to drink* (as [41] might suggest). It also presents the spring water as something pleasant, in a way that either constitutes or brings about some desire, and thus moves us to pursue it.

So desire and discrimination are the two central factors involved in locomotion. Both components come in rational and nonrational

---

[27] On which see for instance [37] and *HA* IX.1 589a4–9. A reading along these lines is also defended in Irwin (1988, 329–33).

[28] Aristotle does allow for their being "different in being" despite being the same—a complicated qualification, on which see *Phys* III.3 202b6ff. One way to approach this difficulty might be to note that for Aristotle animals are essentially perceivers, and that their other capacities, including their capacity to desire, must therefore derive from their capacity to perceive.

forms: I've focused here on the nonrational case. Nonrational discriminations, on Aristotle's view, are both evaluative and instrumental—they tells us what's to be pursued or avoided, and how to pursue or avoid it. In their evaluative role, our discriminations either constitute or serve to generate certain desires, and initiate the chain of physiological changes that lead to locomotion (barring disruption from some other active desire). A thirsty animal might thus see spring water as something pleasant (i.e. feel pleasure at the sight of the spring water), and so desire it. In their instrumental role, our discriminations allow us to recognize things that would help us secure what we pursue—e.g. recognize our going over to the spring and drinking from it as a way to secure the water we desire. Presumably this often happens simultaneously, as Aristotle emphasizes in [41]: an animal sees the spring water as something pleasant, and so desires it, and at once recognizes its going over and drinking from the spring as a way to secure what it desires. But we can imagine cases (which I'll consider in more detail in our next section) where the pursuit is more involved—cases where the subject's perceiving some desirable object will not coincide with its perceiving the means to secure it: a lion might recognize its prey and still need to discriminate how to best hunt it down, perhaps in coordination with the rest of its pride.

Now, to say that nonrational discrimination might play these roles is not yet to say that perception alone would do so. And in fact a number of passages might seem to suggest it does not. In [44] Aristotle tells us thought or *phantasia* initiates the physiological precursors to locomotion—without mentioning perception at all. In [40] he claims that *perception and phantasia*, together, would "hold the same place as thought," rather than singling each of them out as discriminative capacities, as he does in [41]. And in [39] *phantasia* is said to issue from perception or thought and "prepare" desire, seemingly as a necessary intermediate between the two. So it's reasonable to think that *phantasia* must be involved in our discriminations—and in particular in the sort of nonrational evaluative discrimination described above, which serves to solicit some particular behavior from us and prompt our desires.

In our next section I'll consider more closely the role *phantasia* plays in the context of animal locomotion, and what sort of assistance it provides to perceptual discrimination. I'll argue that we should primarily conceive of *phantasia* as a means of storing and associating nonoccurrent perceptions—and not, as is sometimes suggested, as a way of interpreting or enriching what we perceive, or of representing what we perceive as an object of avoidance or pursuit. In doing so I hope to establish that the involvement of *phantasia* in our nonrational behavior does not impugn its broadly perceptual character.

5.2 Perception and *Phantasia*

Aristotle's treatment of *phantasia* is notoriously complex: he assigns *phantasia* a number of different roles in both rational and nonrational cognition, in ways that complicate any attempt at a general account of its role in his psychology, and indeed any singular translation of the term.[29] I won't venture any general account of *phantasia* here. In particular, I will set aside the role *phantasia* plays in assisting rational modes of thought, and questions about the relation nonrational *phantasia* bears to "rational" or "calculating" *phantasia* (*An* III.10 433b29–30). I will also set aside the role *phantasia* plays in accounting for certain forms of error, and Aristotle's discussion of the ways in which *phantasia* and opinion differ. What I aim to defend is a limited claim—namely, that in the context relevant to nonrational learning *phantasia* serves only as means to store and associate nonoccurrent perceptions.[30]

It will be helpful to consider, by way of contrast, some views on which nonrational *phantasia* plays a more substantive role than this. Nussbaum, for instance, suggests that *phantasia* is required in order to recognize certain things as the sorts of things they are:

[29] For a nice overview of the claims Aristotle makes about *phantasia*, see Johansen (2012, 208–9).

[30] A claim that has recently been defended by Johansen (2012, 199–220) and Moss (2012, 51–64). What I have to say here is also, I think, compatible with the treatments of *phantasia* in Corcilius (2008b, 215–40), Frede (1992), and Lorenz (2006).

phantasia is the faculty in virtue of which the animal sees his object as an object of a certain sort, so that we can say the perception has for him some potentially motivating content.[31]

When we perceive a rose by sight, it is not the rose *qua* rose, but the rose *qua* white that acts upon our sight. But to be moved to action an animal has to become aware of something *qua* what-it-is-called; he has to see the man as a man, not just as pale.[32]

On this sort of view, then, perception alone would not allow us to recognize objects *as* substances of some sort or another (*as* roses or *as* humans, say), and this sort of recognition is necessary for it to play any sort of motivating role. Aristotle would thus be invoking *phantasia* as a capacity that interprets perceptual data, and thereby allows animals to selectively respond to certain parts of their environment, rather than passively receiving some indiscriminate array of sensible qualities.

I think the view is mistaken on both counts. I argued in our previous chapter that even the most basic animals must perceptually recognize *objects*, and perceptually recognize that these objects exhibit certain qualities—and that there is good evidence Aristotle thinks they can do this without any assistance from *phantasia*. So perception itself already has more structure than would be involved in the passive, indiscriminate reception of sensible qualities.[33] Indeed, when Aristotle emphasizes perception's role in his inductive account of our learning, he tells us (in [20]) that all animals have an "innate discriminatory capacity called perception," and then immediately points out (in [21]) that not all animals have the *phantasia*-enabled capacity to retain what they perceive. So discrimination must be

---

[31] Nussbaum (1978, 255–56).

[32] Nussbaum (1978, 259). Though these examples emphasize the recognition of *substances* as such, Nussbaum suggests elsewhere that *phantasia* would be required for any sort of apprehension that goes beyond a passive reception of qualities perceptible *per se* (1978, 258). So we not only need *phantasia* to perceive substances as such—we need it to perceive anything at all that isn't a sensible quality as the thing it is (or "*qua* what-it-is-called"). See further Hicks (1907, 416), Morel (2004), and Richardson (1992, 385), and perhaps also Labarrière (1984, 22ff), for views on which *phantasia* is assigned such an interpretive role.

[33] As Dugré (1990, 67–68) and Modrak (1987, 98) are right to point out.

possible without *phantasia*—discrimination of *objects*, that is, since that's what's minimally necessary for animal survival.

In any case, even if we did think animals incapable of perceiving things "as humans" without the assistance of *phantasia*, it doesn't seem right that this sort of recognition is required for perception to play any motivating role. Animals can just as well be motivated to flee or pursue humanoid or human-smelling things, without recognizing them as the humans they are.[34] To be perceptually *responsive* to some universal, as I argued in 4.5, doesn't require any knowledge or recognition of the universal itself, "*qua* what-it-is-called." It's enough to be able to reliably track features associated with the universal in question—and in particular, for lower animals, those relevant to their survival. On my reading of [45], animals can do this on account of the feelings of pleasure and pain associated with their perceptions. Their survival thus depends centrally on their recognizing various entities as objects of pursuit or avoidance in a way that tracks whether or not these entities are good for them in their circumstances. But it does not depend on their recognizing these entities for what they are—e.g. their recognizing humans as humans, or good things as good.

One might, however, still think that the sort of motivational role perception plays for animals depends on *phantasia* in some other way. It's natural to think, for instance, that perception alone could not account for our having desires because desires are inherently future-directed: we perceive things as they presently are, and to desire something we must represent or imagine them as they might be in the future, and recognize that they would supply us something we need. Thus my desire to walk over to the spring might stem from my recognizing that I will be able to drink from it when I get there, and that this will be a pleasant thing to do in my thirsty condition. But perception cannot do this alone, since it does not allow for the sort of projection at play here ("I *will* be able to drink . . ."). If this is right *phantasia* is necessary for perception to play its role in "preparing" desire not because perception does not suffice to identify various objects, but rather because perception only tells us about the present,

---

[34] On which point see Everson (1997, 164–65).

while desires are goal-directed, and therefore require some awareness of what the future might bring.

Now, it's no doubt true that animal desires are frequently future-directed, and so frequently require more than the mere apprehension of our current situation. But some care is needed in spelling out the respective contributions perception and *phantasia* make to these desires. Some interpreters think *phantasia* is needed to reinterpret what perception conveys to us on the basis of the future pleasures and pains we associate with them. Thus, for Modrak, perception "presents an object," and *phantasia* "elaborates on the object, reinterpreting it in the light of anticipated pleasures and pains" in a way that would allow that object to be taken as *desirable*, and thus lead to its pursuit (1987, 97–98). In a similar vein, Pearson suggest that perception would "prompt the creature to have *phantasiai* with the content that some action would be valuable in some way," a necessary component in our being moved to perform the action in question (2011, 103). If this is right perception would not serve as a "mover" on its own because it could not present anything as desirable on its own: only with the assistance of *phantasia* would we be capable of representing certain objects as things we should avoid or pursue. For we do this on the basis of *anticipated* pleasures and pains, which are not available to perception itself.

There is some pressure, however, to think that even without *phantasia* we can perceive things as pleasant or painful in a way that would make us desire them. Recall, first, that in [45] Aristotle assimilates desires with pleasurable perceptions without ever mentioning *phantasia* as an intermediary.[35] Note moreover that Aristotle thinks some animals lack *phantasia*, but that all animals have desires, and that their having desires follows directly from the fact that they can perceive, and so experience pleasures and pains (cf. [42], above). Granted, it's not entirely obvious how we should make sense of desire in animals who cannot anticipate or imagine things, and experience

---

[35] In the lines right after that passage he adds that "*phantasmata* belong to the thinking soul in the same manner as perceptual states ($\alpha i \sigma \theta \eta \mu \alpha \tau \alpha$) [belong to the nonrational]" (*An* III.7 431a14–15). This seems to confirm that perception alone (rather than perception reinterpreted through the use of nonrational *phantasia*) was responsible for our nonrational desires.

only the pleasures and pains of their occurrent perceptions. But it's important to remember that these would be very primitive animals, and that the sorts of desires they would exhibit would presumably be primitive as well: the animals Aristotle has in mind here are sponges, oysters, and other sessile sea-creatures—creatures that essentially rely on water flow and turbulence for their nutrition, and contribute to their survival mostly by pumping water through their internals.[36] So plainly they will not desire the nutrients they filter out in the same way a lion desires its prey: they don't engage in any sort of *hunt*, and thus need not to *anticipate* the pleasures they will derive from some prey once they make a meal out of it. Still, I think we can make sense of the thought that their behavior embodies a certain kind of desire for food: their continued pumping of water through their pores is a sign that they perceive as pleasant certain nutrients they are currently (and continuously) extracting. In a similar vein, Aristotle indicates that sponges contract when we try to detach them—and here too their reaction might be taken to reflect their occurrent pain at being detached, and so their desire to remain (at this very moment) on the sea floor.[37] Thus on this sort of view sponges continuously pump water because they desire its nutrients, even if their desire doesn't stem from any anticipation of the pleasure they *will* feel when they receive these nutrients. They simply desire, moment after moment, to keep feeding as they do and stay attached where they are, in virtue of the occurrent pleasure they feel in this condition. Now, it might be a stretch to say that they *pursue* these things, since sponges are sessile and always feeding, and so not trying to acquire something they do not have or achieve a state different from their own. But to my mind this simply shows Aristotle had an expansive conception of desire, on which desires need not reflect an urge to go after something not already in our possession, and on which we can desire to be in our

[36] Aristotle tells us at *HA* V.16 548b6 and 549a1–3 that sponge nourish themselves in slime, taking in food through their pores, which isn't too far off. Animals like anemones can do a bit more than this, since they latch onto fish and other food that come through their tentacles (*PA* IV.5 681b3, *HA* IV.6 531b5–8), but the movements are still rudimentary, and wouldn't, I take it, qualify as any form of locomotion.

[37] See *HA* V.16 548b10–15, and see also Labarrière (1984, 29) and Lorenz (2006, 138–47) on this example and on the broader possibility of desire without *phantasia*.

very condition without anticipating or imagining any future change to this condition.[38]

The moral here, setting aside the finer points of sponge psychology, is that we should not take our desires to necessarily depend on a reinterpretation of what we perceive in light of anticipated pleasures and pains, achieved through the use of *phantasia*. For in very basic animals there can be perception and desire without *phantasia*, and therefore without any such anticipation. So while anticipation might be necessary for perception to prompt the sort of *locomotion* available to more advanced animals, it is not necessary for the basic environmental responsiveness displayed by sponges and other sessile bottom-dwellers. Of course these are unusual cases—cases where the animals in question are barely responsive enough to count as animals rather than plants (cf. *HA* VIII.1 588b12–16).[39] Thus I think we should grant that for *most* animals, being motivated involves the desiring of something that is not yet there (e.g. the desiring of food that will be acquired once the prey is killed, or the grass chewed, or the nectar collected), and that this cannot be the province of perception alone. But what *phantasia* supplies, in these cases, is not a form of interpretation that is strictly necessary for perception to generate some desire. For by perception alone a perceiver can become aware of something as an object of pursuit or avoidance—or perhaps as something to be tended toward or recoiled from, or responded to in

---

[38] A view along these lines is also defended in Charles (2006, 26).

[39] Johansen claims that these cases are in fact common, and that even human locomotion is possible without *phantasia*. His example is that of someone eating a spoonful of taramosalata, and immediately being motivated to go for another (2012, 216–17n33). This is hard to reconcile with passages like [39], [40], and [44], which all seem to make *phantasia* a key component in locomotion. But it's also counterintuitive to think everything occurs as immediately as his example suggests: I eat the first spoonful, experience the pleasure, and now retain and associate the perception of taramosalata and the resulting pleasure. I am then motivated to go for another spoonful by this (very recent) association, and not by the occurrent experience of my first spoonful—for that occurrent experience lasts only as long as my eating, and I am not motivated *while I eat* to eat more, but only once I'm done enjoying the spoonful. At any rate it seems to me this must be the case, for if a spoonful of something enjoyable motivated more eating *as we were enjoying it*, we would never be motivated to stop eating—and plausibly, there comes a point at which even taramosalata is no longer appealing. (I do think we can allow that sponges are always eating, and always desiring food—so this wouldn't apply to basic sessile animals. My point is only that desires that are not future-directed are the exception, not the rule.)

some even more basic way—and thus desire and be moved toward it, even if the resulting movements are not directed toward some *distal* end, and so fall short of locomotion.

So *phantasia* does not turn perception into a motivational force: the pleasures and pains that accompany perception are enough to solicit some sort of response from a perceiver. What *phantasia* does enable is the much more common case of our appetites or other desires being future-directed, that is, our being moved to behave some way not because of what we currently perceive, but because of what we hope will come from it, based on past experience. This is just the sort of behavior that would paradigmatically constitute a case of locomotion. A good example is the hunting behavior Aristotle ascribes to lions and dogs:[40]

> [47] [Animals don't enjoy sounds or scents in and of themselves].
> For dogs do not delight in the scent of hares, but in the eating of
> them, but the scent told them the hares were there; nor does the lion
> delight in the lowing of the ox, but in eating it; but he perceived by
> the lowing that it was near, and therefore appears to delight in the
> lowing; and similarly he does not delight because he sees 'a stag or
> a wild goat', but because he is going to make a meal of it. (*EN* III.10
> 1118a18–23)

The predators here are described as recognizing their prey as a *source* of pleasure, and so as something to be pursued. But what they actually smell or hear is not itself pleasant: what's pleasant is the recognition that they will serve as food and so satisfy their hunger. And *that* is not something they perceive merely in virtue of recognizing their prey— a lion perceives that there's an ox, associates this with past memories of oxen she's had for dinner, and so recognizes the ox as food, and so as a means to satisfy her hunger. The sorts of desires at play here, and the locomotion they induce, require more than an awareness of present circumstances—and so more than what perception alone can disclose.

---

[40] I adapt the translation in Ross (2009).

This, I suggest, is just the sort of complex, goal-directed behavior *phantasia* is meant to enable. It does so by expanding our temporal horizons, allowing us to retain past perceptions and associate them with our present experience. This role has both backward- and forward-looking dimensions. The backward-looking dimension stems from our capacity to retain and bring back to mind what we've perceived. As Aristotle tells us, *phantasia* is "a motion brought about by active perception," which is "similar to perception," though it "persists" in a way perception does not (*An* III.3 429a1–2, 428b14, 429a4). The way *phantasia* "persists" is usually thought to involve the storing of some perceptual image, which might later be brought to mind by our remembering it (*Mem* 449b28–30, 450a10–13). But *phantasia* can also be put to use in a forward-looking way, as something that would enable us to *expect* what is not yet realized by projecting some image associated with what we currently perceive. In fact, though he says far less about expectation than he does memory, Aristotle typically treats them together as forms of perceptual association—the first concerned with our retrieving the past, the second with our envisioning the future based on the past (see e.g. *Mem* 449b10–15, 449b26–8, *Rhet* I.11 1370a30–35, and [48], below). In both cases, *phantasia* allows us to retain perceptually derived images and relate them to each other. Thus a lion might be reminded of an ox by its lowing, say, and also project the perceptions associated with her hunting it down and feeding on it—for what will be brought to mind is not only the image of the ox, but also a sequence of associated memories that will bear on what the lion presently expects.[41]

Now, remembering and expecting should be distinguished from deliberate forms of recollection and calculation. Recollection, as Aristotle conceives of it, involves a concerted search for something we take ourselves to know, and so depends on our rational capacities (*Mem* 451b18–25, 453a4–14, *HA* I.1 488b25–26). Memory, by contrast, is the province of the perceptual part of our soul, and available to nearly all animals (*Mem* 450a22–25).[42] So the sort of association it requires

---

[41] On the temporal structure and association of memories, see also *Insomn* 461b13–15, *Mem* 451b10–14, and Lorenz (2006, 155–68) and Modrak (1987, 96ff).

[42] Not all animals, since those without *phantasia* presumably do not retain anything they perceive. Because remembering requires an association of retained perceptions *in*

should not be thought of as an intellectual exercise: the associating happens simply by habituation, without any conscious relating of one perceived thing with the other.[43] Nor should its result be conceived of as a form of detached awareness of some series of perceptual images. For in bringing images to mind we not only remember what it is we perceived—we also, to some degree, replicate the motivational force of our initial perceptions:

> [48] Feelings of confidence, fears, sexual excitement, and other bodily affections, painful and pleasant, are accompanied by heating or chilling—in some cases of a part, in others of the whole body. Memory and expectation, using things of this kind as images, are now to a lesser degree, now to a greater, responsible for the same things. (*MA* 8 702a2–7)

So the activity of memory does not simply result in a dispassionate awareness of some past perception. The images brought to mind also replicate the pleasures and pains (and other, more specific affections) attending our past perceptions—and thus reproduce the physiological changes such affections produce.[44] Thus when Aristotle tells us that animals "do many things in accordance with *phantasmata*, because they persist and are similar to perceptions" (*An* III.3 429a4–6), I think we should take the similarity to reflect both the cognitive and affective aspect of our perception: in typical cases we remember with pleasure what we pleasantly perceived, and so are moved by our memories and expectations in much the same way we are by our perceptions.[45]

---

temporal order, it requires the ability to perceive time. As Aristotle tells us, only those animals that can perceiving time remember (*Mem* 449b28–30), and plausibly these are just the animals with *phantasia*.

[43] Aristotle does seem to limit the role habituation plays for animals at *Pol* VII.13 1332b3–4, but his point must be that habituation plays a far lesser role in nonrational animals *than it does in humans*. Any glance at his zoological works makes clear the significance habituation plays in animal life. I'll give some concrete examples below.

[44] Or at least they reproduce heats and chills, and that perhaps only to some degree. We should allow, of course, that remembering something frightening does not always lead to full on flight—though as Aristotle rightly notes, memory and expectation can also *amplify* past pleasures and pains. The important point here is only that memory is not motivationally inert.

[45] In typical cases because Aristotle does allow that we perceive as painful things that wind up being good for us—and thinks we do take pleasure in *those* memories, even

If this is right, *phantasia* allows for the association of past perceptions with each other, as well as the association of some series of associated past perceptions with what we currently perceive—together with the reproduction of the affective changes attending the perceptions in question. Thus in our example in [47], the lion hears an ox lowing, and associates this perception with past memories of lowing. In doing so she remembers not only the lowing itself, but also the subsequent hunting and feeding, and the pleasures associated with the latter. On the basis of these associations she forms an expectation of some future pleasure—which expectation is itself pleasant, and has the potential to activate her appetite and thus (in the right conditions) set her into motion. And once set into motion her past experience hunting down oxen will also come into play, informing her movements, reactions to changes in her environment, coordination with her pride, and so on. So *phantasia* allows us to be motivated by things we do not currently perceive (because we've perceived them before, and associate them with certain pleasures, say), and also makes it possible for our past experiences to inform our behavior in trying to achieve what we are motivated to do (because we've hunted oxen before, we know to avoid the horns, attack them by surprise, and so on).

In defending this sort of view I am aligning myself with readings on which *phantasia* allows us to make use of perceptual information that is not currently presented to us, but does not serve to interpret raw sensory data, or endow our perceptions with motivational force they did not have on their own. Such readings are often presented as defenses of the view that *phantasia* does not "add content" to perception, but rather stores and associates contents that were originally conveyed to us by perceptual means.[46] But one has to be somewhat

---

if they are memories of painful things (*Rhet* I.11 1370a35–b2). Still, as he goes on to note, "for the most part the things we take pleasure in when they're present we also take pleasure in when we expect or remember" (1370b9–10). On this point see also *Phys* VII.3 247a7–14, and Lorenz (2006, 135) and Moss (2012, 57–64).

[46] See for instance Johansen (2012, 216) and Moss (2012, 56–57). It seems to me Lorenz should also be read this way, even if he is sometimes accused of going beyond this view in allowing that animals have the ability to "envisage prospective situations" (2006, 131). But envisaging a prospect need not be taken to involve more than associating various perceptions in the ways outlined above. For a lion to envisage feeding on an

cautious in framing things this way. For plainly *phantasia* does affect perception insofar that it alters what is *conveyed* to us by what we perceive. Presumably a lion doesn't recognize lowing as an indicator of nearby prey by default: it's only thanks to her associations between lowing and oxen (and feeding on oxen) that the lowing becomes salient to her, presenting itself as something to track or pursue when hungry, say. Just as our background theoretical knowledge might make some aspects of our perceptions relevant in certain scientific contexts (as described on p. 119), so too does *phantasia*, through its associative powers, make some aspects of our perceptions relevant in practical ones. It remains true that these are aspects *of our perceptions*, and that *phantasia* is thus best conceived of as making certain types of perceptual content significant in ways they might not be on their own—rather than, say, augmenting or modifying the perceptual contents themselves.[47] But it's important not to understate the impact this has on the sort of practical knowledge Aristotle takes to be available to nonrational animals. Retaining and associating memories is integral to the recognition and tracking of prey, for instance, and for a range of further, more complex behavior I will briefly consider below—and more broadly for the ability animals have to learn to respond coherently to different parts of their environment.

We humans are animals, too, and so often respond to what we perceive in just the same way. Indeed when Aristotle tells us *phantasia* is critical in guiding the behavior of animals, he emphasizes that in doing so it emulates practical modes of thought—and that it does this in both nonrational animals and in humans whose rational capacities are inhibited or for some other reason not currently engaged (*An* III.3 429a4–8; cf. also *An* III.10 433a10). Thus although we can also, as rational creatures, *think* about what to do and how to

---

ox, say, would just be for her to hear lowing, and remember past instances of lowing and the hunt and feeding that ensued, and be motivated thereby to track down the lowing she hears. To "envisage a prospect," so understood, just is to represent, on the basis of past perceptions, something we do not currently perceive. I take it to be relatively uncontroversial that *phantasia* can do *this*, whether or not there is a more involved kind of "envisaging" beyond its reach.

[47] Recall that I'm using "contents" here in a way that doesn't require that contents be conveyed to the perceiver in a way they might use to form beliefs or guide their actions—cf. p. 118.

do it, we often respond to our environment using only the sort of nonrational association described above. We might, for instance, respond to spiders by tensing up, squirming, and wincing away—if personal experience is any guide. These reactions either stem from some internalized association with past, uncomfortable encounters with spiders, or else simply reflect a brute response we naturally have toward potentially dangerous animals. But they are not directly influenced by what we think about spiders: we might squirm without thinking there's any reason to respond to spiders this way, and perhaps even while thinking there's reason not to—and indeed we might squirm without even knowing that what we see is a spider. We simply perceive the spider as *something to be avoided*, and are led to behave as we do by this perception and our basic appetites for pleasure and the avoidance of pain. This is not to say our rational soul *cannot* influence nonrational appetites, or that thought and rational desires cannot be used to overpower perception and nonrational appetites.[48] The point is only that we share with animals an *autonomous* nonrational soul, which does not draw on our rational powers to guide our behavior, and which can often be seen to conflict with what we believe on rational grounds.

So far, then, I've argued that *phantasia* plays an important role in allowing for locomotion and the development of practical, perceptually based forms of knowledge in nonrational animals. Its function is to allow us to retain what we perceive, and associate some past perception (or some series of past perceptions) with what we currently perceive—where the associating does not strip the perceptions of their motivating force, and so has the potential to solicit some behavior on our part, just as our original perceptions did. In doing so *phantasia* allows for perceptual discrimination to be informed by past perceptions, and for the formation of expectations that are based on accumulated perceptual experience—e.g. the expectation of lunch at the sound of lowing. Because it relies only on the information perception affords us, and operates independently of both practical and theoretical modes of thought, *phantasia* can plausibly be considered a nonrational, broadly perceptual power, even if its

---

[48] Aristotle thinks they can be—see for instance *An* III.11 434a14–15.

use results in the same behavior we might undertake on the basis of calculated deliberation.[49]

For all I've said here, however, *phantasia* might seem to yield only a rather limited set of behaviors—pursuing lowing when hungry, squirming at spiders, and so on. In fact Aristotle has a far more expansive conception of its impact on animal life than these examples suggest. I'll consider a few cases from his zoological works below, before drawing some conclusions about their significance for Aristotle's broader account of nonrational learning.

5.3   Animal Experience, Human Experience, and Rationality

Here is Aristotle on dolphins:

[49] Incredible stories are reported about the speed of [the dolphin]. It seems to be the fastest of all animals, whether marine of terrestrial, and it can leap higher than the masts of large ships. This typically happens when dolphins pursue fish they want as food: if some fish tries to escape, their hunger makes them follow it down deep, but when the way back up gets long they hold in their breath, as though calculating (ἀναλογισάμενοι), and then twist themselves around and shoot up like an arrow, striving with all their speed to cover the long way up to catch a breath, and in doing so will leap up high over the masts of any nearby ship. Divers do the same when they plunge in deep waters: they turn around and rise up in accordance with their remaining strength. (*HA* IX.48 631a20–b1)

And on cranes:

[50] Cranes seem to display many forms of intelligence (φρόνιμα). They fly far away and high up to get a broader vantage point, but

---

[49] Again, I am restricting myself here to the sort of *phantasia* that is available to (nearly) all animals. I grant that there is a rational kind of *phantasia*, too, which assists in the sort of thinking and deliberation Aristotle would restrict to humans (cf. *An* III.10 433b29–30).

if they see clouds and storms they fly back down and stay still. They also have a leader, and additional criers among those on the farther edges of the flock, so that the leader's voice be heard. When they settle down they go to sleep with their heads under their wing, standing on one leg, alternating, while the leader stays on the lookout, head uncovered, and signals with a cry when he sees something. (*HA* IX.10 614b18–26)

And panthers:

[51] The panther, it is said, has come to grasp (κατανενοηκυῖαν) that wild animals enjoy its scent. So it hides itself when on the hunt, allowing them to get near, and catching even deer in doing so. (*HA* IX.6 612a12–15)

These are just some examples of the many forms of complex behavior Aristotle ascribes to superior nonrational animals—often in terms he would usually reserve as markers of rationality.[50] It's no surprise that he would describe them in these terms: their behavior is just what we would expect from animals if they could deliberate, or calculate what was good for them to do. Dolphins act like human divers, going just as deep as their air allows, as though calculating the distance to the surface. Cranes react to signs of bad weather, organize their flock around a leader, and know to heed this leader's voice. Panthers recognize that their scent betrays them, and so hide themselves carefully as they hunt. For Aristotle none of these behaviors require any sort of rational thought. But plainly they are intelligent in a way a sponge's constant water suction is not.

So when Aristotle characterizes locomotion in terms of pursuit and avoidance, or our appetites in terms of pleasure and pain, this shouldn't be taken to imply that he only has primitive responses in mind. Likewise his characterization of discrimination: when speaking

---

[50] There are many more cases besides these: deer learning to give birth near roads their predators avoid and habituating their young to stay near their lair (*HA* IX.5 611a15–b23), goats, dogs, and panthers curing themselves of illness (*HA* IX.6 612a1–8), and so on. For Aristotle's usage of rational vocabulary, see also Labarrière (1984, 21), Lennox (2015, 201–11), and Leunissen (2017, 10–11).

in general terms it might be helpful to think of animals as perceiving certain things as objects of avoidance and pursuit, but in many cases their discriminations will be far more specific, and solicit a far broader range of responses than such simplified descriptions might suggest. Thus a dolphin might perceive some fish as worth pursuing just so far, not any farther, and a crane perceive stormy clouds as calling for just so much time on the ground. Their discriminations are meant to be a form of perception—perception informed by past experience these animals accumulate through the sort of retention and associative projection *phantasia* makes possible, and also, in certain cases, by learning from other animals (*HA* IX.1 608a17–21).[51] These resources allow intelligent animals to recognize what is called for by their situation, and also how to best achieve it: the panther sees the deer as a source of food, but also recognizes the need to hide, to stake it out, to pounce at the appropriate moment, and so on, where each of these behaviors is responsive to the particular features of its evolving environment.

It should be clear that this sort of intelligent behavior does not differ, except as a matter of degree, from that of the experienced doctor Aristotle describes in *Met* A1. Recall that this doctor is meant to be successful at recognizing and curing malarials, without yet understanding the nature of the disease, or even thinking of it in general terms. His experience allows him to see the feverish symptoms exhibited by various patients as calling for a cure, and to see leeching as the way to cure them—where the grounding for this experience is meant to be supplied by perception and memory, and the range of associative dispositions and habits they serve to produce. As I noted above (p. 143), and as we would expect, Aristotle allows that animals

---

[51] Aristotle agrees with Plato that there is a kind of teaching that is only possible for those with universal knowledge (cf. *Met* A1 981b7–8). But he also, reasonably, allows that animals with voice can signal things to each other and form habits in their young, and that even bees and ants can display the kind of proto-political organization he ascribes to cranes in [50] (cf. *Met* A1 980b1). So a certain kind of communication is distinctive of humans (communication through words that have some conventional *symbolic* function, cf. *Int* 2 16a19–29), and makes possible human forms of teaching and political organization—but nonrational animals do signal things to each other, and can impart habits and organize themselves into flocks, swarms, and colonies nonetheless. And Aristotle thinks that in doing so they act just as prelinguistic children would (*HA* VIII.1 588a25–b3).

might have some experience. Now, he does qualify this by saying that they only have a "small part" of it (980b26–27). But it's important that the qualification here does not issue from their lack of rational powers. For humans also display certain forms of skillful behavior that stems from habituation alone:

[52] [We think those with causal knowledge superior to those with mere experience.] And this is why we think that the master workers in each craft are more honorable and know in a truer sense than the manual workers, and that they're wiser than them: they know the causes of the things being done. For the manual workers do things in the same way certain lifeless things [τῶν ἀψύχων ἔνια] do things: they act without knowing what they do, as fire burns—though while the lifeless things do each of the things they do by nature, manual workers do them by habit. So it's not in relation to their actions that we consider them wiser, but in relation to their having an account and knowing causes. (*Met* A1 981a30–b6)

Aristotle is being dismissive of manual workers here, comparing their work to the burning of fire—but they are plainly meant to have some sort of experience, acquired through habit, which would allow them to reliably produce certain things (at least under the guidance of some master worker).[52] This is why their inferiority to master workers cannot be understood "in relation to their actions," and must instead be characterized in terms of the craft knowledge the master workers have and the manual workers do not. Presumably these manual workers, for Aristotle, have a less sophisticated form of experience than doctors curing malarials—but they are experienced

---

[52] One shouldn't take this dismissive remark as evidence that Aristotle does not hold the experienced in high regard. First, he is choosing an especially stark case to make his point: the manual workers are presumably meant to be skilled at a very specific task, but we can easily imagine doctors who have experience curing a whole range of diseases. Second, their inferiority is only relative to the epistemic ideal under consideration, which is a form of causal knowledge. Experience could remain valuable in its own right, as Aristotle often tells us it is, even if does not require any knowledge of causes, and so does not constitute the sort of wisdom under consideration in this context. He does add, after all, that the master workers are not any wiser than the manual workers in their actions. So the superiority at play here is only a mark of superior *causal* understanding.

nonetheless, and I take it they do not differ much from the sorts of intelligent animals surveyed above. If this is right animal and human experience are both independent of our rational powers. They differ only because, as Aristotle explains later on, human actions need not always be directed toward "pleasure and the basic necessities for life" (981b21–22), which are central concerns for animals concerned with their survival—so that humans might become experienced in domains that do not "aim at utility" (981b19–20), and eventually develop crafts and theoretical knowledge about them (sculpting and mathematics, say).

Now, it's natural to wonder just what entitles Aristotle to the distinction between sophisticated, intelligent forms of experience, on the one hand, and the sort of practical knowledge that depends on rational thought, on the other. For nonrational *phantasia* and its associative powers are meant to be sufficient to give rise to dispositions to perform just those actions practical thought and deliberation would prescribe—and yet practical thought is meant to be the province of craft knowledge, and a marker of wisdom Aristotle would deny to those with experience only. But why draw such a stark line between nonrational, associative animal psychology and rational forms of thought? The right conclusion might seem to be that there is no line to be drawn here—that what appears to be craft knowledge or reflect the operation of practical thought is, at bottom, nothing but a more elaborate form of perceptual association, amplified perhaps by a greater capacity for retention and anticipation, and the freedom—of some—to use them for something other than their self-preservation.

I think Aristotle has good reasons to resist this more extreme, reductive form of empiricism. I noted above (4.5) that universal knowledge, for Aristotle, treats in explicit terms the causal underpinnings of our various successful practices.[53] For the most part, I focused on the development of *theoretical* knowledge (knowledge of the nature of malaria, and of its effects, say) rather than *practical* knowledge (knowledge how to return malarial patients to health). But a similar point can be made in the latter case as well: a physician with both experience and craft knowledge understands *why* she prescribes as

---

[53] Recall (p. 99) the connection between universals and explanations in this context.

she does in a way a merely experienced doctor does not. Thus the experienced doctor sees a malarial patient as someone to cure, and to be cured by leeching—and in leeching them this doctor is indeed taking the means to her end. However she need not (*qua* experienced) recognize the means as such—though she acts with purpose and reliably takes the right means, she does this thanks to the habits she has developed, without taking herself to be doing so, or consciously grasping the means *as means to an end.*[54] So it may be that if we were to consider only their prescriptions of malarials, there would be no discernible difference between the physician and an experienced doctor. But there plainly is a difference in the knowledge that led each of them to prescribe as they did.

The difference is not only that those with craft knowledge know the "why" where the experienced only know the "that" (cf. [35]). It also reflects the synoptic, reflective character of the sort of knowledge Aristotle takes to be distinctive of rational creatures like ourselves. Recall that theoretical understanding requires knowledge of explanations, but also requires an understanding of the broader role one's explanations play in some scientific domain, and thus knowledge of the domain's structure, and of the extent of one's understanding of it (cf. p. 21). To understand some fact scientifically is to know why it must be so, where our grasp of the relevant explanation is sensitive to its theoretical role—that is, to what else it explains, and what explains it. So too for practical understanding, which requires knowledge why one acts as one does, but also requires an appreciation of our ends (and the means taken to achieve them) sensitive to their broader practical role. Thus a physician with craft knowledge of medicine will recognize leeching as the right remedy for malarials, but also as the wrong remedy for pneumonia, say—and her understanding of the remedial powers of leeching will be informed by some general appreciation of a range of different diseases and their effects, and

---

[54] I take the argument to this effect Lorenz (2006, 179–85) to be decisive. See also Fernandez (2014, 186–97). In what follows I will treat productive craft knowledge as a form of *practical* knowledge. Though Aristotle does seek (in *EN* VI.4–5) to distinguish the practical wisdom of the virtuous from craft knowledge, the differences he points to will not affect what I say here. More below (pp. 220–21) on practical wisdom and craft knowledge.

which of these disease leeching will and will not be able to cure (I take this to be part of what is required to think of malarials as "marked off in one class," as Aristotle puts it in [34]). She will also recognize curing malarials as an end rather than a means toward something else, in the same way an expert scientist recognizes her definitions as an indemonstrable explanatory bedrock, rather than something we might try to demonstrate.[55] This kind of knowledge might not make a physician any more successful at curing malarials (though it will probably make her better at curing other, related diseases).[56] But it does mark a significant difference between the physician with craft knowledge and the merely experienced doctor: only the former performs actions with a synoptic appreciation of their role as means or ends in her various pursuits, and thus acts in a manner that manifests a reflective understanding of the structure of her medical practice.[57]

---

[55] Thus the physician recognizes that her ends do not admit of deliberation (cf. *EN* III.3 1112b11–15), and the expert scientist that her definitions do not admit of demonstration (cf. 3.1). There are of course differences, too: in the theoretical case definitions express the essences of certain kinds, while the starting points of practical deliberation typically do not (cf. *EE* I.5 1216b16–25 and Lorenz and Morison (2019), where this point is connected with Aristotle's ascription of theoretical and practical rational thought to different parts of the soul). And of course practical knowledge deals with particulars, while theoretical knowledge concerns universals only, and the necessary connections between them (*EN* VI.7 1141b8–16, VI.8 1142a14–15). So the *sort* of explanation grasped in each of these case is different, though both forms of knowledge are explanatory, synoptic, and reflective (on which latter point see also *EN* I.5 1095b2–13).

[56] It is often argued (e.g. by Johansen (2017, 131) and Moss (2014, 226)) that Aristotle should not be taken seriously when he claims that a physician with both causal knowledge and experience would be no better at curing patients than a doctor with experience only. This seems to me unnecessarily dismissive. Aristotle can allow that the physician is more flexible and better at curing patients *in general* than the doctor, yet still hold that *when it comes to malarials* they are equally successful (on which point see *EN* X.9 1180b16–20). He can also allow that the physician is more *efficient* at curing malarials, being better able to assess the merits of various cures and pick the superior one in cases where there are many viable options (cf. *EN* III.3 1112b15–20). Still, the flexibility at play here need not make any practical difference if we hold the target ailment fixed—and increased efficiency does not make any difference to the outcomes achieved.

[57] I myself think it plausible that this sort of understanding involves a *conceptual* mastery of medicine a merely experienced doctor would not possess (cf. p. 89), though of course this depends on a specific conception of concept possession. See Bengson (2016) for a recent view in this direction, and see also Bengson (2017) for a recent account of practical and theoretical understanding that seeks to preserve some of the commonalities described in the main text.

Just as scientific understanding is meant to mirror the structure of an objective, natural explanatory order, so too is an understanding of the means and ends relevant to one's practices meant to mirror the structure of an objective, natural hierarchy Aristotle takes to hold between means and ends.[58] In both cases, our epistemic progress involves making better known to us what is better known "by nature," or better known *simpliciter*, as Aristotle sometimes puts it—coming to recognize the ultimate causes whose effects we are familiar with (in the theoretical case); or coming to appreciate the means-end relations that we implicitly grasp when engaging in our various pursuits (in the practical). It is just this sort of appreciation that Aristotle denies nonrational animals—an appreciation which might not make any difference to our outward behavior, or to the actions we perform, but which does modify our relationship to these actions when we perform them, and so affects the sort of activity these actions manifest.[59]

So Aristotle is not a reductive empiricist: he thinks there is a clear distinction between rational and nonrational knowledge. But he plainly has an ambitious view of the sort of nonrational knowledge perception (together with perceptual *phantasia*) allows us to achieve. For he thinks perception allows for an appreciation of what our situation calls for, and a recognition of how best to achieve it—both of which are informed by our own past experiences, as well as the dispositions others have inculcated in us by habit. This sort of experience is perceptually grounded and nonrational: nonhuman animals can and do become experienced, though perhaps to a lesser degree than humans (or at least, humans of leisure). And it remains operative even in humans with rational forms of knowledge, and the capacity to

[58] See for instance *EN* I.7 1097a19ff, VI.13 1144b1–16, and *Pol* VII.13 1332a21–25, and see also [15], where the theoretical and practical are explicitly assimilated. On the objective structure of means and ends in our practices, see Lear (2004, 15–23).

[59] Allowing, as above, that it might make a difference to the *range* of activities we engage in, and our ability to cope with situations of a type we haven't yet encountered. Of course this is not an iron-clad response to the sort of objection considered above: one might further press Aristotle, in Humean spirit, about our grasp of causal and means-end relations, and what our grounds are to think them distinct from internalized associations. Still, it does show that Aristotle's views on rational knowledge are systematically motivated by his background metaphysical views, as well as his empirical zoopsychology—and so not easily undermined by more targeted forms of skepticism.

engage in thoughtful deliberation how to achieve their ends—the fact that we humans can *also* grasp the causal underpinnings of our practices in a comprehensive and reflective way does not itself transform or otherwise suppress our animal responses to the situations we face. Thus while theoretical or practical forms of rational knowledge often inform our perceptions, allowing us to recognize the broader scientific significance of some observation, say, or recognize something as the best means to achieve some end, our background *nonrational* knowledge informs our perceptions, too, and allows for the sophisticated sorts of associative responses Aristotle describes throughout his zoological works—associative responses that might emulate the discriminations of practical thought and deliberation, and typically produce the same outward behavior by purely nonrational means.

What I hope to have shown in this chapter is that Aristotle had good grounds to consider the learning necessary to form such responses perceptual in nature. These grounds stem from his account of the psychological and physiological underpinnings of animal locomotion. The two central components of this account are desire and discrimination—in nonrational animals, basic appetites for pleasure and the avoidance of pain, and perception, respectively. Perception's discriminative role is both evaluative and instrumental: it allows us, thanks to the pleasures and pains that attend it, to recognize something as an object of avoidance or pursuit, and also allows us to recognize ways to realize an end we pursue. Perception can do this much on its own, without any assistance from *phantasia*. But *phantasia* does remain necessary for anything but the most basic forms of animal behavior, and in particular for the sort of locomotion that is Aristotle's focus in *MA*. It makes possible the retention of past perceptions as memories, and the association of these past perceptions with an occurrent perception—and thus supplies the mechanism by which *past* perceptions would inform our present and future behavior, and yield the sorts of complex, goal-directed dispositions we find in experienced humans and intelligent nonrational animals alike. It's on these grounds, I submit, that Aristotle motivates his nuanced empiricism, on which perception allows for sophisticated responses to some situation without thereby being assimilated to or tacitly influenced by rational modes of thought.

6

Perception in Aristotle's Ethics

In the above, I've argued that perception contributes to more advanced forms of knowledge by putting us in touch with particular things in a way that's responsive to the universals governing their behavior: perceptible particulars possess certain features because they instantiate certain universals, and perception allows us to discriminate these features and experience them as action-guiding aspects of our environment. Aristotle thinks (on broadly zoopsychological grounds) that we can develop a coherent, sophisticated sort of practical experience in certain domains on the basis of this sort of perceptual discrimination. And he thinks that we can develop a rational understanding of the causal structure of such domains on the basis of this experience. We do so by induction—a cognitive process that eventually yields the sort of scientific understanding that constitutes our highest epistemic accomplishment. Though induction is the work of rational creatures, experience is an inherently perceptual state, and thus available in some degree to nearly all animals (with exceptions for sponges and other sessile bottom-dwellers unendowed with *phantasia*).

So far I've mostly been concerned with the development of craft knowledge and scientific understanding (τέχνη and ἐπιστήμη) from these perceptual beginnings. In this chapter I'll be considering more closely what Aristotle's views on perception and perceptual learning might tell us about his moral epistemology. I'll focus in particular on the relation between perception and practical wisdom (φρόνησις); a relation often invoked by commentators (call them *particularists*) who find in Aristotle a rejection of the view that general moral rules could play any significant role in governing ethical behavior.[1]

---

[1] Below I will spell out in more detail what the rules are supposed to be, and what significant role they are denied. As will become clear, I think some particularist readings of Aristotle are correct, and some not.

Aristotle's Empiricism. Marc Gasser-Wingate,
Oxford University Press (2021). © Oxford University Press.
DOI: 10.1093/oso/9780197567487.003.0006

Particularists conceive of Aristotle's virtuous agent as someone who *sees* what to do in the many particular situations they face, without reasoning at a more general level about the sorts of behavior that might be required of them, or about how their actions might accord with some conception of the human good. On some versions of their view, this is because there simply are no codifiable rules that govern ethical behavior—what we should do is always, ultimately, a matter of what we should do *in the particular situation we're in*. Thus ethics, unlike other disciplines, is not a subject matter Aristotle thought we could understand scientifically, or of which there might be a craft. For universals are the proper objects of scientific understanding or craft knowledge, while virtuous behavior is irreducibly particular, and thus the province of perception.

If this sort of particularist view is right, it provides a counterexample to the general thesis I've been defending: in the ethical domain, perception does not contribute to our developing any advanced knowledge of universals. For in the ethical domain there simply is no advanced knowledge of universals to be found. Thus perceptual learning cannot operate as I have suggested so far—or at least not in general, and not when it comes to working out how we should live. Perception would still play a critical ethical role, of course, but it wouldn't supply the basic knowledge necessary for the sort of inductive progress we can achieve in other domains, and which results in forms of understanding that serve to explain what we can learn from perception alone.

I will argue in this chapter, however, that Aristotle's remarks about perception in the *Ethics* do not support particularist views that would rule out universal ethical knowledge, or indeed any sort of particularist view that would conflict with Aristotle's account of perceptual learning.[2] More broadly, I will argue that Aristotle assigns no *special* role to ethical perception: the importance perception has in guiding our behavior and coping with the many particular situations we face is no different in the ethical domain than it is in productive domains

---

[2] I'll mostly be focusing on *EN*, but the main interpretive points I'll be making are consistent with Aristotle's discussion in *EE* (many of the key passages appear in the common books). Unless otherwise noted, references in this chapter are from *EN*, and translations of *EN* are adapted from Ross (2009).

like carpentry or medicine. In all these cases Aristotle emphasizes that perception is an indispensable source of practical knowledge, and that it provides a grasp of particulars that cannot easily be achieved by purely theoretical means. And in all these cases it might be right to characterize the skilled practitioner as someone who simply *sees* what's to be done in the particular situations she faces. But in none should we infer that universal rules governing the practice are not to be found, or that the things we perceive are not coherent or determinate enough to be treated in the context of a theoretical science. To the contrary: for Aristotle the very possibility of perceptually grounded practical wisdom would serve as evidence that a theoretical treatment of virtuous behavior is possible.

So I think we should reject the stronger formulations of particularism, on which virtuous behavior is uncodifiable in principle, and universal ethical knowledge useful only as a summary of the particular perceptual judgments of the virtuous. Still, particularists are right to emphasize the indispensable role perception and perceptually grounded experience play in the development and deployment of practical wisdom. For, as I will further argue, while it might be possible to approach ethics theoretically, ethical theory offers no guidance how to act—or does so only indirectly, and not *qua* theoretical. If this is right, the indispensable perceptual aspects of practical wisdom are not indispensable because ethical theory is impossible or hopelessly vague or imprecise, but rather because theorizing about virtue does not alone make anyone virtuous, any more than theorizing about various diseases and their cures makes anyone a doctor. In all practical and productive domains, our learning depends on first-hand, personal experience in a way theoretical expertise does not—personal experience which, on Aristotle's view, must be acquired by broadly perceptual means, and not by reason alone.

6.1 Strong Particularism: Ethics and Rules of Conduct

Aristotle announces at the beginning of *EN* that he intends his investigation as a study of "fine and just things," and, therefore, as part of the science of politics (I.2 1094b14–15). His investigation proceeds in a familiar way: Aristotle offers a definition of the highest human good, and then goes on to discuss what this definition might tell us about the features of a flourishing human life. He tells us that the highest human good is virtuous activity of the soul (I.7 1098a16–17), and that a flourishing human life is a life characterized by such activity—as it manifests itself in practical thought and deliberation, and in the virtuous character displayed by the temperate, courageous, generous, and so on (I.13 1103a3–10).[3]

Yet Aristotle doesn't say much about what exactly would count as an exercise of these virtues. He does of course go on to describe the character virtues as dispositions to hit the mean between two extremes, and the intellectual virtues in terms of the sort of deliberative thinking involved in our various virtuous activities. But it's natural to wonder how any of this is supposed to teach us how we should live our lives, or how reading it would help make us *better*, as Aristotle claims it should (*EN* II.2 1103b27–29, X.9 1179a35–b2, *EE* I.5 1216b16–25). All the more so since a central point of his account is precisely that the actions that constitute our hitting the mean will depend on the particulars of our circumstances, and so must ultimately be determined by perceptual means (II.9 1109b14ff). So while we do seem to get from Aristotle certain general ethical principles (a conception of the good life, of the place of various goods in this life, and so on), we get very little concrete advice how to act. And much of what he says makes it seem that this is because he simply didn't consider it possible to give any such advice at a general level—that is, that Aristotle didn't *omit* a detailed account of what virtue would call for in various situations, but that he simply didn't think such an account could be given.

Apart from the lack of concrete advice in *EN*, two pieces of evidence are typically invoked to support this conclusion. The first is Aristotle's frequent insistence (see e.g. *EN* I.3 1094b11–27, I.7 1098a26–33, II.2 1104a1ff) that we not expect from ethics the sort of *exactness* we find in sciences like geometry. He takes this to follow from the nature of the

---

[3] I set aside Aristotle's later discussion of the contemplative life, and how this discussion bears on his account of the human good. Those issues are largely orthogonal to what I have to say here—though of course if we think happiness is found in contemplation only, practical wisdom will not have much of a role to play.

subject matter of ethics: it would be absurd to expect mathematical exactness when it comes to virtuous conduct, just as it would be absurd for geometers to be satisfied with the sort of approximate right angles a carpenter uses in her work (I.7 1098a29–31). For (as Aristotle explains) we should only ever seek as much exactness as the subject matter we're investigating demands, and ethics and politics do not demand much: there is considerable "variety and fluctuation" in our characterizations of good conduct, and so we must be satisfied with an account that holds "for the most part," and seeks to describe things "roughly and in outline" only (I.3 1094b19–22).

The second piece of evidence is Aristotle's emphasis on the perceptual judgment of the virtuous. This emphasis is present in his discussion of character virtues, where he notes that perception is necessary to determine what rules like "hit the mean" might dictate in some given situation (see e.g. II.9 1109b14ff and IV.6 1126a32ff). It's also present in his later discussion of practical wisdom, where Aristotle argues that the virtuous rely on their (perceptually based) *experience* to determine how to act, and that their practical wisdom is concerned with perceptible particulars, rather than focusing exclusively on the sorts of universals studied in some demonstrative science (VI.8 1142a12–30). In both cases, he plainly thinks perception must supply a form of discernment theoretical modes of thought do not— and that this is one of the key features that distinguishes practical wisdom from a state like scientific understanding.

This is of course not to say that nothing general can be said on ethical matters. I take it even the most extreme particularists wouldn't deny that Aristotle offers us a general account of human happiness, or that he intends his conclusions about the nature of courage, friendship, or practical wisdom as generic, universal claims about these virtues. The motivating thought is, rather, that there are no such claims specific or precise enough to be of any use in determining how to act. Thus we might hold that happiness is virtuous activity, and (a bit more specifically) that courage and friendship are virtues, and (more specifically still) that the courageous stand their ground in battle and good friends give each other what they're due. But even then, the corresponding prescriptions ("stand your ground in battle," "give your friends what they're due") are context-sensitive, open to exceptions, and vague: if they have any content that would serve to guide our actions, this content would ultimately depend on some individual, situation-specific judgment what to do. For instance, one might need to assess whether there is really still a *battle* going on, or whether we should stand our ground even when our friend has been cornered and needs our help, or whether we should really return a sword to a friend who has gone mad. Even relatively specific prescriptions must still be applied, balanced against each other, and sometimes rejected. So while we can formulate certain rules of conduct and make broader, general claims about the nature of happiness and the virtues, it may seem these would be useful only as an imperfect shorthand for the various particular judgments of the practically wise, from which any normative authority must ultimately derive.

Here is how some prominent particularists put the point:[4]

> Principles [of conduct] are perspicuous descriptive summaries of good judgments, valid only to the extent to which they correctly describe such judgments. They are normative only insofar as they transmit in economical form the normative force of the good concrete decisions of the wise person and because we wish for various reasons to be guided by that person's choices.[5]

> [Aristotle's] point is that, *in this case*, the universal is nothing over and above the particular instances, in that there is nothing more to grasping the universal than being able to identify instances of the specific sorts that comprise it: there is nothing more to a grasp of what the good life is in general than the ability to produce correct identifications of the virtuous actions that go to constitute happiness. Intuition has no role to play analogous to its role in the theoretical sphere: it is involved in making judgements about individual cases, and if someone is able to do that, nothing more is needed, or indeed possible.[6]

---

[4] See further, in a similar vein, Wiggins (1980).
[5] Nussbaum (1986, 299–300). See also Nussbaum (1990, 68).
[6] Woods (1986, 160), emphasis the author's.

Aristotle's scepticism about universal truths in ethics implies that the content of [the correct general conception of what doing well is] cannot be definitively written down, in a shape suitable for deduction of particular practical conclusions. [...] If having the correct conception of doing well [...] cannot be identified with acceptance of a set of universal rules or principles, something whose correctness we could try to make out independently of their application to particular cases, then there is really nothing for it to be except the capacity to get things right occasion by occasion.[7]

Now, there are a number of subtle differences between the versions of particularism endorsed by these authors, to which I cannot fully do justice here. But as I see it, they share a common motivating idea, namely, that virtuous activity requires confronting various situations and "getting things right occasion by occasion," and nothing more— and that this is so because Aristotle thinks that what constitutes "getting things right" *cannot* be characterized in general terms. So any textbook rule or characterization of virtue or happiness will be useful only insofar as it provides "perspicuous summaries" of the various particular judgments of the virtuous, and not, for instance, because it provides a set of standards we might use to decide what to do. In this respect, the ethical domain is supposed to be unique: an expert scientist's understanding of other domains is based on her noetic grasp of the fundamental explanatory grounds proper to that domain, but a virtuous agent's knowledge consists only in her ability to discern the right course of action in any given particular situation. To know what the virtues are, or what human happiness is, just is to correctly discern what would constitute virtuous behavior in this way—anything beyond such discernment might be helpful as a heuristic, but would not itself have any normative significance.

This is a particularly strong formulation of particularism. After all, one might allow that certain rules of conduct are helpful in deciding how to act, even if they don't *entirely* determine our actions, and require some judgment to apply to some given situation.[8] One

---

[7] McDowell (1988, 93–94). See also McDowell (1998).
[8] On which point see Curzer (2016, 66–73).

might also allow that perception has a critical role to play for the virtuous without concluding that it must serve as an *exclusive* source of normative authority, upon which any sort of justification of our actions would depend.[9] Indeed, I will be defending a more moderate view in this direction below.

My reason for focusing on such strong formulations of particularism is primarily dialectical: only strong formulations pose a threat to the general account of perceptual learning I've been defending. Recall that the challenge to this account depends on the idea that there is no knowledge of ethical universals of the sort we find in other disciplines—so that perception cannot in this case play the role I claim it does in Aristotle's inductive account of our learning. If one allows knowledge of ethical universals (that is, knowledge of ethical universals that is not mere shorthand for the particular judgments of the virtuous, or a matter of "getting things right" on various occasions), perception might still be taken to play the foundational role it does everywhere else—even if it also plays *other* roles in guiding the conduct of the virtuous.[10]

So my argument in what follows will have two parts. I'll first try to show that Aristotle doesn't rule out a theoretical, scientific treatment of ethical universals—though he does make it clear such a treatment would be unhelpful in certain ways.[11] I'll then argue that the role perception plays in ethics is akin to the role it plays in crafts like medicine and navigation, and that our knowledge of universals should be understood on the same model in both cases—as a form of knowledge that is practical and informed by our personal experience, but is nonetheless more than a mere summary of this experience, and so not only a matter of reliably getting things right.

[9] On which point see Irwin (2000, 118–27).

[10] I do in fact think all the particularists mentioned above would deny the possibility of such knowledge. But I will not insist on this: if they do not deny this possibility, then their position will simply be closer to the sort of view I defend in what follows.

[11] I do not think we have any clear-cut evidence that Aristotle thought we *could* develop a science of ethics. But to my mind the burden of proof is on those who would deny it. My claim is that our evidence does not support this denial.

6.2 Against Strong Particularism

Consider, first, Aristotle's many cautionary remarks about the subject matter of ethics.[12] Here is one characteristic warning Aristotle offers after presenting his substantive conception of happiness:

> [53] And we must also remember what has been said before, and not look for precision in all things alike, but in each class of things such precision as accords with the subject matter, and so much as is appropriate to the inquiry. For a carpenter and a geometer investigate the right angle in different ways; the former does so in so far as the right angle is useful for his work, while the latter inquires what it is or what sort of thing it is; for he is a spectator of the truth. We must act in the same way, then, in all other matters as well, that our main task may not be subordinated to minor questions. (*EN* I.7 1098a26–33)

This passage is meant to explain why we shouldn't expect an exact, fully worked-out account of human happiness, and be satisfied instead with an "outline of the good" whose details might be filled later on (I.7 1098a20–22, cf. I.3 1094b19–22). But in doing so it makes clear that the disciplines best treated inexactly might nonetheless deal with objects that *could* be treated exactly: a carpenter's healthy disregard for exact angles does not imply the *impossibility* of treating angles in an exact manner, as a geometer would.

So when Aristotle tells us that some subject matter shouldn't be treated exactly, he doesn't mean that there are certain things—the carpenter's angles, the just person's actions and deliberations, and so on—that are such that they simply don't admit of any sort of exact treatment. What he means is that *given the aims of some discipline* (housebuilding, living well) it would be inappropriate to treat the discipline's objects in an overly exact manner. Thus, for someone who wants to live a good life, it may well be a waste of time to seek definitions of all the virtues, and an exact, demonstrative understanding

---

[12] I will discuss these remarks only briefly, since a number of commentators have made the case that they should not be taken as evidence that Aristotle thought ethical science impossible—see for instance Anagnostopoulos (1994), Henry (2015), Irwin (2000), Nielsen (2015), and Striker (2006).

of the relations between them. But this does not preclude such an investigation for someone who primarily seeks to understand the truth about a good human life.[13]

A similar thought motivates the warning that precedes his account of the various virtues of character:

> [54] The whole account of matters of conduct must be given in outline and not exactly, as we said at the very beginning that the accounts we demand must be in accordance with the subject matter; matters concerned with conduct and questions of what is good for us have no fixity, any more than matters of health. The general account being of this nature, the account of particular cases is yet more lacking in exactness; for they do not fall under any craft or precept, but the agents themselves must in each case consider what is appropriate to the occasion, as happens also in the craft of medicine or of navigation. (*EN* II.2 1104a1–10)

In this passage Aristotle compares his investigation of virtue with an investigation of crafts like medicine and navigation. He tells us, first, that any *general* account of ethical matters ("matters concerned with conduct and questions of what is good") will have to be inexact. For ethical matters, like matters of health, "have no fixity." An account of *particular* cases, he adds, will have to be even less exact than any such a general account: in ethical matters the agents will always have to determine "what is appropriate to the occasion," as is the case also for doctors and captains when they practice their craft.

But note that this already indicates that we can investigate both ethical and medical matters more exactly than we do when focusing on particular cases. Medicine is, after all, the very sort of subject we

---

[13] To be clear, I do not deny that learning the truth about how to live well, for Aristotle, might contribute to our living well. My point is only that the pursuit of truth is not the ultimate aim of our investigation (the ultimate aim is to live well). If the truth about living well were our end, then a deeper grasp on the nature of virtue would always be a mark of progress, whatever its impact on our conduct. If, however, living well is our end, then concerning oneself too much for an exact account of the virtues might be counterproductive: learning about the virtues might still be helpful, but the scope and character of our investigation will be structured by our concern for our actually living well, rather than merely understanding what it would take to do so.

can come to know in more exact, universal terms, as Aristotle makes explicit in *Met* A1, and as he suggests here when alluding to a more exact (but not *overly* exact) general account of matters of health. Note also that Aristotle's admonition against seeking too much exactness in any general account of ethical or health-related matters need not be taken as an indication that such exactness is *impossible*, or that these are matters that could not be treated in a more exact manner. His point, as I understand it, is only that a fully exact theory is not *helpful* unless our aims are purely theoretical ones. And this is true for any practical or productive domain: a physician would be ill-advised to seek a full account of the nature of malaria and its consequences before curing her patients, and a captain would be ill-advised to seek a full account of tides and currents before setting out to sea.[14] Likewise, we would be ill-advised to try and spell out exactly what courage is, and demonstrate on this basis what courage would require in various situations. Ill-advised not because this is a hopeless task, but simply because it would get in the way of our actually becoming virtuous, which Aristotle presents as a key aim of his investigation right before the passage above (II.2 1103b26–28).

Similar pragmatic considerations motivate the limits Aristotle sets on the politician's investigation of psychology. Since the political scientist aims to make his fellows citizens good (I.13 1102a9), and since the human good is an activity of the soul, Aristotle thinks the political scientist will have to study the soul. But not too closely. For as Aristotle puts it:

[55] The student of politics must study the soul [...] with these objects in view, and do so just to the extent which is sufficient for the questions we are discussing [=what laws will make citizens good]; for further exactness is perhaps something more laborious than our purposes require. (*EN* I.13 1102a23–26)

---

[14] In the case of medicine, Aristotle tells us explicitly at *Sens* 436a17–21 that a natural scientist (or a doctor approaching her craft philosophically) could investigate the principles of health and disease. But presumably one need not have a worked-out demonstrative account of such principles to have craft knowledge of medicine. Aristotle suggests a similar point would apply to the student of politics: she can approach her subject philosophically, but should take care not to be led into some digression or extraneous argument when she does so (*EE* I.6 1216b35–1217a9).

So seeking an overly exact account of the soul is a mistake because it's an ineffective, overly laborious way to realize the aims of political science—not because a more exact account of the soul is impossible in principle (Aristotle's psychological works are good evidence it is not).[15] The limitations on exactness in political science are therefore a reflection of the *aims* of political science, rather than some irreducibly particular feature of its subject matter.

In all these cases, then, I take Aristotle's point to be that there is a degree of exactness that it would be superfluous to seek given the aims of some investigation. If this is right, his emphasis on the inexactness of his account in *EN* need not be taken as evidence that virtuous conduct (or "fine and just things" more broadly) are inherently uncodifiable, as particularists would have it.[16] It could simply reflect the fact that his account is not intended as a purely theoretical study of the human good, but rather as something that might be put to practical use—e.g. as an account that would inform the laws a legislator might seek to enact (*EN* X.9 1179b31ff), or afford the virtuous a more reflective and systematic appreciation of their existing virtuous practices (as I will suggest below). So I don't think Aristotle's remarks about the inexactness of ethics support the strong particularist views under consideration.[17]

---

[15] This is not to say Aristotelian psychology is anywhere close to a demonstrative science. The point is only that one can study the soul with a greater degree of exactness than is advisable in the political context—and that nothing Aristotle says rules out a perfectly exact demonstrative science of the soul.

[16] I will not investigate in detail the other claims Aristotle makes about ethics— e.g. the claim that noble and just things "exhibit much variety and fluctuation," or that claims about them hold only "for the most part" (I.3 1094b15–16, 1094b21). For Aristotle, the fact that certain phenomena hold "for the most part" does not mean they cannot be treated scientifically (cf. Irwin (2000, 105–13), Henry (2015)). And even if there is more disagreement or "fluctuation" about what counts as noble or just than there is about (say) what counts as a healthy person or a good shoe, this need not be a sign of any indeterminacy in the noble or just things themselves. The problem could be with us: we might not be able to escape our limited conception of nobility, and appreciate it for what it is. This would leave it open that it is in principle possible to codify what is (objectively) noble and just, even if disagreement on these points often seems intractable.

[17] I don't think they support our *rejecting* these views, either. But one would need a separate argument to show that virtuous conduct is uncodifiable, rather than just overly laborious to codify exactly given that Aristotle's aims are not purely theoretical. And any such an argument would have to contend with the fact that Aristotle sometimes seems to

Now, one might object here that on the picture I've advanced theoretical science must be developed on the basis of practical experience, and that if this is right there could be no "purely theoretical" grasp of virtuous conduct: any understanding of virtue must issue from our experience acting virtuously, and so could not be theoretical only. But one should be careful to distinguish the possibility of theoretical knowledge *tout court* from the possibility of some individual's engaging with some subject matter theoretically. Recall (from 3.2) that Aristotle's inductive account of our learning is intended to show how it would be possible for advanced universal knowledge to come about, where that knowledge did not exist beforehand. According to this account, virtuous conduct must indeed precede its treatment in theoretical terms—in the sense that no theoretical treatment of virtuous conduct would have been possible (on anyone's part) absent some coherent body of virtuous practices (on the part of some individual or collective). But it does not follow from this that the theorist must *herself* be virtuous before developing her theory. She might theorize about the virtuous conduct of others, just as an astronomer might seek out explanations for observations that aren't her own—allowing of course that it might be more controversial what counts as virtuous conduct than what counts as an eclipse or other astronomical phenomenon.

So just as a studious physician could "have an account without experience" (cf. [16]), so too could someone learn about the nature of the virtues, the relations between them, and have an account of "fine and just things" in general without any concern for her own behavior—even if what she learns is a form of understanding that could not have been developed without someone's (or some collective's) having acted virtuously. It is just this sort of possibility that Aristotle is guarding against in [55]: his concern is that those requiring exactness in the ethical or political realm would be seeking an understanding of ethics as "spectators of the truth" (cf. [53]), and not an understanding of ethics that would inform and shape their own actions. That would be a wrong-headed way to approach the study of

treat the virtues as he would any other scientific subject—as for instance in his treatment of magnanimity at *APo* II.13 97b17–25, on which see Nielsen (2015, 36–37).

ethics, where, as Aristotle tells us, "we inquire not in order to know what virtue is, but in order to become good" (II.2 1103b27–28). But again, this is not because one could not, in principle, understand what virtue is scientifically: the point is that one should seek the sort of knowledge of virtue that would manifest itself in our own conduct, in the same way a physician should seek the sort of knowledge of diseases and cures she might put to use in treating her patients, rather than the sort of exact, purely theoretical understanding she might achieve in the context of a demonstrative system (cf. [54]).

Let's turn now to the second piece of evidence invoked in favor of particularist views: Aristotle's frequent emphasis on the role perception plays in the cognitive life of the virtuous. Again, I do not think this evidence is sufficient to establish the strong formulations of particularism under consideration. Here, for instance, is how Aristotle describes the role perception plays in making an indeterminate end like "hit the mean" (or "be good-tempered") issue in some concrete, practical guidance how to act in our circumstances:[18]

[56] But this [=hitting the mean] is no doubt difficult, and especially in particular cases; for it is not easy to determine both how and with whom and on what provocation and how long one should be angry; for we too sometimes praise those who fall short and call them good-tempered, but sometimes we praise those who get angry and call them manly. But the one who deviates little from goodness is not blamed, whether he do so in the direction of the more or of the less— only the one who deviates more widely is blamed, for he doesn't go unnoticed. But up to what point and to what extent one must deviate before becoming blameworthy it is not easy to determine by reasoning, any more than anything else among the things we perceive: such things belong to the particulars, and the discernment rests with perception. (*EN* II.9 1109b14–23)

For Aristotle, then, those with a good temper hit the mean between excessive anger and excessive meekness. But as he tells us here, determining how much anger one's circumstances call for (and toward

---

[18] For a similar point see also IV.6 1126a31–b11.

whom to direct it, and for how long) is a form of discernment that's most naturally exercised by perceptual means, rather than through some form of reasoning—which is why ascriptions of praise or blame are also hard to make by rational means alone. For the discernment concerns particulars, and particulars are the province of perception, and "not easy to determine by reasoning."

Now, Aristotle does not say which particulars perception would help us discern, or what about them we are supposed to learn perceptually. We could understand the claim in different ways: perception might make salient to us the features of our situation that call for anger. Or it might reveal to us what our situation calls for *overall*— that is, it might reveal to us which of the morally salient features we are confronted with should take precedence over the others, and thus dictate which end we should seek to realize in our circumstances. Or it might be necessary simply because it supplies us with the background experience needed to determine how some rule of conduct would apply to our situation, where someone without experience would grasp it as an abstraction only. But let's suppose that perception plays all of these different roles. And let's suppose, further, that it *must* play these roles—that is, that perception alone can supply the sort of discernment that would serve to guide our actions on various particular occasions.[19] Even then, it doesn't follow that virtuous conduct does not admit of codification, or that our perception of particular cases has a special form of normative authority in the ethical realm which general rules do not.

---

[19] It's not entirely clear this is the case: in [56] Aristotle is careful to say that it's *not easy* (rather than *impossible*) to determine how much anger some situation calls for by reason alone (οὐ ῥᾴδιον τῷ λόγῳ ἀφορίσαι, 1109b21). In the same spirit he says it's not easy to define or give an account of such things in *EN* IV.6 (οὐ γὰρ ῥᾴδιον διορίσαι τὸ πῶς καὶ τίσι καὶ ἐπὶ ποίοις καὶ πόσον χρόνον ὀργιστέον, 1126a32–34; οὐ ῥᾴδιον τῷ λόγῳ ἀποδοῦναι, 1126b3). So when Aristotle says that perception is the capacity that tells us how much anger some situation calls for, he need not be taken to discount the possibility that we come to the same conclusion by painstaking reasoning about virtuous conduct and the features of our situation. His point might just be that the reasoning would indeed be painstaking, and that it's an unnatural way for someone to decide how to act—that *paradigmatically* this is a kind of judgment we reach by perceptual means, because perception is far better suited to the task than any form of reasoning that would involve general definitions and accounts.

Take the latter point first. It is true that, for Aristotle, any general principle concerning virtuous behavior would have to cohere with the judgments of the practically wise: if the courageous deviate from some purported rule of courage ("stand your ground in battle"), then we should follow the judgments of the courageous, and give up or revise the rule. In practical matters, "the agents themselves must in each case consider what is appropriate to the occasion," as Aristotle tells us in [54], and "actions are called just and temperate when they are such as the just or temperate would do" (II.4 1105b5–7), making the virtuous "the norm and the measure" of the good (III.4 1113a33). Here is how Aristotle puts it in his discussion of justice and equity (ἐπιείκεια):

> [57] When the law speaks universally and a case arises on it which is not covered by the universal statement, then it is right, when the legislator fails us and has erred by over-simplicity, to correct the omission—to say what the legislator himself would have said had he been present, and would have put into his law if he had known. (*EN* V.11 1137b19–24)

Thus Aristotle is well aware that laws are imperfect guides, and thinks an equitable person will recognize this and know how to apply them to new cases, upholding the spirit of the law in scenarios not covered by its letter. To do so is a way to say what the legislator "would have said had he been present," and thus ostensibly a way to give precedence to some particular judgment over an imperfect codification of virtuous behavior.[20]

But this does not imply any *special* sort of authority for ethical perception over general rules of conduct. Recall (from [12], [13], and [14]) that Aristotle disapproves of natural scientists and astronomers who cling to their principles in the face of conflicting evidence, and that he thinks what we perceive should serve as a standard of

---

[20] For laws (and justice more broadly) as a codification of virtuous behavior, see Striker (2006, 134–36). Strictly speaking, and *contra* Nussbaum (1986, 301), [57] does not describe a case where some particular judgment takes precedence over a general prescription, but rather a case where some particular judgment has weight on an issue the general prescription does not address. Still, in context it seems clear Aristotle would also endorse the correction or qualification of laws were they to conflict with some particular judgment.

correctness for our demonstrative theories. So the view that perceptual evidence serves as an authority against which general principles must be measured is one Aristotle holds for theoretical and nontheoretical disciplines alike. And (as I've argued) this view does not imply that our perceptual knowledge would serve as a *unique* source of justification, or that the sort of priority ascribed to general principles would derive from their being perceptually grounded. For perception is a "primitive" source of knowledge in one sense only (primitive to us, not by nature), and is not the *only* source of justification for the principles we derive on its basis (cf. 2.4). Barring any clear evidence to the contrary, it's natural to think this would hold in the ethical case as well: the perceptual judgments of the virtuous serve as a standard of correctness for moral principles, but do not serve as a unique source of normative authority, or as the sole justification one might give for our actions.

Indeed, Aristotle makes a number of methodological remarks which seem to indicate that perception's role as a standard is the same in the ethical case as it is in other disciplines. After offering his general account of the character virtues, he tells us that

[58] among statements about conduct those which are general apply more widely, but those which are particular are more true, since conduct has to do with individual cases, and our statements must harmonize with the facts in these cases. (*EN* II.7 1107a29–32)

And toward the end of his discussion of contemplation, he notes that

[59] the truth in practical matters is discerned from the facts of life; for these are the decisive factor. We must therefore survey what we have already said, bringing it to the test of the facts of life, and if it harmonizes with the facts we must accept it, but if it clashes with them we must suppose it to be mere theory. (*EN* X.8 1179a18–22)

Aristotle's point here is the same as it is for any sort of inquiry, namely that our theories must harmonize with the facts. If the facts are facts about the conduct and judgments of the virtuous, then our theories must adequately describe and explain the conduct and judgments of the virtuous. But it does not follow from this constraint that general rules would have no "normative force" whatsoever. Perceptual judgments might vindicate general rules of conduct which the practically wise would nonetheless appeal to as grounds for their decisions—just as our observations vindicate the scientific principles an expert invokes to explain what we observe.

And it's natural to think general rules would in fact have some normative role to play, since the practically wise are often described as relying on both universal and particular knowledge in their deliberations—for instance, knowledge that "light meats are healthy" and "chicken is a light meat" (*EN* VI.7 1141b18–21), or that "heavy liquids are bad" and "this liquid is heavy" (*EN* VI.8 1142a20–23).[21] Now, the particularist line on these universals is that our knowledge of them simply consists in our correctly identifying their particular manifestations: for the virtuous to know that light meats are healthy just is for them to see that chicken is healthy, turkey is healthy, and so on, and be disposed to respond to these meats in the right sort of way, as temperance requires. But while it seems right to say that the practically wise see that they should opt for various light meats, we shouldn't infer from this that there is nothing more their grasp of the relevant universal ("light meats are healthy") could possibly be.[22] Indeed Aristotle's views about our perceptual responsiveness to universals suggest the opposite. For as I argued in 4.5, the fact that one can become perceptually responsive to some range of phenomena shows that there is some universal our perceptions are "of," and which

[21] The exact reasoning in these deliberations is left unclear, but presumably the wise decide to eat chicken and avoid the liquid in question, however exactly they reach this decision. My point here is that it's natural to think they would invoke the fact that light meats are healthy if pressed to justify their behavior. Of course this is compatible with the idea that they learned this fact through perception and experience, rather than any sort of theoretical demonstration (cf. [62], below). And it's compatible with their *also* invoking, in justifying themselves, the fact that they perceived that the meat was light. It seems to me natural to think both rules *and* perception have some normative role to play in these contexts, with neither being a "sole normative authority." But just as talk of "justification" is not easily squared with Aristotle's epistemological writings, so too is talk of some unique "normative authority" not easily squared with his ethics—and so I think we would probably do best to resist framing his views in those terms.

[22] It seems right to say that they "see" what to do on the basis of Aristotle's description of experience and the trained perception of the practically wise—on which more below.

we *could* come to understand in its causal role, even if perception does not supply any such understanding itself. Thus if the temperate can respond appropriately to light meats "occasion by occasion," and thus become experienced, virtuous meat eaters, this simply shows that there are certain universal features (of meat, or of healthy foods more broadly) their eating decisions are tracking—features we could study in the context of some science or craft, even if our dietary practices do not depend on our having engaged in any such study.

So the perceptual responsiveness invoked by particularists seems to me, if anything, to count against strong formulations of their view. It is right to say that the practically wise reliably determine what virtue requires of them, and that this is a paradigmatically perceptual exercise: they see what to do in the various particular situations they face. But this simply shows that virtuous conduct *can* be treated systematically, in the same way the skill some people display in argument shows rhetoric can be treated systematically (cf. [36], where, again, those skilled at argument need not understand what makes them skilled).[23] Now, no doubt there are certain ways of treating virtuous conduct that will be too exact to be of any practical use (for instance, attempts at a *demonstrative* treatment of virtue). But one need not conclude from this that *any* general treatment of virtue would have no practical relevance whatsoever, or that it would be devoid of normative authority, serving at best as a summary of particular perceptual judgments. In the same way craft knowledge of medicine might deepen our understanding of certain successful healing practices, and provide an explanation for these practices, so too will an (inexact, nondemonstrative) investigation of ethics deepen our understanding of our own virtuous behavior, and provide us with an explanation of some of the features of this behavior—in a way that does have practical implications. Or so I will argue in what follows.

---

[23] Maybe I haven't convinced you that we should think of our perception of universals in this manner. But even if our reliably getting things right doesn't serve as evidence that some universal might serve to explain our success, it doesn't serve as evidence against this, either—and so doesn't serve as evidence in favor of the strong particularist views under consideration, on which the universal in question would simply not exist.

For now, I hope to have shown that what Aristotle says about the inexact character of ethics and the reliance of the virtuous on perceptual modes of discernment does not support the sort of particularism considered thus far. For all Aristotle says, ethics could be investigated exactly by those with purely theoretical aims. And the perceptual judgments of the virtuous, while no doubt of central importance, are not required because virtuous conduct is uncodifiable in principle, or because these judgment are the only norm one could invoke to account for virtuous behavior. If anything, the fact that the virtuous can coherently get things right on various occasions shows there is some explanatory structure underlying their virtuous practices. Nonetheless, and for all these criticisms, I do think particularists are right to emphasize the central role perception plays in guiding the conduct of the virtuous. In what follows I will consider more closely the role perception and experience play in the cognitive life of the practically wise, and defend a more moderate form of particularism. My hope is that this more moderate particularism will preserve some of the motivating insights outlined above without positing theses about ethical uncodifiability our evidence does not warrant.

6.3 Perception, Experience, and Practical Wisdom

Aristotle thinks we count as virtuous in the strict sense only when we possess practical wisdom in addition to a virtuous character (VI.13 1144b14ff). Practical wisdom is an intellectual virtue that (at a minimum) reveals to the virtuous how best to achieve their ends— for instance, the virtue that reveals to someone who sees a fellow soldier in need of rescue how best to rescue the soldier.[24] In a case like this, Aristotle tells us, the virtuous person's character supplies an end ("rescue the soldier," "be courageous"), and practical wisdom supplies the "things toward" this end (see e.g. III.3 1112b11–20, VI.12 1144a7–9, 1144a20–22, and VI.13 1145a5–7). So practical wisdom is a kind of instrumental reasoning. But not instrumental reasoning in

---

[24] I leave it open here whether virtue includes practical wisdom as a component, or rather as a necessary condition for its full development.

a narrow sense, which would imply a sharp division between means and ends, or make our intellect a mere form of executive cleverness, subservient to some task independently supplied. An agent seeking to "be courageous," in choosing the "things toward" this end, is simply *being courageous*: she is taking a course of action that constitutes a realization of her end.[25] What this looks like will of course depend on her circumstances—whence the need for perception Aristotle mentions in [56], and in the further passages we will discuss below. So practical wisdom is a way to realize certain ends, but is also itself what makes an end like "be courageous" determinate enough that it could issue in some concrete action on our part.

Suppose, to take a simple example, that a courageous person recognizes a wounded soldier as a salient aspect of the battlefield, and judges that the soldier should be helped (or that helping the soldier is what courage requires, that it would be hitting the mean, that it is what's fine here and now). Because of her courageous character, this is not a dispassionate thought—she also *desires* to help the wounded soldier, despite the obvious dangers involved. Depending on the situation, further deliberation might be required about how best to proceed: does she create a diversion? Does she sneak by this enemy soldier, or confront him head-on? What are the tools at her disposal? Would she do best to mobilize others? Let's suppose she decides to create a diversion.[26] On Aristotle's view, this decision, together with her recognizing a specific way to divert the enemy, results in an action—a rational counterpart to the sort of behavior resulting from

---

[25] Put differently, she is working out what "hitting the mean" would require in her specific circumstances, or what is fine for her to do (cf. III.7 1115b13–14, IV.1 1120a23–24). See for instance Irwin (1975, 567–71), McDowell (1998, 108–10), Moss (2011, 241–51), or Wiggins (1980, 224–25) for defenses of (various versions of) this interpretation. It would take us too far afield to consider these variants in any sort of detail, but what I say here should be relatively uncontroversial, because it does not rule out that practical wisdom does *more* than what I have suggested so far—e.g. that it is also put to use when we reflect on our virtuous ends and the reason why we have them, or where they fit in our broader conception of human happiness.

[26] Assuming she is practically wise, this is the best way to be courageous in her situation. Presumably there are some cases where deliberation of this sort will not be required: if a diversion is the only way to rescue the soldier, then the courageous person simply decides, without deliberating, that she should create a diversion, and creates a diversion. That too would be a display of practical wisdom.

an animal's appetite for drink and recognition of something to drink, in [41].[27]

Now, note that none of the reasoning here seems to depend on her grasping in any sort of systematic way what the necessary features of courage (or human happiness) are, or how she could demonstrate from certain basic principles that it has the features in question. Which is a good thing, because it's not at all clear how *that* kind of reasoning would ever result in any sort of action. For suppose someone had a complete demonstrative theory of happiness—and so full scientific understanding of the highest human good (which, as I argued, Aristotle does not rule out in principle). And suppose this expert demonstrated from first principles that courage (in some set of circumstances, for a certain kind of person, etc.) requires rescuing our fellow soldier by creating a diversion. It seems to me this sort of demonstration would do nothing at all that would result in an *action* on her part, even if she were the kind of person in question, facing the circumstances in question. The problem is not only that she would have to recognize the set of circumstances as her own, and know to apply her demonstrated conclusion to herself. Even if she understood what courage requires of someone in her circumstances *and* knew that the circumstances were her own, it seems to me still open that the expert not act in accordance with this application of her theory—not because of any sort of akratic failure on her part, but simply because understanding scientifically why virtue requires something of her does not yet mean she will act on this understanding.[28] What would be

---

[27] Though I won't attempt an account of the practical syllogism here, I take it this process is meant to mirror Aristotle's cloak example at *MA* 7 701a17–22, with our decision supplying the "premise of the good," and our recognition of a way to realize it the "premise of the possible." On this point see Cooper (2020), Fernandez (2014), Lorenz and Morison (2019), and Price (2016).

[28] Thus, though I am sympathetic with his rejection of strong forms of particularism, I do not find satisfying the alternative proposed in Reeve (2012, 193), where "practical reasons that guide action directly" are said to have the following form: "why will this bird meat further happiness? Because it is light and all light meats are healthy." This leaves it quite unclear how knowing that some bird meat promotes happiness (and why) would have any bearing on my actions. Likewise (though again with sympathies for the broader view) I do not find convincing the thought that a doctor could not produce health without an account of the nature of health (Nielsen (2015, 40)). Surely we should allow that a doctor can heal without a worked-out definition of health: though some doctors might approach their work "more philosophically" (*Sens* 436a20–21), those who

required is a form of thought that does not have purely theoretical aims—knowledge of what's required of her that would motivate her in the right way and result in some action on her part.

It seems clear that Aristotle did not think demonstrative science motivating in this way. At *MA* 7 701a10–13, for instance, he contrasts practical and theoretical modes of thought, telling us that the former yields action and the latter contemplation.[29] In general, "thought moves nothing unless it's practical and directed toward an end," where the end is either a product or an action (*EN* VI.2 1139a35–b1). I take it this is one of the central motivating features of particularist views: practical wisdom is meant to be, well, *practical*, and thus reflect the sort of thought that would result in our acting as the virtuous would. Demonstrations about the human good, even if possible, do not seem to yield knowledge of the right sort—it's not clear how they would lead anyone to act (or even be motivated to act) some way or another, and so it's not clear how the sort of understanding they provide would serve to guide or justify our actions. And so particularists conclude that practical forms of knowledge must be understood only in terms of our discerning what's good on various occasions, rather than our grasping some general conception of the human good, and what follows from it.[30]

But I think we can preserve what's attractive about this line of thought without endorsing this conclusion. For we can allow that there is no purely theoretical, demonstrative approach to working out how we should act that would yield action on our part, and nonetheless

don't might presumably be quite effective at healing their patients. This is not to say that an account of health will be useless to a doctor—only that understanding the nature of health *scientifically* (having νοῦς of health) does not in itself have any direct practical ramifications.

[29] Or "speculation," or "seeing why something is true" (θεώρημα). For these renderings see Corcilius (2008a, 264–65) and Morison's translation of Primavesi (forthcoming). Aristotle does of course allow for a kind of *practical* truth as well (*EN* VI.2 1139a21–30, on which see Broadie (1991, 220–25), Lear (2004, 102–3), Olfert (2014), and Pakaluk (2010)). But this is not the truth we aim at when contemplating, or would secure by demonstration.

[30] Thus McDowell's rejects pictures of practical wisdom as a deductive understanding of moral prescriptions and their application (1998, 110–12), and Woods tells us that "there is no question of *justifying* the virtues by appeal to some conception of the good life, since one's grasp of what that is manifested in, and does not transcend, the ability to recognize goodness in particular cases" (1986, 164).

resist the thought that practical wisdom could only be the habituated disposition to rightly perceive what to do in particular cases, and act occasion by occasion as the virtuous would. For Aristotle thinks we can treat certain subjects in universal terms without treating them *theoretically*—that is, without treating them in a manner that would seek to articulate essence-giving definitions, and appreciate their explanatory consequences. In fact, conceiving of practical wisdom on the model of crafts like medicine and navigation, as Aristotle often does, suggests just this sort of picture—a picture on which first-hand, perceptually grounded experience plays a critical role in our knowing how to act, but does not preclude a general, practically-oriented (and thus nondemonstrative) appreciation of the explanatory structure underlying our practices.

Before filling out some of the details of this picture, a note on the association between craft knowledge and practical wisdom. I've been categorizing both of these as *practical* forms of knowledge, and contrasted them with their theoretical counterparts. That may seem a bit cavalier. For Aristotle is careful to distinguish practical wisdom and craft: "acting is not producing and producing is not acting," as he puts it, the key difference being that producing "has an end other than itself," while acting, at least in the technical sense at play here, is meant to be an end in itself, and not a means to something further (*EN* VI.4 1140a5–6, VI.5 1140b6–7).[31] But although this distinction plays an important role in Aristotle's conception of virtuous activity, and in his broader argument about the relationship between such activity and human happiness, I do not think it threatens the sense in which both forms of knowledge are practical.

---

[31] Another key difference is that "in the case of craft he who errs willingly is preferable, but in the case practical wisdom, as for the virtues, the reverse is true" (VI.5 1140b22–24). But that difference concerns our attitudes about craft and practical wisdom more than it does the states themselves, or the cognitive powers on which they depend. It also reflects the fact that the virtuous do not misuse their practical wisdom, while those with craft knowledge might bring about some result just as well as its opposite. Thus a physician's craft knowledge might be used to produce health or illness, and a musician's to play the right or wrong note—and in each case the ability to do either thing is a sign of technical wisdom (*Met* Θ2 1046b5–25). The practical wisdom of the virtuous, by contrast, is such that it is only ever put to good use (*Rhet* I.1 1355b2–7). Thanks to Gisela Striker for raising these points.

Both craft knowledge and practical wisdom are practical, as I see it, in the sense that they depend on the sort of goal-directed thinking that normally leads us to act (VI.2 1139a35–b1).[32] Part of what makes this possible is that these states concern themselves with "what can be otherwise," as opposed to what cannot (VI.4 1140a1–2, VI.3 1139b20–21), that is, with particular entities, as they appear to us at some time and place, rather than their necessary, universal features, and the relations that obtain between them (cf. 4.4). Thus we are not moved by the sort of thinking that would result from a demonstration—coming to recognize that triangles have 2R, and seeing how this follows from basic geometrical principles, say (cf. VI.5 1140b14–16).[33] But we *are* moved both by our thinking about what's to be done here and now to produce a cloak or a house, say, and by our thinking about what's to be done where our acting is itself the end we seek to achieve (*MA* 7 701a16–22; *EN* VI.2 1139a31–36). Of course there are substantial questions about exactly how practical thinking might do this, and how we should understand the relationship between such thinking and our desires and broader character. My claim here is only that, cognitively speaking, craft knowledge and practical wisdom share the core features that make them count as *practical* forms of knowledge: both states deal with particulars, and do so in a way that normally elicits some action on our part.[34]

To get a better sense of perception's contribution to such practical forms of knowledge, recall that Aristotle tells us in *Met* A1 that those

[32] By "normally" I mean in cases where there is no disruption from some desire or extraneous force. Arguably such practical thinking would be a constituent part of the sort of acting undertaken on its basis—on which point see Fernandez (2014, 179n50) and Price (2016, 456). But the exact relationship between virtuous activity and practical thought is more than I can hope to tackle here.

[33] Aristotle's example is geometrical, but I take it the mode of thought is what's critical here, rather than the subject matter. One could make the same point about recognizing that happiness is virtuous activity, and seeing how this follows from basic principles drawing on human psychology and the means-end structure of various goods and pursuits. That sort of thought would not move us in itself, even if it might lead to conclusions relevant to our conduct. (Likewise carpenters are left unmoved by a geometrical demonstration concerning the angular sum of triangles, even if such a demonstration establishes a conclusion highly relevant to their craft.)

[34] On this point see also Cooper (1975, 1–2) and Joachim (1951, 3–4). On the connection between particularity and practicality, see further Hasper and Yurdin (2014, 142) and Jimenez (2019, 381–83).

with medical experience but no causal knowledge succeed more than those with causal knowledge but no experience, and that this is so because actions and productions concern particulars like Socrates and Callias, rather than universals like "human," which would be studied in the context of a craft (981a13–20). He makes the same point in the case of practical wisdom:

[60] Practical wisdom is not concerned with universals only—it must also recognize the particulars; for it is practical, and practice is concerned with particulars. This is why some who do not know, and especially those who have experience, are more practical than others who know; for if someone knew that light meats are digestible and healthy, but did not know which sorts of meat are light, they would not produce health. But the person who knows that chicken is healthy is more likely to produce health. (*EN* VI.7 1141b14–21)

This passage is part of Aristotle's broader attempt to distinguish practical wisdom from scientific understanding and philosophical wisdom. The key difference alluded to here is that scientific understanding doesn't concern itself with particulars, and so doesn't have any direct bearing on our practices.[35] Just as we cure Socrates and Callias and not the universal "human," so too must we eat this and that chicken or other light meat and not the universal "light meat." And that kind of experience requires an acquaintance with many particular cases, which Aristotle thinks we must acquire over time: merely learning from dietary guidelines that light meats are healthy is no help without the ability to recognize that some particular meat (some meat as it appears to us here and now, cf. 4.4) is light, and so healthy. In fact, Aristotle tells us that in terms of health outcomes simply knowing that chicken is healthy (without knowing why) would be better than merely knowing such a guideline—just as he tells us in [35] that perception does not teach us the "why," but yields authoritative knowledge of particular "thats."

---

[35] Another, related difference is that practical wisdom deals with matters that have practical, human significance, while scientific understanding deals with matters "remarkable, admirable, abstruse, and divine—but useless" (VI.7 1141b6–7). The same point is also made at *Met* A1 981b13–25.

In depending on accumulated experience in this way, the development of practical wisdom differs from the sort of learning possible in fields like geometry:

[61] What has been said [=that practical wisdom requires knowledge of particulars, and not just universals] is confirmed by the fact that while the young become geometers and mathematicians and wise in matters like these, they do not seem to become practically wise. The cause is that such wisdom is concerned [not only with universals but] also with particulars, which become familiar from experience. But a young person has no experience, for it is length of time that yields experience. Indeed one might ask this question too, why a boy may become accomplished in mathematics, but not in wisdom or natural science. Or isn't it because the objects of mathematics exist by abstraction, while the first principles of these other subjects come from experience? The young have no conviction about the latter, though they might speak about them, while the essence of mathematical objects is plain enough to them. (*EN* VI.8 1142a11–20)

So some kids might be good at geometry, but kids are never wise—they just haven't lived enough to form the sort of experience practical wisdom requires. Later on Aristotle will echo this point when he tells us that "a particular age brings with it insight (νοῦς) and good judgment" (VI.11 1143b8–9), and that we therefore

[62] ought to attend to the undemonstrated sayings and opinions of experienced and older people or of people of practical wisdom not less than to demonstrations: they see things right, because experience has given them an eye. (*EN* VI.11 1143b11–14)

As noted above (p. 209), Aristotle's point in these passages cannot be that practical wisdom depends on perception and experience in the same way more advanced cognitive states are said to depend on perception and experience in *APo* II.19. For that much is true for any field—even the objects of geometry are abstracted from our perceptually grounded experience with the shapes of physical things (cf. *Met* M3 and [18], where our knowledge of abstractions is said to be acquired inductively). His point must be, rather, that *personal* experience is not required in the case of geometry, while it is in the case of practical wisdom: an expert geometer's understanding of triangles doesn't depend on her personally seeing many triangles, while practical wisdom, plausibly enough, is something we develop over time, and whose development depends in large part on our personally confronting many different situations (and being brought up under the right laws, that reward and punish the right responses to these situations—cf. II.3 1104b8–13, X.9 1179b23ff).[36]

Particularists, then, are right to emphasize the central role perception plays in practical wisdom—which is distinct from the role it plays, for Aristotle, as the origin of all our knowledge. Perception and perceptual experience are needed because they inform our knowledge of general claims like "light meats are healthy," "heavy liquids are bad," and also, presumably, our knowledge of the various prescriptions implicit in Aristotle's discussion of moral virtues.[37] Our knowledge of these claims and prescriptions must be informed by perception to be of practical significance to us: learning medicine from a textbook does not itself teach us how to produce health, and hearing arguments about the human good does not alone make anyone virtuous (X.9 1181b2–3; 1179b4–10).[38] Direct, *personal* experience is needed to produce the right affective dispositions, and train ourselves to recognize the situations we face as relevant to certain broader background commitments, and as opportunities to act on these commitments— where the commitments must therefore not be mere theoretical

[36] As similar point is made at I.3 1095a2–11. See further Striker (2006, 138–39), who also emphasizes our personal experience in practical and productive forms of knowledge, and contrasts this experience with the sort involved in our learning from systematic observation.

[37] Pay back your debts where possible (VIII.13 1163a1–2, IX.2 1165a2–3), give up your seat for the elderly (IX.2 1165a27–29), spend lavishly, but with good taste, if you have the means (IV.2 1122a34–35), and so on—broad principles useful only to those practiced in their application. These and Aristotle's more general axiological claims are of course not presented as imperatives of this sort: the right upbringing is necessary to grasp them as action-guiding in the way the imperative mood suggests (likewise for more general claims like "courage is a virtue," "happiness is virtuous activity," etc).

[38] See also *EE* I.6 1216b40–1217a10, where Aristotle indicates that one might be skilled at producing arguments on ethical matters "without any disposition or even capacity for practical or architectonic thought."

positions, or understood as we might understand demonstrative conclusions, but rather known in the manner of a "premise of the good" (as in *MA* 7 701a23–25) or its nonrational analogue (as in [41]). This sort of experience and perceptual training is, initially at least, a largely nonrational matter: Aristotle thinks we are typically habituated into our background commitments through pleasure and pain, under the compulsion of the law. This is as we would expect, since, as I argued in our last chapter, Aristotle thinks our perceptions of pleasure and pain are motivating and action-guiding, and can yield often sophisticated forms of experience which, in turn, inform what's conveyed to us by our perceptions—and would presumably allow us to see what to do (and be motivated to do it) as the virtuous would.

Where particularism goes wrong is in thinking that this is all practical wisdom could possibly be, and that our knowledge of general prescriptions would be exhausted by our trained perception what to do.[39] That would simply be to deny the parallel Aristotle clearly intends to draw with craft knowledge, which is after all a form of *universal* knowledge, and contrasted with experience for that reason. And while inexperienced doctors are ineffective, Aristotle clearly thinks experienced doctors do benefit from understanding their craft universally:

[63] They try, anyway, to stipulate not only the treatments but also how particular classes of people can be cured and should be treated, distinguishing the various states. It seems this is helpful to experienced people, but useless to the inexperienced. (*EN* X.9 1181b3–7)

[39] Some particularists do take such perception to be an intellectual exercise, even if it results from nonrational habituation (cf. McDowell (1998, 114)). But *prima facie* this is hard to square with the view that experience is available to nonrational animals (cf. p. 143), and requires only perception and the assistance of *phantasia*, operating independently of our intellectual capacities (cf. p. 186). If practical wisdom is just perception trained to track what's fine, together with appropriate motivational propensities, then it seems to me to amount to a form of experience—and if that's right more would have to be said about why practical wisdom requires the intellect, while experience ostensibly does not.

This is why Aristotle thinks anyone wishing to master a craft must "go to the universal, and come to know it as well as possible" (1180b21–22), and why a politician must likewise come to appreciate universally the laws and prescriptions that will make good citizens.

Appreciating such prescriptions universally benefits the citizens, too—or at least those the laws have successfully trained into acting virtuously. The benefit is just the sort of synoptic, reflective appreciation of their practices characterized in 5.3: an appreciation of the structure of their various virtuous pursuits, and of the role certain goods play as means and ends in these pursuits. This is a distinctly practical way of knowing universals, and so should not be taken to depend on any sort of scientific understanding of the means and ends in question (though, as I've argued, it might be possible to achieve that as well). And this is so even if it requires knowing some fact that *could* be demonstrated. For instance, Aristotle might think it demonstrable that the highest human good is virtuous activity.[40] But practical wisdom would not depend on our understanding such a demonstration scientifically— that is, on our knowing why that fact must obtain, and how it depends on the explanatorily basic definitions from which it derives. What it would require is an appreciation of this fact as it bears on our practical decisions. Thus if we're practically wise, knowing that the highest human good is virtuous activity rules out certain possible responses to our situation: we need not, in our deliberations, consider virtuous activity as a means toward something else. And knowing that courage is a form of virtuous activity will likewise allow us to rule out its pursuit for the sake of honor, or pleasure, say. It will also inform our encounter with situations we have *not* experienced first-hand: as Aristotle tells us in [57], equity requires good judgment in scenarios not covered by some general rule, and as he tells us in X.9 1180b7–29, our personal experience, because personal, will not always help us cope with cases that are not specific to us. It's natural to think that an appreciation of

---

[40] A point also raised in Lorenz and Morison (2019), and which may seem supported by the sort of argument Aristotle gives in *EN* I.7. But even if he is approaching ethics theoretically in that context, his doing so should not be taken as evidence that such a theoretical approach would be of any direct practical significance: it might be helpful for the practically wise to know the conclusion of a demonstration, even if they need not understand this conclusion scientifically, or appreciate its place in ethical science.

the broader structure of our practices would be relevant in such cases, and thus make us more flexible than those relying on their experience only.

Making room for a practically oriented knowledge of universals of this sort does not conflict with the central role Aristotle assigns perception and experience. I've argued here that the sort of understanding of general ethical claims Aristotle has in mind is non-theoretical: demonstrations do not guide our actions, and the sort of understanding they supply would be only of indirect assistance to the virtuous. The practically wise might rely on the *content* of some demonstrated claim in their deliberations, but they would not rely on it *qua* demonstrated, or theoretical, even if they themselves have demonstrated it. And to rely on it as they do they would have to be practiced in recognizing how the claim would apply to various situations, and how it would play out in their deliberations—which is something that requires personal experience, and is thus never found in kids, as Aristotle tells us in [61]. So perception and experience are needed to develop the sort of knowledge of ethical claims that would "have a great influence on life" and serve as something we might aim at in our pursuits (I.2 1094a22–24). And it's because ethics aims at this sort of knowledge that it would be a waste of time to seek an overprecise treatment of the human good.[41]

Still, the knowledge in question is universal, and goes beyond a habituated disposition to get things right occasion by occasion, and recognize what is just and good as the practically wise would. That disposition is just the knowledge "that" from which we must seek the "why," in ethics as everywhere else (I.4 1095b2–8, cf. [35] and [15]). The knowledge "why" we seek is non-theoretical, and need not be taken to provide an "external validation" that our knowledge "that" did not possess, or affect whether or not we would count something as just and good in the first place.[42] But it does allow for a synoptic, reflective

---

[41] Ethics can aim at this sort of knowledge even if action is its *ultimate* end: the extent and nature of the knowledge sought is shaped by its realization in our activities.

[42] McDowell's particularism is motivated in part by a rejection of the possibility of providing such a validation for the judgments of the practically wise (see in particular McDowell (1998, 117–19)). I agree there is no such external validation for Aristotle. But it doesn't follow from this that there is nothing ethical knowledge could be besides the

appreciation of our existing virtuous behavior—an appreciation that does have practical consequences, benefiting us in our deliberations and decisions in the ways described above. It's this sort of appreciation, as I see it, that would distinguish practical thinking from a mere habituated disposition to see what to do in our situation, and respond to it as the virtuous would.

So Aristotle, as I've now argued at length, thinks highly of our perceptual capacities. What we perceive plays an essential role in the development of sophisticated states like experience, and in the more advanced practical and theoretical knowledge we might derive from it. Indeed, as far as ethics and productive crafts go, those with experience and a trained eye might be just as successful (though perhaps not as efficient or flexible) as those with a deeper understanding of their practices. This much is right about the particularist view.

What we should resist is the further thought that there is something irreducibly particular about the subject matter under consideration, or that our perceptual capacities only serve us so well because our intellectual ones cannot. It's right to say that the virtuous simply *see* what their situation calls for, and that our perceptual capacities are uniquely suited for this sort of discernment, and that living a full life is the best way to get better at discerning things the right way. But it does not follow that virtuous activity doesn't admit of theoretical treatment— even if we grant, as I think we should, that ethical theory does not directly inform how we act. Nor does it follow that the universal knowledge of the practically wise would amount *merely* to their seeing things correctly (and with the appropriate motivational propensity) in the various particular situations they face. Just as mastering a craft

various judgments and motivations of the practically wise. I am also disagreeing here with readings of the *Ethics* on which ethical knowledge proper is only the knowledge "that" we get from experience, and any knowledge "why" would be the province of metaphysics, physics, or psychology (see Achtenberg (2002, 61–95) for this reading). As I see it, there is ethical knowledge "why," which is just the sort of synoptic understanding of the structure underlying one's pursuits described above, and which does have a transformative effect on our conduct. There is also pure ethical theorizing, which might indeed involve some mix of metaphysics, physics, and psychology, and which would not in itself have any effect on our conduct (at least not *qua* theoretical). See Burnyeat (1980, 81) for a view in this direction, and see also Whiting (2002, 188), who takes practical wisdom to inform the perceptions of the virtuous, allowing them to recognize perceptually what is noble and just.

requires knowing the "why," so too does practical wisdom—even if personal experience is needed to appreciate its practical significance, and make our knowledge "why" pertinent to our conduct. What we gain in both cases is not an external validation for our productive methods and virtuous practices, but rather a form self-knowledge: an appreciation of the practical role of the various goods we pursue, and of the means-end structure underlying our pursuit of them.[43] Such knowledge is indeed practical in a way scientific understanding is not, and allows for a reflective form of deliberative thought that is the province of rational creature alone—even if its manifestation in our virtuous behavior will inevitably depend on forms of perceptual learning we share with other animals.

[43] For a recent view along these lines, see Velleman (2000, 11–12).

7

Final Thoughts

Here is Aristotle encouraging us to study lower animals:

> [64] We've already discussed celestial things and stated our views about them. Now onto our treatment of animals, omitting none of them if we can help it, however base they may be. For even if some hardly charm the senses, nature made them, and made their study a source of immense pleasure for those who can recognize causes and are philosophically minded. [...] So we shouldn't be childish and turn away from an examination of the lower animals: in every realm of nature there is something wonderful. And just as Heraclitus is said to have called out to visitors who wanted to meet him but stopped as they saw him warming himself by the kitchen stove ("come on in, don't be scared," he urged, "there are gods here too"), so too should we approach our investigations of animals of all sorts without any sort of shame, knowing that nature and beauty are to be found in each and every one of them. (*PA* I.5 465a4–23)

These are the words of someone with a deep fascination for the variety and richness of animal life, in even its most basic manifestations. What all these forms of animal life have in common, cognitively speaking, is the capacity to perceive—a capacity we humans share with intelligent animals, but also with sponges and other primitive bottom-dwellers. Thus while Aristotle thinks only we humans can think about causes and reflect on our perceptual responses to the world, he is not dismissive of the cognitive achievements of (so-called) lower animals. As he puts it a bit later, "anyone who thinks the study of other animals an unworthy pursuit must think the same about studying themselves" (465a27–28). After all, though we might by some measures be better off than other animals, Aristotle thinks we are still

Aristotle's Empiricism. Marc Gasser-Wingate,
Oxford University Press (2021). © Oxford University Press.
DOI: 10.1093/oso/9780197567487.003.0007

rather basic creatures, at least in relation to celestial bodies and other divine beings (cf. *EN* VI.7 1141a33–b2).

Of course, Aristotle *also* thinks that causal understanding is our highest cognitive achievement: humans want to understand things rationally, and live by craft and reasoning where nonrational animals get by with only perception, memory, and some degree of experience (*Met* A1 980b25–28). In his more Platonic moments, he characterizes the happiest human life as a life freed as much as possible from its animal needs and impulses, and enjoins us to not think mortal thoughts, but strive instead toward the sort of immortality found in pure contemplative study (*EN* X.7 1177b31–34). Remarks of this sort might make it seem as though perception and perceptual knowledge are valuable only in an instrumental way, as prerequisites for the unfettered exercise of rational contemplation—just as the "summoners of the understanding" we find in Plato's middle dialogues.

What I hope to have shown is that this sort of inference would be a mistake. For Aristotle, perceptual knowledge is valuable in its own right. It serves as a key part of our inductive advance toward definitional principles, affording us (with the assistance of *phantasia*) a nonrational form of experience of the very domains we might go on to understand in rational terms. That perceptual knowledge would allow for the development of such experience is an idea supported by a broad range of epistemological and zoopsychological considerations: Aristotle's generous conception of perceptual contents, the central role he assigns perception in purposive animal locomotion, and his allowing that our background knowledge might inform what's conveyed to us by what we perceive, and that we might reliably respond to universal causes without yet recognizing them as such. Together, these considerations motivate a moderate form of empiricism—a view on which our perceptual powers serve as an autonomous and independent source of practical knowledge, but on which our intellectual faculties are nonetheless necessary to develop any reflective understanding of the causes that would explain what we learn from perception alone.

Nor is perceptual knowledge dispensable once such an understanding is achieved. Even for an expert scientist, perception remains a non-intellectual source of conviction, and supplies the basic evidence demonstrative principles must recover and explain. In productive and practical fields, it also provides the sort of first-hand, personal experience necessary to recognize any piece of universal knowledge as relevant to the situations we face, so that we might use it in our deliberations and actions. So while there are epistemic achievements that exceed the reach of our perceptual powers, these achievements do not undermine the authority of perception, or make dispensable the knowledge it affords us.

What all of this suggests is a view on which we share a good deal of our cognitive lives with nonrational animals. We humans might perceive better than certain other creatures, and some of us might have the leisure to learn for purposes other than our own survival. As rational beings we desire to understand things, and not just get them right—and so take pleasure in developing a reflective, synoptic appreciation of the world and our practices. But perception, memory, and experience are the sorts of things we share with nonrational animals of all kinds, and on which we depend just as they do, whatever our rational powers allow us to do besides. To understand these nonrational animals is thus to understand an important and ineliminable part of ourselves. As I see it, this conception of our shared cognitive lives marks an important departure from innatist views Aristotle sought to reject. But it also gives rise to a brand of empiricism that remains worth our full consideration today—a brand of empiricism on which our rationality does not serve as the sole measure or source of epistemic dignity.

Bibliography

Achtenberg, Deborah (2002). *Cognition of Value in Aristotle's Ethics: Promise of Enrichment, Threat of Destruction.* State University of New York Press.

Ackrill, J. L. (1973). "Anamnesis in the *Phaedo*: Remarks on 73c–75c." In *Exegesis and Argument* (Gregory Vlastos, Edward N. Lee, Alexander P. D. Mourelatos, and Richard Rorty, eds.), Phronesis Supplementary Volume I, Van Gorcum.

Ackrill, J. L. (1981). "Aristotle's Theory of Definition: Some Questions on Posterior Analytics II 8–10." In *Aristotle on Science: The Posterior Analytics, Proceedings of the Eighth Symposium Aristotelicum* (Enrico Berti, ed.), 359–384, Editrice Antenore.

Adamson, Peter (2010). "Posterior Analytics II.19: A Dialogue with Plato?" In *Aristotle and the Stoics Reading Plato* (Verity Harte, Mary M. McCabe, Robert W. Sharples, and Anne Sheppard, eds.), 1–19, Institute of Classical Studies.

Alston, William P. (1993). "Epistemic Desiderata." *Philosophy and Phenomenological Research*, 53, 527–551.

Anagnostopoulos, Georgios (1994). *Aristotle on the Goals and Exactness of Ethics.* University of California Press.

Anagnostopoulos, Georgios (2009). "Aristotle's Methods." In *A Companion to Aristotle* (Georgios Anagnostopoulos, ed.), 101–122, Blackwell.

Angioni, Lucas (2014). "Aristotle on Necessary Principles and on Explaining X Through the Essence of X." *Studia Philosophica Estonica*, 7, 88–112.

Angioni, Lucas (2016). "Aristotle's Definition of Scientific Knowledge (*APo* 71b 9–12)." *Logical Analysis and History of Philosophy*, 19, 79–104.

Annas, Julia (2011). "Practical Expertise." In *Knowing How: Essays on Knowledge, Mind, and Action* (John Bengson and Marc A. Moffett, eds.), 101–113, Oxford University Press.

Auffret, Thomas (2011). "Aristote, *Métaphysique* A 1-2: un texte 'éminemment platonicien'?" *Elenchos*, 32, 263–285.

Barnes, Jonathan (1993). *Aristotle: Posterior Analytics.* Clarendon Press.

Bayer, Greg (1997). "Coming to Know Principles in *Posterior Analytics* II 19." *Apeiron*, 30, 109–142.

Bedu-Addo, J. T. (1991). "Sense-Experience and the Argument for Recollection in Plato's Phaedo." *Phronesis*, 36, 27–60.

Bengson, John (2016). "Practical Perception and Intelligent Action." *Philosophical Issues*, 26, 25–58.

Bengson, John (2017). "The Unity of Understanding." In *Making Sense of the World: New Essays on the Philosophy of Understanding* (Stephen Grimm, ed.), 14–53, Oxford University Press.

Biondi, Paolo C. (2004). *Aristotle, Posterior Analytics II.19: Introduction, Greek Text, Translation and Commentary Accompanied by a Critical Analysis*. Les Presses de l'Université Laval.

Block, Irving (1960). "Aristotle and the Physical Object." *Philosophy and Phenomenological Research*, 21, 93–101.

Bolton, Robert (1987). "Definition and Scientific Method in Aristotle's *Posterior Analytics* and *Generation of Animals*." In *Philosophical Issues in Aristotle's Biology* (Allan Gotthelf and James G. Lennox, eds.), 120–166, Cambridge University Press.

Bolton, Robert (1991). "Aristotle's Method in Natural Science: *Physics* I." In *Aristotle's Physics: A Collection of Essays* (Lindsay Judson, ed.), 1–29, Clarendon Press.

Bolton, Robert and Alan Code (2012). "Aristotle on Knowledge." In *Epistemology: The Key Thinkers* (Stephen Hetherington, ed.), 50–71, Continuum.

Bostock, David (1986). *Plato's Phaedo*. Clarendon Press.

Boyle, Matthew (2012). "Essentially Rational Animals." In *Rethinking Epistemology* (Günter Abel and James Conant, eds.), volume 2, 395–427, De Gruyter.

Boyle, Matthew (2016). "Additive Theories of Rationality: A Critique." *European Journal of Philosophy*, 24, 527–555.

Broadie, Sarah (1991). *Ethics With Aristotle*. Oxford University Press.

Bronstein, David (2012). "The Origin and Aim of Posterior Analytics II.19." *Phronesis*, 57, 29–62.

Bronstein, David (2016a). *Aristotle on Knowledge and Learning: The Posterior Analyics*. Oxford University Press.

Bronstein, David (2016b). "Aristotle's Critique of Plato's Theory of Innate Knowledge." *Logical Analysis and History of Philosophy*, 19, 126–139.

Burnyeat, Myles (1980). "Aristotle on Learning to Be Good." In *Essays on Aristotle's Ethics* (Amélie Oksenberg Rorty and Martha C. Nussbaum, eds.), 69–92, University of California Press.

Burnyeat, Myles (1981). "Aristotle on Understanding Knowledge." In *Aristotle on Science: The Posterior Analytics, Proceedings of the Eighth Symposium Aristotelicum* (Enrico Berti, ed.), 97–139, Editrice Antenore.

Burnyeat, Myles (2011). "Episteme." In *Episteme, etc.* (Benjamin Morison and Katerina Ierodiakonou, eds.), 3–29, Oxford University Press.

Cashdollar, Stanford (1973). "Aristotle's Account of Incidental Perception." *Phronesis*, 18, 156–175.

Caston, Victor (1996). "Why Aristotle Needs Imagination." *Phronesis*, 41, 20–55.

Caston, Victor (2015). "Perception in Ancient Greek Philosophy." In *The Oxford Handbook of Philosophy of Perception* (Mohan Matthen, ed.), 29–50, Oxford University Press.

Caujolle-Zaslawsky, Françoise (1987). "Étude préparatoire à une interprétation du sens aristotélicien d'ἐπαγωγή." In *Biologie, logique et métaphysique chez Aristote* (Daniel Devereux and Pierre Pellegrin, eds.), 365–387.

Charles, David (2000). *Aristotle on Meaning and Essence.* Oxford University Press.

Charles, David (2006). "Aristotle's Desire." In *Mind and Modality: Studies in the History of Philosophy in Honour of Simo Knuuttila* (Toivo J. Holopainen Vesa Hirvonen and Miira Tuominen, eds.), 19–40, Brill.

Charles, David (2010). "Definition and Explanation in the *Posterior Analytics* and *Metaphysics*." In *Definition in Greek Philosophy* (David Charles, ed.), 286–328, Oxford University Press.

Charles, David (2015). "Aristotle on Practical and Theoretical Knowledge." In *Bridging the Gap between Aristotle's Science and Ethics* (Devin Henry and Karen Margrethe Nielsen, eds.), 71–93, Cambridge University Press.

Cooper, John (1975). *Reason and the Human Good.* Hackett.

Cooper, John (1999). "Some Remarks on Aristotle's Moral Psychology." In *Reason and Emotion: Essays on Ancient Moral Psychology and Ethical Theory*, 237–252, Princeton University Press.

Cooper, John (2020). "*De Motu Animalium 7* (through 701b1): The Role of Thought in Animal Voluntary Self-locomotion." In *Aristotle's De Motu Animalium, Proceedings of the Symposium Aristotelicum* (Christof Rapp, ed.), Oxford University Press.

Corcilius, Klaus (2008a). "Praktische Syllogismen Bei Aristoteles." *Archiv für Geschichte der Philosophie*, 90, 247–297.

Corcilius, Klaus (2008b). *Streben und Bewegen: Aristoteles' Theorie der animalischen Ortsbewegung.* De Gruyter.

Corcilius, Klaus (2011). "Aristotle's Definition of Non-rational Pleasure and Pain and Desire." In *Aristotle's Nicomachean Ethics: A Critical Guide* (Jon Miller, ed.), 117–143, Cambridge University Press.

Corcilius, Klaus (2015). "Faculties in Ancient Philosophy." In *The Faculties: A History* (Dominik Perler, ed.), 19–58, Oxford University Press.

Curzer, Howard J. (2016). "Rules Lurking at the Heart of Aristotle's Virtue Ethics." *Apeiron*, 49, 57–92.

Dugré, François (1990). "Le rôle de l'imagination dans le mouvement animal et l'action humaine chez Aristote." *Dialogue*, 29, 65–78.

Engberg-Pedersen, Troels (1979). "More on Aristotelian Epagoge." *Phronesis*, 24, 301–319.

Evans, Gareth (1982). *The Varieties of Reference.* Oxford University Press.

Everson, Stephen (1997). *Aristotle on Perception.* Oxford University Press.

Ferejohn, Michael (1988). "Meno's Paradox and De Re Knowledge in Aristotle's Theory of Demonstration." *History of Philosophy Quarterly*, 5, 99–117.

Ferejohn, Michael (1991). *The Origins of Aristotelian Science*. Yale University Press.

Ferejohn, Michael (2009). "Empiricism and the First Principles of Aristotelian Science." In *A Companion to Aristotle*, 66–81, Blackwell.

Fernandez, Patricio A. (2014). "Reasoning and the Unity of Aristotle's Account of Animal Motion." *Oxford Studies in Ancient Philosophy*, 47, 151–204.

Fine, Gail (2003). *Plato on Knowledge and Forms*. Clarendon Press.

Fine, Gail (2010). "Aristotle on Knowledge." In *La scienza e le cause a partire dalla* Metafisica *di Aristotele* (Francesco Fronterotta, ed.), *Elenchos*, 121–155.

Fine, Gail (2014). *The Possibility of Inquiry: Meno's Paradox from Socrates to Sextus*. Oxford University Press.

Frede, Dorothea (1992). "The Cognitive Role of *Phantasia* in Aristotle." In *Essays on Aristotle's* De Anima (Amélie Oksenberg Rorty and Martha C. Nussbaum, eds.), 279–296, Oxford University Press.

Frede, Dorothea (2012). "The Endoxon Mystique: What Endoxa Are and What They Are Not." *Oxford Studies in Ancient Philosophy*, 43, 185–215.

Frede, Michael (1987). *Essays in Ancient Philosophy*. University of Minnesota Press.

Frede, Michael (1990). "An Empiricist View of Knowledge: Memorism." In *Companions to Ancient Thought 1: Epistemology* (Stephen Everson, ed.), 225–250, Cambridge University Press.

Frede, Michael (1996). "Aristotle's Rationalism." In *Rationality in Greek Thought* (Michael Frede and Gisela Striker, eds.), 157–173, Oxford University Press.

Freeland, Cynthia A. (1994). "Aristotle on Perception, Appetition, and Self-Motion." In *Self-Motion: From Aristotle to Newton* (Mary Louise Gill and James G. Lennox, eds.), 35–63, Princeton University Press.

Frege, Gottlob (1884). *The Foundations of Arithmetic: A Logico-Mathematical Enquiry Into the Concept of Number*, Second Revised edition. Northwestern University Press. 1950.

Gasser-Wingate, Marc (2020). "Aristotle on Self-Sufficiency, External Goods, and Contemplation." *Archiv für Geschichte der Philosophie*, 102, 1–28.

Goldin, Owen (2013). "Circular Justification and Explanation in Aristotle." *Phronesis*, 58, 195–214.

Goldman, Alvin I. (1976). "Discrimination and Perceptual Knowledge." *Journal of Philosophy*, 73, 771–791.

Gotthelf, Allan (1987). "Aristotle's Conception of Final Causality." In *Philosophical Issues in Aristotle's Biology* (Allan Gotthelf and James G. Lennox, eds.), 204–242, Cambridge University Press.

Gregorić, Pavel and Filip Grgić (2006). "Aristotle's Notion of Experience." *Archiv für Geschichte der Philosophie*, 88, 1–30.

Grimaldi, William M. A. (1957). "A Note on the Pisteis in Aristotle's Rhetoric, 1354–1356." *American Journal of Philology*, 78, 188–192.

Gupta, Anil (2006). *Empiricism and Experience*. Oxford University Press.

Hamelin, Octave (1900). "Sur l'induction." In *L'année philosophique* (Félix Alcan, ed.), volume 10, 40–53, Paris.

Hamlyn, David W. (1976). "Aristotelian Epagoge." *Phronesis*, 21, 167–184.

Hankinson, Robert J. (2011). "Avant *nous* le Déluge: Aristotle's Notion of Intellectual Grasp." In *Episteme, etc.* (Benjamin Morison and Katerina Ierodiakonou, eds.), 30–59, Oxford University Press.

Harte, Verity (2002). *Plato on Parts and Wholes: The Metaphysics of Structure*. Oxford University Press.

Harte, Verity (2010). "What's a Particular and What Makes It So? Some Thoughts, Mainly About Aristotle." In *Particulars in Greek Philosophy* (Robert W. Sharples, ed.), 97–125, Brill.

Hasper, Pieter Sjoerd (2013). "Between Science and Dialetic: Aristotle's Account of Good and Bad Peirastic Arguments in the *Sophistical Refutations*." *Logical Analysis and History of Philosophy*, 15, 286–322.

Hasper, Pieter Sjoerd and Joel Yurdin (2014). "Between Perception and Scientific Knowledge: Aristotle's Account of Experience." *Oxford Studies in Ancient Philosophy*, 47, 119–150.

Henry, Devin (2015). "Holding for the Most Part: the Demonstrability of Moral Facts." In *Bridging the Gap between Aristotle's Science and Ethics* (Devin Henry and Karen Margrethe Nielsen, eds.), 168–89, Cambridge University Press.

Hicks, Robert D. (1907). *Aristotle: De Anima*. Cambridge University Press.

Hintikka, Jaakko (1980). "Aristotelian Induction." *Revue internationale de philosophie*, 34, 422–439.

Irwin, Terence (1975). "Aristotle on Reason, Desire, and Virtue." *The Journal of Philosophy*, 72, 567–578.

Irwin, Terence (1988). *Aristotle's First Principles*. Clarendon Press.

Irwin, Terence (2000). "Ethics as an Inexact Science." In *Moral Particularism* (Brad Hooker and Margaret Olivia Little, eds.), 100–130, Clarendon Press.

Jimenez, Marta (2019). "Empeiria and Good Habits in Aristotle's Ethics." *Journal of the History of Philosophy*, 57, 363–389.

Joachim, Harold H. (1951). *Aristotle, the Nicomachean Ethics: A Commentary*. Oxford University Press.

Johansen, Thomas Kjeller (2012). *The Powers of Aristotle's Soul*. Oxford University Press.

Johansen, Thomas Kjeller (2017). "Aristotle on the *Logos* of the Craftsman." *Phronesis*, 62, 97–135.

Johnson, Monte Ransome (2008). *Aristotle on Teleology*. Oxford University Press.

Kahn, Charles (1981). "The Role of *Nous* in the Cognition of First Principles in *Posterior Analytics* II 19." In *Aristotle on Science: The Posterior Analytics, Proceedings of the Eighth Symposium Aristotelicum* (Enrico Berti, ed.), 385–414, Editrice Antenore.

Kahn, Charles (1992). "Aristotle on Thinking." In *Essays on Aristotle's De Anima* (Amélie Oksenberg Rorty and Martha C. Nussbaum, eds.), 359–79, Oxford University Press.

Karbowski, Joseph (2016). "Justification 'by Argument' in Aristotle's Natural Science." *Oxford Studies in Ancient Philosophy*, 51, 119–160.

Keil, Geert and Nora Kreft (2019). "Introduction." In *Aristotle's Anthropology* (Geert Keil and Nora Kreft, eds.), 1–22, Cambridge University Press.

Kelsey, Sean (2000). "Recollection in the Phaedo." *Proceedings of the Boston Area Colloquium in Ancient Philosophy*, 16, 91–121.

Kornblith, Hilary (1999). "Knowledge in Humans and Other Animals." *Philosophical Perspectives*, 13, 327–346.

Kosman, L. A. (1973). "Understanding, Explanation and Insight in the Posterior Analytics." In *Exegesis and Argument; Phronesis supplementary volume I* (Edward N. Lee, Alexander P. D. Mourelatos, and Richard M. Rorty, eds.), 374–392, Van Gorcum.

LaBarge, Scott (2006). "Aristotle on Empeiria." *Ancient Philosophy*, 26, 23–44.

Labarrière, Jean-Louis (1984). "Imagination humaine et imagination animale chez Aristote." *Phronesis*, 29, 17–49.

Labarrière, Jean-Louis (2004). "Désir, sensation et altération." In *Aristote et le mouvement des animaux: Dix études sur le De motu animalium* (André Laks and Marwan Rashed, eds.), 149–165, Presses universitaires du Septentrion.

Le Blond, Jean-Marie (1939). *Logique et méthode chez Aristote*. Vrin.

Lear, Gabriel Richardson (2004). *Happy Lives and the Highest Good*. Princeton University Press.

Lee, Henry D. P. (1935). "Geometrical Method and Aristotle's Account of First Principles." *The Classical Quarterly*, 29, 113–124.

Lennox, James G. (1987). "Divide and Explain: The *Posterior Analyics* in Practice." In *Philosophical Issues in Aristotle's Biology* (Allan Gotthelf and James G. Lennox, eds.), 90–119, Cambridge University Press.

Lennox, James G. (2011). "Aristotle on Norms of Inquiry." *Hopos: The Journal of the International Society for the History of Philosophy of Science*, 1, 23–46.

Lennox, James G. (2015). "Aristotle on the Biological Roots of Virtue." In *Bridging the Gap between Aristotle's Science and Ethics* (Devin Henry and Karen Margrethe Nielsen, eds.), 193–213, Cambridge University Press.

Lennox, James G. (2021). *Aristotle on Inquiry: Erotetic Frameworks and Domain Specific Norms*. Cambridge University Press.

Lesher, James H. (1973). "The Meaning of ΝΟΥΣ in the Posterior Analyics." *Phronesis*, 18, 44–68.

Lesher, James H. (2010). "'Just as in Battle': The Simile of the Rout in Aristotle's *Posterior Analytics* II 19." *Ancient Philosophy*, 30, 95–105.

Leunissen, Mariska (2010). *Explanation and Teleology in Aristotle's Science of Nature*. Cambridge University Press.

Leunissen, Mariska (2017). *From Natural Character to Moral Virtue in Aristotle*. Oxford University Press.

Lorenz, Hendrik (2006). *The Brute Within*. Oxford University Press.

Lorenz, Hendrik and Benjamin Morison (2019). "Aristotle's Empiricist Theory of Doxastic Knowledge." *Phronesis*, 64, 431–464.

Lyons, John (1963). *Structural Semantics: An Analysis of Part of the Vocabulary of Plato*. Blackwell.

Marmodoro, Anna (2014). *Aristotle on Perceiving Objects*. Oxford University Press.

McDowell, John (1988). "Comments on T.H. Irwin's 'Some Aspects of Incontinence.'" *The Southern Journal of Philosophy*, 27 (suppl.), 89–102.

McDowell, John (1998). "Some Issues in Aristotle's Moral Psychology." In *Companions to Ancient Thought 4: Ethics* (Stephen Everson, ed.), 107–128, Cambridge University Press.

McKirahan, Richard D. (1983). "Aristotelian Epagoge in Prior Analytics 2.21 and Posterior Analyics 1.1." *Journal of the History of Philosophy*, 21, 1–13.

McKirahan, Richard D. (1992). *Principles and Proofs: Aristotle's Theory of Demonstrative Science*. Princeton University Press.

Mignucci, Mario (1975). *L'Argomentazione Dimostrativa in Aristotele*. Editrice Antenore.

Modrak, Deborah (1981). "Aristotle On Knowing First Principles." *Philosophical Inquiry*, 3, 63–83.

Modrak, Deborah (1987). *Aristotle: The Power of Perception*. University of Chicago Press.

Modrak, Deborah (2001). *Aristotle's Theory of Language and Meaning*. Cambridge University Press.

Morel, Pierre-Marie (2004). "Volontaire, involontaire et non-volontaire dans le chapitre 11 du *DMA* d'Aristote." In *Aristote et le mouvement des animaux: Dix études sur le* De motu animalium (André Laks and Marwan Rashed, eds.), 167–183, Presses universitaires du Septentrion.

Moss, Jessica (2011). "'Virtue Makes the Goal Right': Virtue and Phronesis in Aristotle's Ethics." *Phronesis*, 56, 204–261.

Moss, Jessica (2012). *Aristotle on the Apparent Good: Perception, Phantasia, Thought, and Desire*. Oxford University Press.

Moss, Jessica (2014). "Right Reason in Plato and Aristotle: On the Meaning of Logos." *Phronesis*, 59, 181–230.

Moss, Jessica and Whitney Schwab (2019). "The Birth of Belief." *Journal of the History of Philosophy*, 57, 1–32.

Nehamas, Alexander (1985). "Meno's Paradox and Socrates as a Teacher." *Oxford Studies in Ancient Philosophy*, 3, 1–30.

Nielsen, Karen Margrethe (2015). "Aristotle on Principles in Ethics: Political Science as the Science of the Human Good." In *Bridging the Gap between Aristotle's Science and Ethics* (Devin Henry and Karen Margrethe Nielsen, eds.), 29–48, Cambridge University Press.

Nozick, Robert (1981). *Philosophical Explanations.* Harvard University Press.

Nussbaum, Martha C. (1978). *Aristotle: De Motu Animalium.* Princeton University Press.

Nussbaum, Martha C. (1986). *The Fragility of Goodness: Luck and Ethics in Greek Tragedy and Philosophy.* Cambridge University Press.

Nussbaum, Martha C. (1990). *Love's Knowledge: Essays on Philosophy and Literature.* Oxford University Press.

Olfert, C. M. M. (2014). "Aristotle's Conception of Practical Truth." *Journal of the History of Philosophy*, 52, 205–231.

Owen, G. E. L. (1961). "Tithenai ta phainomena." In *Aristote et les problèmes de méthode: communications présentées au Symposium Aristotelicum tenu à Louvain du 24 août au 1er septembre 1960*, 83–103, Louvain.

Pakaluk, Michael (2010). "The Great Question of Practical Truth, and a Diminutive Answer." *Acta Philosophica*, 19, 145–162.

Pearson, Giles (2011). "Aristotle and Scanlon on Desire and Motivation." In *Moral Psychology and Human Action in Aristotle* (Michael Pakaluk and Giles Pearson, eds.), 95–118, Oxford University Press.

Popper, Karl R. (1959). *The Logic of Scientific Discovery.* Routledge.

Price, A. W. (2016). "Choice and Action in Aristotle." *Phronesis*, 61, 435–462.

Primavesi, Oliver (forthcoming). *Aristoteles: De motu animalium. Ein neues Bild der Überlieferung und ein neuer Text.* De Gruyter.

Quine, W.V.O. (1961). *From a Logical Point of View*, 2nd edition. Harvard University Press.

Rabbås, Øyvind (2015). "*Eudaimonia*, Human Nature, and Normativity: Reflections on Aristotle's Project in *Nicomachean Ethics* Book I." In *The Quest for the Good Life: Ancient Philosophers on Happiness* (Øyvind Rabbås, Eyjólfur K. Emilsson, Hallvard Fossheim, and Miira Tuominen, eds.), 88–112, Oxford University Press.

Reeve, C. D. C. (2012). *Action, Contemplation, and Happiness: An Essay on Aristotle.* Harvard University Press.

Richardson, Henry S. (1992). "Desire and the Good in De Anima." In *Essays on Aristotle's De Anima* (Amélie Oksenberg Rorty and Martha C. Nussbaum, eds.), 381–399, Oxford University Press.

Robin, Léon (1942). "Sur la conception aristotélicienne de la causalité." In *La pensée hellénique, des origines à Épicure*, 423–485, Presses Universitaires de France.

Rodriguez, Evan (2020). "Aristotle's Platonic Response to the Problem of First Principles." *Journal of the History of Philosophy*, 58, 449–469.

Ross, W. D. (1949). *Aristotle: Prior and Posterior Analytics*. Clarendon Press.

Ross, W. D. (1961). *Aristotle: De Anima*. Oxford University Press.

Ross, W. D. (1995). *Aristotle*, 6th edition. Routledge.

Ross, W. D. (2009). *Aristotle: The Nicomachean Ethics*. Oxford University Press. Revised with notes by Lesley Brown.

Salmieri, Gregory (2014). "Aristotelian *Epistēmē* and the Relation Between Knowledge and Understanding." *Metascience*, 23, 1–9. Published as part of a Book Symposium: "*Episteme*, Demonstration, and Explanation: A Fresh Look at Aristotle's Posterior Analytics" (James G. Lennox, ed.).

Sartwell, Crispin (1991). "Knowledge is Merely True Belief." *American Philosophical Quarterly*, 28, 157–165.

Scheiter, Krisanna M. (2012). "Images, Appearances, and *Phantasia* in Aristotle." *Phronesis*, 57, 251–278.

Schiefsky, Mark J. (2005). *Hippocrates on Ancient Medicine*. Brill.

Scott, Dominic (1995). *Recollection and Experience*. Cambridge University Press.

Sedley, David (2006). "Form-Particular Resemblance in Plato's *Phaedo*." *Proceedings of the Aristotelian Society*, 106, 311–327.

Sedley, David (2007). "Equal Sticks and Stones." In *Maieusis: Essays in Ancient Philosophy in Honour of Myles Burnyeat* (Dominic Scott, ed.), 68–86, Oxford University Press.

Shields, Christopher (2016). *Aristotle: De Anima*. Oxford University Press.

Siegel, Susanna (2010). *The Contents of Visual Experience*. Oxford University Press.

Smith, Angela (1998). "Knowledge and Expertise in the Early Platonic Dialogues." *Archiv für Geschichte der Philosophie*, 80, 129–161.

Sorabji, Richard (1992). "Intentionality and Physiological Processes: Aristotle's Theory of Sense-Perception." In *Essays on Aristotle's De Anima* (Amélie Oksenberg Rorty and Martha C. Nussbaum, eds.), 195–225, Oxford University Press.

Sorabji, Richard (1996). "Rationality." In *Rationality in Greek Thought* (Michael Frede and Gisela Striker, eds.), 311–334, Oxford University Press.

Sorabji, Richard (2010). "The Ancient Commentators on Concept Formation." In *Interpreting Aristotle's Posterior Analytics in Late Antiquity and Beyond* (Frans A.J. de Haas, Mariska Leunissen, and Marije Martijn, eds.), 3–26, Brill.

Sosa, Ernest (1985). "Knowledge and Intellectual Virtue." *The Monist*, 68, 226–245.

Stein, Nathanael (2009). "After Literalism and Spiritualism: The Plasticity of Aristotelian Perception." In *Ancient Perspectives on Aristotle's De Anima* (Gerd Van Riel and Pierre Destrée, eds.), 17–33, Leuven University Press.

Striker, Gisela (2006). "Aristotle's Ethics as Political Science." In *The Virtuous Life in Greek Ethics* (Burkhard Reis, ed.), 127–141, Cambridge University Press.

Taylor, C. C. W. (1990). "Aristotle's Epistemology." In *Companions to Ancient Thought 1: Epistemology* (Stephen Everson, ed.), 116–142, Cambridge University Press.

Tuominen, Miira (2007). *Apprehension and Argument: Ancient Theories of Starting Points for Knowledge*. Springer.

Tuominen, Miira (2010). "Back to Posterior Analytics II 19: Aristotle on the Knowledge of Principles." *Apeiron*, 43, 115–144.

Tuominen, Miira (2014). "Naturalised versus Normative Epistemology: An Aristotelian Alternative." In *New Perspectives on Aristotelianism and Its Critics* (Miira Tuominen, Sara Heinämaa, and Virpi Mäkinen, eds.), 66–91, Brill.

Tuozzo, Thomas (1994). "Conceptualized and Unconceptualized Desire in Aristotle." *Journal of the History of Philosophy*, 32, 525–549.

Vasiliou, Iakovos (2014). "Apparent Goods: A Discussion of Jessica Moss, *Aristotle on the Apparent Good*." *Oxford Studies in Ancient Philosophy*, 46, 353–381.

Velleman, David (2000). *The Possibility of Practical Reason*. Oxford University Press.

Wedin, Michael (1988). *Mind and Imagination in Aristotle*. Yale University Press.

Whiting, Jennifer (2002). "Locomotive Soul: The Parts of Soul in Aristotle's Scientific Works." *Oxford Studies in Ancient Philosophy*, 22, 141–200.

Whiting, Jennifer (2014). "Fools' Pleasures in Plato's *Philebus*." In *Strategies of Argument: Essays in Ancient Ethics, Epistemology, and Logic* (Mi-Kyoung Lee, ed.), 21–59, Oxford University Press.

Wiggins, David (1980). "Deliberation and Practical Reason." In *Essays on Aristotle's Ethics* (Amélie Oksenberg Rorty, ed.), 221–240, University of California Press.

Williamson, Timothy (2000). *Knowledge and Its Limits*. Oxford University Press.

Woods, Michael (1986). "Intuition and Perception in Aristotle's Ethics." *Oxford Studies in Ancient Philosophy*, 4, 145–156.

Index-Locorum-Aristotle

De Anima (An)
402a10–22 42
402a16–17 79
402b22–403a2 19, 96
403a3–b19 139
404a25ff ix
410b18–20 161
413b23–24 165
414a29–b16 110
414b1–6 160
414b3–6 165
414b4–9 139
414b6–10 115
414b19–33 122
416b33–34 160
418a11–16 116
418a15 110, 115
418a16 110
418a20–24 113
418a25 109
420b5ff 112
421a7ff 144
424a2–10 172
424a28–b3 172
424a29 109
425a20ff 106
425a25–27 113
425a26 113
425b12–25 106
427b6ff ix
427b11–12 6
427b11–16 82
427b22–24 137
428a8–11 160
428a10–11 153
428a18ff 9
428a19–24 123, 151

428a20 34
428b10ff 144
428b14 183
428b18–19 6
428b18–22 129
428b21 129
428b21–22 116
428b21ff 111
428b22–23 115
428b24–30 111
429a1–2 111, 183
429a4 183
429a4–6 184
429a4–8 122, 186
429b10ff 137
429b12–18 117, 138–39
430b27–29 129
430b29–30 110
430b29–31 114
431a8–14 168
431a8ff 106
431a12 168
431a14–15 179
431b5–6 118
432a17 161
432b7–19 162
432b8 161
432b19–25 162
432b19–26 161
432b25–433a6 162
432b26–433a1 163
432b29–433a1 160
433a1–3 163
433a6–8 164
433a10 186
433a13 161
433a28–29 162

433a31–b1 162
433b8–10 162
433b11–12 162
433b13–18 162
433b29–30 176, 188
433b31–434a5 161
434a12–14 164
434a14–15 187
434a30ff 109
434b30 160
435b19–24 147

De Caelo (Cael)
275b5–11 137
278a10–11 137
278b3–7 134
293a25–27 36
306a11–17 35

De Generatione Animalium (GA)
731a30–34 5
760b27–33 36
777b24–778a2 145

De Generatione et Corruptione (GC)
316a5–10 36

De Insomniis (Insomn)
458a33–b2 144
458a33–459a10 121
458b31–33 116
459a8ff 144
459b1ff 160
460b3–8 173
461b13–15 183

De Interpretatione (Int)
16a19–29 190
17a16–26 168
17a38–40 133

De Memoria et Reminiscentia (Mem)
449b4–8 121
449b5ff 160
449b10–15 183
449b13–15 5
449b22–23 153
449b24–30 153
449b26–8 183
449b28–30 183, 184
450a9–11 5
450a10–13 183
450a14 153
450a16–19 153
450a22–25 183
451a14–16 153
451a16–17 153
451b10–14 183
451b18–25 183
453a4–14 183

De Motu Animalium (MA)
698a11–14 36
700a8 161
700a26 161
700b17–22 161
700b23–25 162
701a10–13 41, 163, 219
701a16–22 221
701a17–22 218
701a23–25 164, 225
701a28–29 166
701a32–33 164
701b16 160
701b16ff 160
701b24–6 167
701b28–32 160, 167
701b33–702a1 167
701b36 167
702a2–7 184
702a17–19 160
703a4–5 162
703b8ff 161

De Partibus Animalium (PA)
465a4–23 230
465a27–28 230
639a1ff 42
646a8–12 28, 96
661a6–8 165
666a11–13 171
681b3 180

De Sensu et Sensibilibus (Sens)
436a17–21 207
436a17–b1 141
436a20–21 218
436b18–437a3 109, 145
437a11–15 112
442b4–9 116
443b20–26 110, 173
443b27ff 167

Eudemian Ethics (EE)
1014a18–19 78
1216b16–25 141, 194, 200
1216b26–35 7
1216b26–1217a10 37
1216b35–1217a9 207
1216b40–1217a10 224
1227b5–11 20
1247a3ff 142

Historia Animalium (HA)
488b25–26 183
491a7–14 28, 96
531b5–8 180
535a29ff 112
536b14–17 152
548b6 180
548b10–15 180
549a1–3 180
555a23–26 152
558a30 146
571a4–6 152
578a22–24 146
588a18ff 122
588a25–b3 190

588b12–16 181
589a4–9 174
608a17–21 190
611a15–b23 189
612a1–8 189
612a12–15 189
614b18–26 188–89
631a20–b1 188

Magna Moralia (MM)
1201b6 37
1208a13–21 123

Metaphysics (Met)
980a20–27 123, 144
980a22–27 167
980a24–27 4
980a27 151
980a27–29 82
980a27–b25 6
980a28–b28 82, 122
980b1 190
980b23–24 6
980b25–28 231
980b26–27 144, 191
980b28–a1 142
981a4–5 68
981a5–7 91
981a7–8 125
981a7–12 89, 130, 140
981a13–15 43, 67
981a13–20 222
981a13ff 89
981a14 140
981a15–16 83
981a16 91
981a24–28 43, 91
981a24–30 140
981a30–b6 91, 141, 191
981a30ff 42
981a31 92
981b2–3 91
981b5 142
981b6 90

981b7-8 190
981b7-10 78
981b10-13 4, 91, 101, 127, 140
981b13-25 222
981b19-20 192
981b21-22 192
982a10ff 42
982a11-12 viii, 127
982a12-14 78
982a24-25 101
983a26 12
992b24ff 28
992b30-33 51
993b9-11 151
993b19-31 7
993b20-21 41
993b23-24 10
1009b12-13 ix
1010b2ff 116
1015a32-33 37
1018b30-34 29-30
1019a1ff 30
1027a20-22 78
1029b3-8 41
1029b3ff 28
1035b32ff 117
1036a2-7 137
1036a7-8 137
1036b33ff 137
1046b5-25 220
1051b17ff 129
1070a9ff 137
1073b5-6 134
1087a19-20 111

Nicomachean Ethics (EN)
1094a22-24 227
1094b11-27 200
1094b14-15 199
1094b15-16 208
1094b19-22 201, 205
1094b21 208
1095a2-11 224
1095b2-8 227

1095b2-13 194
1097a19ff 195
1097a25-34 70
1098a16-17 200
1098a20-22 205
1098a26-33 200, 205
1098a29-31 201
1102a9 207
1102a23-26 207
1103a3-10 200
1103b26-28 207
1103b27-28 41, 210
1103b27-29 200
1104a1-10 206
1104a1ff 200
1104b8-13 224
1105b5-7 212
1106b36 20
1107a29-32 213
1109b14-23 210
1109b14ff 200, 201
1109b21 211
1112b11-15 194
1112b11-20 216
1112b15-20 194
1113a1 106
1113a33 212
1115b13-14 217
1118a17ff 106
1118a18-21 109
1118a18-23 182
1119b8-10 162
1120a23-24 217
1122a34-35 224
1126a31-b11 210
1126a32-34 211
1126a32ff 201
1126b3 211
1137b19-24 212
1139a6-8 152
1139a21-30 219
1139a31-36 221
1139a35-b1 219, 221
1139b20-21 221

1139b31–32 20
1140a1–2 221
1140a5–6 220
1140b6–7 220
1140b11–21 122
1140b14–16 221
1140b22–24 220
1141a7 76
1141a33–b2 231
1141b6–7 222
1141b8–16 194
1141b14–21 222
1141b18–21 214
1142a11–20 79, 223
1142a12–30 201
1142a14–15 194
1142a20–23 214
1142a28–29 106
1143a35–b5 20
1143b8–9 223
1143b11–14 67, 223
1144a7–9 216
1144a20–22 216
1144b1–16 195
1144b14ff 216
1145a5–7 216
1147a34–35 162
1147b3–5 127
1149a24–b2 163
1149a35 106
1163a1–2 224
1165a2–3 224
1165a27–29 224
1174b14ff 171
1175b30–35 172
1177b31–34 231
1179a16–22 36
1179a18–22 213
1179a35–b2 200
1179b4–10 224
1179b23ff 224
1179b31ff 208
1180b7–29 226
1180b16–20 194

1180b21–22 226
1181b1–12 79
1181b2–3 43, 224
1181b3–7 225
1181b5 90

Physics (Phys)
184a12 12
184a21–b14 148–49
184a22 87
184b12–14 125
189a5–8 101
195a28ff 112
202b6ff 174
247a7–14 185
247a16–17 171

Politics (Pol)
1253a7–18 120
1253a7ff 112
1253a10–18 170
1332a21–25 195
1332b3–4 184

Posterior Analytics (APo)
71a1–2 48
71a8–9 48
71a11–16 28
71a21–24 98
71a24ff 48
71b9–12 12
71b10–12 76
71b15 12
71b16–25 13–14
71b27 31
71b29–33 27
71b31 10, 12, 31
71b33–72a5 27
72a7 31
72a15ff 15
72a25 10
72a25–32 33
72a29–30 77
72a37–b4 33

72b5–15 75
72b13 10
72b18–21 13
72b18–22 75
72b20 31
72b23–25 76
72b24 83
73a34ff 48
73b33ff 101
74a25–32 101
74a29 136
75a28 19
75a32 10
75b24–26 134, 152
75b39 31
76a41 15
78a31ff 16
78a33–35 106
78a34–35 102
79a10–15 141
79a16 10
81a38–b9 50–51
81b6 128
83a1–4 113
83a1–17 113
83a1ff 113
83a14–17 113
83b35 10
85b23–27 101
85b27–35 12
87b28–35 133
87b29–30 106
87b33–35 80
87b35–39 134–35
87b38 133
87b39–88a5 50
88a1 106
88a2 128
88a4 133
88a12–17 27
88a13 119
88a15 106
88b36 76, 83
89a23–b6 23

89b10 104
89b11–13 120
89b29–31 28, 96
90a26–29 119
90a28–29 100
90b3–4 15
90b14 34
92a34–b1 85
92a37 102
92b2–3 80, 138
92b17–19 15
93b30–31 150
97b17–25 209
97b28–29 103
99b17–30 6
99b25–32 64–65
99b28–29 6
99b29 58
99b32–35 31, 65, 130
99b35 68
99b36–100a3 81
100a3 58
100a3–9 82
100a4–6 142
100a10–14 83
100a14–b5 84
100a16–b1 106
100a17 128
100b1 127
100b1–3 102
100b4 51, 66, 80
100b5–17 77
100b15 76, 83

Prior Analytics (APr)
43a33 113
46a17–27 28, 96
46a27 96

Rhetoric (Rhet)
1354a4–11 141–42
1354a15 34
1355a4–5 34
1355b2–7 220

1356a6 34
1366a11 34
1370a30-35 183
1370a35-b2 185
1370b9-10 185
1393a26 98
1393b4-8 98

Sophistical Refutations (SE)
171b38-172a21 37

Topics (Top)
101a37-b4 51

105a13-14 97
105a15-16 98
130b16 37
131b21-30 134
131b23-28 4
133b29ff 37
134a1ff 37
134a35ff 37
134b16 37
141b36ff 28
146b9-12 165

Index-Locorum-Plato

Gorgias
448c6–7 68
465b 68
500e4–501b1 67–68

Meno
81c 57
85c–d 65

Phaedo
62b 57
64e–67a 57
73c4–d11 53–54
73e5–74a1 54
74a5–8 57
74b6–c3 54, 59
74c4–d3 55
74d4–8 54
74e1 56
75a–b viii
75a2 56
75a5–10 57
75a7 58
75a11 58
75a11–b8 56
76a1–6 55
76c12 57
82d–83a 57
96b5–8 69
100c–d 55

Phaedrus
249c–251a 61
250a 57

Philebus
58a–d 64

Republic
476c 57
518d–519b 57
521d3–4 59
523a10–b4 59
523b5–8 59
523b9–c4 59
523c5–6 59, 63
523e 59
524b3–5 60
524b4–5 59
524c6–8 59
524d1–5 viii
524e4 68
525a1 60
525a4–5 60
525d6–7 60
582a5 68
582d 68

Theaetetus
163b1–c3 112
186b8ff 68
207e5–208a5 19

Timaeus
51e1–4 37

Index Nominum

Achtenberg, D. 169, 171, 228
Ackrill, J. L. 6, 53
Adamson, P. 69
Alston, W. 44
Anagnostopoulos, G. 22, 33, 125, 205
Angioni, L. 17
Annas, J. 141
Auffret, T. 68
Barnes, J. x, 6, 12, 13, 16, 30, 49, 78, 81, 83, 84, 86, 100, 101, 125, 128
Bayer, J. 74, 81
Bedu-Addo, J. T. 56
Bengson, J. 194
Biondi, P. 125
Block, I. 112
Bolton, R. 6, 9, 22, 51, 87
Code, A. 6
Bostock, D. 53, 80
Boyle, M. 121
Broadie, S. 169, 219
Bronstein, D. 6, 10, 12, 17, 29, 35, 48, 51, 65, 74, 81, 83, 87, 91, 99, 103, 104, 128, 131, 150, 151
Burnyeat, M. x, 4, 6, 10, 13, 19, 35, 228
Cashdollar, S. 112, 114, 117
Caston, V. 125, 128
Caujolle-Zaslawsky, F. 98
Charles, D. 12, 17, 83, 90, 91, 98, 104, 150, 160, 166, 168, 171, 172, 181
Cooper, J. 122, 144, 160, 163, 218, 221
Corcilius, K. 123, 160, 168, 169, 170, 172, 173, 176, 219
Curzer, H. 203

Dugré, F. 177
Engberg-Pedersen, T. 98, 100
Evans, G. 129
Everson, S. 112, 114, 117, 153, 178
Ferejohn, M. 6, 18, 22, 104, 128
Fernandez, P. 160, 193, 218, 221
Fine, G. 3, 6, 9, 22, 40, 80, 146, 151
Frede, D. 23
Frede, M. ix, 3, 22, 24, 81, 176
Freeland, C. 146, 173
Frege, G. 25
Gasser-Wingate, M. 142
Goldin, O. 23, 35, 125, 129, 130
Goldman, A. 8
Gotthelf, A. 22
Gregorić, P. 81, 90
Grgić, F. 81, 90
Grimaldi, W. M. A. 34
Gupta, A. 44
Hamelin, O. 102
Hamlyn, D. W. 81, 85, 98
Hankinson, R. J. 81, 87
Harte, V. 19, 137
Hasper, P. S. 37, 83, 91, 101, 221
Henry, D. 205, 208
Hicks, R. D. 109, 112, 123, 177
Hintikka, J. 98
Irwin, T. x, 3, 22, 24, 29, 33, 74, 131, 174, 204, 205, 208, 217
Jimenez, M. 221
Joachim, H. H. 120, 221
Johansen, T. K. 91, 114, 126, 141, 176, 181, 185, 194
Johnson, M. R. 123
Kahn, C. 49, 74, 109, 112, 120, 125, 129
Karbowski, J. 6, 37

Keil, G. 121
Kelsey, S. 56
Kornblith, H. 8, 9
Kosman, L. A. 6, 13, 18
Kreft, N. 121
LaBarge, S. 6, 91
Labarrière, J. 163, 165, 177, 180, 189
Le Blond, J. 22, 74, 83
Lear, G. 195, 219
Lee, H. D. P. 51
Lennox, J. G. 25, 42, 94, 97, 104, 189
Lesher, J. H. 16, 83
Leunissen, M. 123, 189
Lorenz, H. ix, 121, 122, 161, 169,
    176, 180, 183, 185, 193, 194,
    218, 226
Lyons, J. 13
Marmodoro, A. 126
McDowell, J. 203, 217, 219, 225, 227
McKirahan, R. D. 18, 22, 35, 83, 98,
    128
Mignucci, M. 48
Modrak, D. 49, 81, 98, 104, 112, 114,
    128, 131, 153, 177, 179, 183
Morel, P. 177
Morison, B. 102, 194, 218, 219, 226
Moss, J. 9, 34, 91, 110, 112, 118, 128,
    131, 144, 160, 164, 166, 169,
    171, 176, 185, 194, 217
Nehamas, A. 19, 80
Nielsen, K. M. 205, 209, 218
Nozick, R. 8
Nussbaum, M. C. 125, 160, 165, 176,
    177, 202, 212
Olfert, C. 219
Owen, G. E. L. 23
Pakaluk, M. 219
Pearson, G. 179

Popper, K. R. 25
Price, A. W. 218, 221
Primavesi, O. 219
Quine, W. V. O. 44
Rabbås, Ø 121
Reeve, C. D. C. 112, 218
Richardson, H. S. 169, 177
Robin, L. 12, 101
Rodriguez, E. 104
Ross, W. D. 22, 51, 83, 97, 100, 103,
    112, 182, 198
Salmieri, G. 33
Sartwell, C. 8
Scheiter, K. M. 112, 125
Schiefsky, M. J. 91
Schwab, W. 9, 34, 118
Scott, D. 53, 57, 80, 127, 128, 149
Sedley, D. 53, 57
Shields, C. 109, 112, 113
Siegel, S. 118
Smith, A. 19
Sorabji, R. 49, 110, 112, 128
Sosa, E. 7, 8, 9
Stein, N. 125
Striker, G. 99, 205, 212, 220, 224
Taylor, C. C. W. 6, 49, 112,
    125, 129
Tuominen, M. 22, 72, 81, 83
Tuozzo, T. 109, 110, 114, 169, 171
Vasiliou, I. 171
Velleman, D. 229
Wedin, M. 125, 133
Whiting, J. 120, 123, 166, 171, 228
Wiggins, D. 202, 217
Williamson, T. 8
Woods, M. 202, 219
Yurdin, J. 83, 91, 101, 221

Thematic-Index

account, *see* λόγος
action
  and practical knowledge 42–43,
    193–96, 222–27
  and production 220–21
akrasia 163–64, 218
animal, animals 81, 90, 123–24,
    144–46, 230–32
  behavior, *see* locomotion
  and intelligence 145, 188–92,
    195–96
  nonrational 1–2, 8–10, 107–08,
    120–26, 130, 143–46, 173–76,
    186–88, 230–31
  survival 109–10, 123–25, 144–48,
    178, 181, 192
better known 14–15, 27–29, 33,
    41–42, 149, *see also* priority
causes, *see* explanations
cognition, cognitive 2, 4–10, 117,
    124, 126, 176, *see also*
    knowledge
  achievements 40–46, 67–70, 86,
    130, 230–31
  of animals 122, 144, 158, 230–32
  capacities 81, 89, 104, 107, 111
  development 23–25, 51, 66,
    71–75, 78–79, 88, 95, 125,
    137, 152, 154, *see also*
    induction
  factive, as knowledge 6–10
  penetration 119–20, 123
  states 48, 64, 71–73, 84, 88, 119,
    138–39
concepts, conceptual ability 48–49,
    129–32, 169

contemplation 123, 200, 213, 219,
    231
conviction (πίστις) 1, 33–40,
    44–45, 71, 77, 123, 231
craft knowledge (τέχνη) 42–44,
    67–68, 83, 89–94, 130, 139–43,
    191–94, 197–98, 206–07, 215,
    220–22, 225–26, 228, 231
definition 15, 51, 149–50, 194, 205,
    218, 220, 226
deliberation 196, 200, 205, 214,
    217–18, 226–29
demonstration 13–21, 26–27,
    33–34, 49–52, 93–97, 101,
    133–35, 207–08, 214–15,
    218–20, 223, 225–27, *see also*
    scientific understanding
    (ἐπιστήμη)
desire 160–76, 178–82, 187, 196,
    217, 221
  as future-directed 178–82
  and locomotion 160–76, 186–88,
    see also locomotion
  and pleasurable
    perceptions 168–74, 178
discrimination 65, 68, 107, 138–39,
    148–52, 154–55, 160–66,
    174–76, 177–78, 187, 189–90,
    196
disposition (ἕξις) 20, 47, 141, 192,
    195–96, 200, 214, 220, 224,
    227–28
empiricism 192–96, 230–32
essence 17, 45, 96, 117, 138–39, 147,
    150, 154, 220
ethical particularism 197–204, 216,
    224–28

ethical perception, *see* perception
experience (ἐμπειρία) 67–68,
    82–83, 89–93, 139–48, 196,
    109–11, 222–27, 231
    and perception 67, 139–48, 154,
        199, 201
    and practical success 43–44,
        67–68, 89–90, 190–96, 204,
        222–29
expertise 11–12, 18–21, 37–39,
    44–45, 79, 199
    and conviction 33–40
    demonstrative 21, 49, 76–77
    and explanation 12, 17, 21, 32,
        49, 76–79
    and justification 22–26, 32,
        40–46
    scientific 11–12, 20–21, 78–79,
        203, 226–28, 231
explanations 12–13, 17–21, 26–32,
    38–39, 43–45, 49, 75–77,
    91–97, 119, 137, 147, 193–95
    and explanatory knowledge, *see*
        knowledge
    and universals, *see* universals
Forms (Plato) 53–61, 65, 128
Foundationalism 22–26, 32, 70–72
geometry 21, 78–79, 223–24
habit 141–42, 184, 189–91, 195,
    225, 227–28
happiness 201–03, 205, 217–18
holism 16–21, 44–45, 193–94,
    226–28, 232
immediate, *see* primitive
induction (ἐπαγωγή) 37, 50–52,
    66, 73–75, 79, 82–104, 137, 154,
    197–98, 204, 209, 224, 231
    as an advance (ἔφοδος) 97–99
innatism 47, 53–69, 72, 79–81,
    107–08, 127, 146, 148, 155–57,
    232

justification 3, 22–26, 29, 32, 34–35,
    39–46, 70–72, 204, 213–14, *see*
    also normative authority
knowledge
    craft, *see* craft knowledge (τέχνη)
    explanatory 11–12, 45, 66, 92–94,
        100–04, 132, 137, 144,
        146–47, 155–57, 193–96, 231
    innate 53, 60, 62–64, 65–67, *see*
        also innatism
    noetic, *see* νοῦς
    of particulars 84, 92, 98–102,
        106–07, 127–29, 133–38, 140,
        147, 148–51, 201–04, 214,
        222–26
    perceptual 7–11, 45, 51, 66–72,
        80, 90, 105–08, 121, 156,
        213–15, 231
    practical 120, 190–96, 218–24,
        see also experience
        (ἐμπειρία), *see also* practical
        understanding, *see also*
        practical wisdom
        (φρόνησις)
    of principles 24, 26–32, 38–39,
        50, 64–66, 73, 75–82
    of propositions 6, 16–17, 19–21,
        33, 48–49, 78, 99
    scientific, *see* scientific
        understanding (ἐπιστήμη)
    theoretical 11, 20–21, 41–42, 120,
        138–39, 141, 145, 186,
        192–96, 201, 204, 208–10,
        219–20, *see also* scientific
        understanding (ἐπιστήμη)
    of universals 91–94, 97–104,
        127–38, 151, 154–55, 199,
        204, 214–15, 222–23, 226–28
learning 6, 10, 13, 16, 28, 31–32,
    41–45, 47–53, 61–72, 74,
    79–80, 105, 112, 118–19,
    152–57, 196, 209, 223–24

by induction, *see* induction
(ἐπαγωγή)
nonrational 159, 176, 195–96
from perception 1, 4–6, 56–64,
    66–67, 70–72, 154–57, 198,
    211, 224–27
by recollection, *see* recollection
locomotion 158–59, 161–67,
    174–75, 181–82, 187, 189–90,
    196
λόγος
    as account 138–39, 140–45,
        148–52, 191
    as speech 112, 120
    as reason 37, 81–82, 140, 148
memory 82–83, 89–91, 118, 121,
    142–44, 152–53, 159, 182–86
methodology 35–37, 42, 51, 94, 213
middle term 14–17, 27, 49, 76, 95,
    105
moral rules 198–99, 202–03,
    211–12, 214, 224, 226
motivation 20, 164, 170–71,
    176–78, 181–82, 184–87, 219,
    225, 228
normative authority 202–04,
    212–15
νοῦς 16, 22, 23, 73–82, 94–97, 103,
    223
nutrition 122, 162, 180
particulars 43, 50–52, 56, 83–85,
    88–92, 97–104, 106–07,
    126–29, 133–38, 148–50, 154,
    198, 201, 206, 208, 210–14,
    222–26
and tokens 98–99, 133–38
perceptibles, perceptible
    objects 106, 108–19
    per se (καθ᾽ αὑτό) 105, 109–11,
        124–26, 153–54
    accidental (κατὰ
        συμβεβηκός) 105, 108,
        110–19, 124–26, 152–54

and perceptual experience 109,
    112, 117–18, 124, 128–32
pursuit and avoidance of 110,
    121–22, 145–47, 160, 166–76,
    189–90, 196
perception
    as action-guiding 170–71, 173,
        186–87, 192, 198–99, 202,
        210–11, 216, 225, 227, 229
    and perceptual knowledge, *see*
        knowledge
    and animals 65–66, 81–82, 107,
        109–11, 165–77, 188–90
    as a capacity 5, 65–66, 68, 72, 109
    and conceptual content 126–33,
        147, 194
    as deficient 54–56, 58, 62–63,
        67–68, 156–57
    ethical 199, 210–16, 222–27
    as a material process 137, 154
    motivational role of 171, 177–78,
        181, 184, 185–87
    and pleasure 67–68, 110, 120,
        162, 165–76, 178–87, 196
    and perceptual
        recognition 114–20, 122,
        124, 127, 129, 131, 148–57
    as a standard 39, 44–45, 71, 204,
        212–14
    as a summoner of
        knowledge 58–64, 231
    of universals 88, 106, 126–32,
        138–48, 151, 154, 214–15
phantasia 110–11, 125, 144, 153,
    155, 159–62, 164, 167, 175–90,
    192, 195–96, 231
pleasure, *see* perception
practical understanding 192–96,
    219–21, 227–29, *see also*
    practical wisdom (φρόνησις)
practical wisdom (φρόνησις) 42,
    145, 193, 197, 199, 201, 216–29

primitives 14, 18, 22, 26, 31–33, 35, 73, 76–78, 84, 94, 213, see also priority

principles, first principles (ἀρχαί) 14–18, 22–24, 26–39, 50–51, 64–66, 73–80, 84, 96–97, 103, see also primitives, see also scientific understanding (ἐπιστήμη), see also νοῦς

priority 13–15, 26–32, 49–50, 70, 87–88, 102, 213, see also primitives

rationalism 3–4, 11, 22–26, 29, 32, 34–35, 39–40, 44–46, 67, 69–71

reason, rational capacities 107, 114, 118–26, 129, 139, 144, 155, 169, 186–88, 192–96, see also λόγος 1,05,000

recollection 53–58, 60–62, 64–65, 69, 80–81, 156

scientific understanding (ἐπιστήμη) 3, 9, 12–21, 26, 32, 40–43, 45, 49–50, 66, 75–76, 78–80, 100, 133–34, 136, 141, 154, 195, 198, 201, 218, 222, 226, 229, see also expertise
as a cognitive ideal 11, 19–21, 40–41, 44, 156, 191, 230–31

syllogism 14–18, 49, 98, 164, 218, see also middle term

teaching 48, 79–80, 151, 190, see also learning

teleology, teleological 122–23, 147, 158, 165, 174

trust, trustworthiness, see conviction (πίστις)

universals 27–28, 30, 50–52, 74, 80, 82–88, 94–104, 106–07, 111, 128–32, 134, 138–39, 141, 144–49, 201–04, 214, 222–23
as eternally recurring 134, 136–37
and ethical knowledge 199, 202, 204, 214, 226–27
and explanation 66, 93, 95–104, 138, 145
generality of 85–86, 102–03, 133
perception of, see perception
and universal knowledge, see knowledge

virtue, virtuous 20, 198–204, 206–17, 220, 224–29
behavior or conduct 199, 201, 203, 209, 212, 215
of character 200–01, 206, 213, 216–17
and exactness 200–01, 206–10, 215–16
as a mean 200–01, 210–11